SCOTTISH

*Published with financial support from the estate of
the late Miss Vera M.M. Watt, Guelph, Canada
and from an anonymous donor.*

Scottish Studies

The Journal of the
School of Scottish Studies
University of Edinburgh

Vol. 31 1992-93

Edited by
Alexander Fenton
Assistant Editor: Ian Fraser

Published by Canongate Academic
for
The School of Scottish Studies
University of Edinburgh
1993

Scottish Studies is published annually

Address for editorial correspondence:

Editor, *Scottish Studies,*
27 George Square,
Edinburgh EH8 9LD

Address for subscriptions:
Canongate Academic,
14 Frederick Street,
Edinburgh EH2 2HB

The annual subscription rate is £10. Postage is extra.

Printed by The Alden Press, Oxford.

ISBN 1 89410 070

Editorial

The last issue of *Scottish Studies*, Volume 30, appeared in 1991. We apologise to subscribers, who should be getting an issue each year, and our intention is that Volume 32 should follow the present one very quickly, to try to catch up. Delays were due to publishing difficulties. We now have in Canongate Academic a new publisher and distributor, and look forward to continuing collaboration with them.

The previous editor of *Scottish Studies*, Miss Daphne Hamilton, retired in 1992, after a long association with the Journal. She deserves full thanks for her standard of meticulous editing. She will continue to have a link with the forthcoming volume, which is to be dedicated to the late Eric Cregeen. Meantime, editing has been taken over by Alexander Fenton, Director of the School, with the assistance of Ian Fraser, Head of the School's Place-Name Survey of Scotland.

Volume 31 includes Alexander Fenton's inaugural lecture following the setting up of the first established Chair of Ethnology in the British Isles. The University of Edinburgh deserves much praise for this pioneering move, which now brings Scotland into line with most countries of Europe, including Southern Ireland. It also includes the sermon delivered by Donald Meek on the occasion of a University church service to mark the School's fortieth anniversary in 1991. The remaining papers, and the *Notes and Comments* section (revived from an earlier practice), reflect the work of the School, whether it relates to traditional forms of oral and material culture, or emigrant experiences, or the languages of Scotland. In Susan Storrier's contributions on *Jewish Cuisine in Edinburgh* and on *Bunning*, we are looking at aspects of contemporary ethnology.

Another new feature is the information on Postgraduate Theses by students of the School of Scottish Studies, and the Departments of Celtic and of Scottish History. These three bodies together form what is called the—Scottish Studies' Planning Unit, within the Faculty Group of Arts, Music and Divinity. This and subsequent volumes of *Scottish Studies* will act as a voice for all three, and for any other departments with Scottish interests, as part of the promulgation of the concept of 'Scottishness' as a major feature of the attraction of students to the University of Edinburgh.

Another new feature is the organisation of *Books Noticed* according to the classification system of the International Ethnological Bibliography (Internationale Volkskundliche Bibliographie—IVB). This is seen as an aid to comparative international ethnological studies. Even if there is not room to review all books received, it seems to us that a short notice, with an indication of the main points of importance, is a worthwhile service that allows us to mention many more books than would otherwise be possible.

The Editors

Contents

Notes and Comments

Contributors

Margaret Bennett, School of Scottish Studies, University of Edinburgh, 27 George Square, Edinburgh.

Ronald I. M. Black, Department of Celtic, University of Edinburgh, David Hume Tower, Edinburgh.

Dr Alan Bruford, School of Scottish Studies, University of Edinburgh, 27 George Square, Edinburgh.

Kerry Cardell, Faculty of Social Sciences, Deakin University, Geelong, Victoria, Australia 3217.

Hugh Cheape, Department of History and Applied Art, National Museums of Scotland, Queen Street, Edinburgh.

Cliff Cumming, Faculty of Social Sciences, Deakin University, Geelong, Victoria 3217.

Professor Alexander Fenton, School of Scottish Studies, University of Edinburgh, 27 George Square, Edinburgh.

Jane George, Honours Graduate, School of Scottish Studies.

Owen Hand, Honours Graduate, School of Scottish Studies.

David Heppell, Department of Natural History, National Museums of Scotland, Chambers Street, Edinburgh.

Alyne Jones, Honours Graduate, School of Scottish Studies.

Roger Leitch, 58 Seafield Road, Dundee.

Dr Emily Lyle, School of Scottish Studies, University of Edinburgh, 27 George Square, Edinburgh.

Donald A. MacDonald, School of Scottish Studies, 27 George Square, Edinburgh.

Professor John W. Sheets, Department of History and Anthropology, Central Missouri State University, Warrensburg, Missouri 64093, USA.

Dr Christopher Smith, Department of Archaeology, the University, Newcastle-upon-Tyne.

Susan Storrier, School of Scottish Studies, University of Edinburgh, 27 George Square, Edinburgh.

David Sydeserff, 1 Ross's Close, Haddington, East Lothian.

Scottish Ethnology: Crossing the Rubicon

Inaugural Lecture for the Chair of Scottish Ethnology

ALEXANDER FENTON

When Caesar crossed the Rubicon, he took a decisive step that led to war. War is not in question with Scottish ethnology, but at least the University of Edinburgh, in setting up a Chair of Scottish Ethnology as the first such Chair in Britain, took a decisive and pioneering step. This enterprising move has brought Scotland into line with nearly every other country in Europe.

It is a privilege to be the holder of this Chair, but it is important at this time to remember what lies behind it. It is not so many years ago that the word 'ethnology' would hardly have been understood in academic contexts in this country, at least not as it had come to be understood in the surrounding countries of Europe. The basis for the new situation has been laid by work from two overlapping directions, both of them stemming from the 1950s.

The first was the founding of the School of Scottish Studies in 1951. The School's tremendous work in the collection of oral traditions and the building up of the Sound and Photographic Archives was complemented from the 1970s by postgraduate teaching and then by undergraduate teaching. Now it is possible to take a single Honours four-year degree in Scottish Ethnology, and the School also has a good number of outstanding postgraduate students. There is no doubt that this academic activity played a major role in the University of Edinburgh's decision to establish the Chair of Scottish Ethnology within the School of Scottish Studies, which is a full department within the Faculty of Arts, as well as continuing its role as the centre for the national Sound Archive.

The second was the setting up in 1959 of the Country Life Section of the former National Museum of Antiquities of Scotland. Through its subsequent series of exhibitions on major topics of Scottish rural life, its eventual founding of the Scottish Agricultural Museum, its establishment of the Scottish Country Life Archive (now the Scottish Ethnological Archive), and its series of publications, it became a focal point for material culture studies, thus complementing in a great degree the work of the School of Scottish Studies. After the Royal Scottish Museum and the National Museum of Antiquities of Scotland amalgamated in 1985, the Country Life Section became the Working Life Section, and its remit was broadened to encompass urban and industrial as well as rural conditions of life.

These two centres of activity have done a great deal to raise the level of understanding of what 'ethnology' means, in European terms, within Britain, and in this inaugural lecture I shall look at the provision of ethnological 'centres' in Europe, outline the phases of development of this complex discipline, and look a little to the future. A survey published in 1967 showed that there were then in Europe 65 university chairs dealing with ethnology, as well as 13 related institutes. Germany, with 13 chairs in the West and two in the East, was far and away in the lead. Poland came next with seven, then Hungary and Switzerland with four each. (E.E. 1.4 (1967), Introduction).

The survey revealed the great depth of ethnological teaching in Germany and elsewhere in Middle Europe. From a British viewpoint, this was perhaps unexpected. We are accustomed to looking to Scandinavian countries for a lead in ethnology and have benefited greatly from contact with them. The Archives of the School of Scottish Studies owe much in their form to those of the Archive for Dialect and Folk Traditions in Uppsala, as also do those of the Department of Irish Folklore in University College, Dublin. Our open-air and folk museums, whether national like the Welsh Folk Museum or serving more local needs like the Highland Folk Museum at Kingussie or the Glenesk Museum in Angus, also owe much to the earlier developments in Scandinavian countries. In both the theory and the practice of ethnology, Scandinavian ethnologists continue to be in the van. Like all good scholars they are quick to grasp or test ideas and theories emanating from neighbouring disciplines, for ethnology is above all a method of approach to the study of the cultural history of mankind and is prepared to make progress by all possible means. But the Scandinavians do not stand alone. We ignore Middle Europe now at our peril. Unfortunately the German scholars are less kind to us than the Scandinavians, who have always used a good deal of English in their academic work. An immense depth of solid and pioneering research work in ethnology exists in Germany. Any growing generation of ethnologists in this country must get to grips with German in order to be able to keep up properly with current theory and practice. Linguistic isolation may still be a British characteristic, though no doubt the pace of events in the Europe of today will—given time—lead to a cure.

Where exactly do we stand in these islands? We now have a Chair in Scottish Ethnology, based on and in the School of Scottish Studies. The only direct equivalent is the Chair of Irish Folklore, held by Professor Bo Almqvist at University College, Dublin. England trails behind though all honour is due to the Centre for English Cultural Tradition and Language in Sheffield, led by Professor John Widdowson. For a time there was also the Institute of Dialect and Folk Life Studies at Leeds University, founded in 1960 as part of the English Department. Its Director was the School's former secretary and archivist, Stewart Sanderson. But in 1984 the Institute fell victim to the first round of the major reorganisation of the British university system, which in translation means government cuts—surely a concrete example of the negative impact of politics on the study of our cultural heritage. Not surprisingly, the Institute's organisational models were the School of Scottish Studies, the Department of Irish Folklore in Dublin and the Institute of Dialect and Folk Traditions in Uppsala (for some of the background see Lysaght 1990, 27-51; Lysaght 1993, 49-61; Sanderson 1991, 5-18).

The academic name of the subject was long a matter of debate. Names *are* important, as Professor Anthony Cohen, Department of Social Anthropology, made clear in his inaugural lecture on Rites and Identity, Rights of the Self on 22 November 1990. He spoke of names, naming and associated rituals in relation to the concepts of selfness and socialness, and the meaning of having a 'right to be oneself'. Translating this to the level of academic disciplines, I believe that ethnology has now gained the right to be itself, and in this the name itself plays a role. Efforts to find a generally accepted name and thereby an accepted identity have been part of the growth of the subject. But when the Institute in Leeds was being set up, Sanderson said of it: 'We felt we couldn't use the word *ethnology* in English studies, as we probably wouldn't have got that through the Senate and other committees' (J.F.I. VII, 2/3 (1970), 104).

If this was true of academic Britain in the 1960s, what of other parts of Europe? There was a multiplicity of names: the Scandinavian *folkliv* and its English parallel *folk life*, Germanic *Volkskunde*, the term *folklore* itself, the Greek-based *laography* and others. These were seen as concealing (as language differences helped to do also) what was recognised to be a substantive discipline of general validity. Scandinavian and Finnish scholars were amongst the first to grasp the nettle. At a joint meeting at Jyväskylää in Finland in 1969, it was agreed that 'etnologi' should replace 'folkliv' as the official academic term for the subject. Following this initiative, and influenced by it, German scholars undertook a plebiscite on the name, under the aegis of the Deutsche Gesellschaft für Volkskunde, in 1970. The conclusion was: 'The term "European Ethnology" appears to have a real chance of coming into common general use. It would be a great benefit in encouraging the better integration of national and regional "ethnologies", in stimulating associated comparative studies, in deepening the discussion on the theoretical side, and in defining the character and function of the subject. The great majority of the scholars and institutions that were consulted favoured the adoption of "European Ethnology", if not outright, at least as a by-name—for example, in German, "Volkskunde (europäische Ethnologie)". This is a compromise that preserves the "Volkskunde" tradition, and at the same time emphasises the international aspect of the subject. The widespread demand for an international term can now be realised' (Wiegelmann 1971).

There is still an aftermath of older terms in European countries, but the hoovering up of other terms by 'ethnology' has proceeded rapidly. Even in the USSR, the Ethnographical Institute in Moscow has just become the Institute of

Ethnology and Anthropology, and its journal, long edited by my old friend Kyril Čistov in Leningrad as *Sovietskaya Etnografia*, has become *Sovietskaya Etnologiya ii Antropologiya*. There is now an accepted general international name for the discipline. The cluster of older terms is becoming no more than a marker on the path of development. To this extent, in the identification of the 'selfness' of ethnology as a generally recognised discipline, the Rubicon has been crossed.

But not all the troops have crossed the bridgehead yet, and here I want to touch on a subject that could be as controversial as monetary union in Europe. What are we to do with folklore and all that it involves? Though enshrined in the title of the august Folklore Society, founded in London in 1878, it has never achieved full academic recognition, in spite of all the work and efforts of British folklorists (usefully summed up in Dorson 1968 (a) and 1968 (b)). Anthropology, for instance, did not open its doors to folklore, even though Sir Edward B. Tylor, first Professor of Anthropology in Oxford, was active at the same time as the Folklore Society was making its presence felt.

Striving for greater academic acknowledgement remains. An editor of a new journal, *Rural History: Economy, Society and Culture*, observed in 1989 that: 'for long the concerns of rural historians and folklorists have been separated, as if the study of virtually all aspects of folklore (particularly, for some reason, that of England) was considered something less than respectable . . . despite the fact that very original research has often been done by scholars with the expertise and breadth to incorporate folklore study into a wider disciplinary framework' (Snell 1989, 218).

Similarly, Professor John Widdowson, Sheffield, deplored the fact in 1990 that England had no major academic or public institution to 'function, amongst other things, as an official forum for fostering a sense of regional identity and a proper pride in community and in maintenance of tradition', though Scotland, Wales and Northern Ireland were better off (Widdowson 1990, 209). These are comments from a rural historian and a linguist. They demonstrate continuing unease, at least in England.

I should here clarify my own position, and in doing so may touch on the beginnings of a solution. As I see it, folklore is part of the wider field of ethnology as the term is now construed by agreement between European scholars. It is normal for any discipline to have branches within it, sometimes even substantial ones. Those who concentrate their work in such branches may well feel that they are concerned with the whole tree, whether they are or not. Of course there are differences in emphases between the study of spiritual or oral, and the material aspects of culture, but as often as not, these amount to technicalities. Put in an over-simplified way, you need a tape-recorder for one and a measuring tape for the other.

But objects can also be made to speak in their own way, like oral traditions. They have regional characteristics and individual properties due in part to techniques of use and resultant wear. They are themselves symbols that can be subjected to analysis. This need not be very different from that applied to songs, tales, proverbs, all the audible symbols of humankind. They can be used to interpret and re-interpret this history of cultural areas and of interactions between areas, as they are and as they have been changing through time in a continuous kaleidoscopic process. This is why I shall be doing my best to ensure that students in the School of Scottish Studies—on whom the future practice and development of the subject in Scotland depends—are given every opportunity to realise that major branches like folklore and material culture are not separable from the greater tree of ethnology, which is itself a part of the limitless forest of the cultural history of mankind.

The title I have chosen for my lecture is influenced by the inaugural lecture of my Danish equivalent in the University of Copenhagen, Professor Bjarne Stoklund. His title was 'European Ethnology between Scylla and Charybdis' (Stoklund 1971 and 1972). The Chair he took over, by the way, was founded in 1959 as the Chair in Material Folk Culture, but, soon after Stoklund took over from Professor Axel Steensberg in 1970, the name was changed to the Chair in European Ethnology. Nevertheless the Institute associated with the Chair has retained its older name: Institut for europæisk folkelivsforskning (Institute for European Folk Life Research).

Stoklund's inaugural lecture presented ethnology as a growing organism, still finding its feet in the world and surrounded by dangers. One of these, the Scylla of his title, was the danger of too-ready specialisation, or of too great concentration on narrow aspects, with research links only or mainly with like-minded colleagues at home and abroad practising similar methods of approach in the same or in related disciplines (Fenton 1985, 51). I do not think this is a real danger. It is, of course, entirely natural for scholars to get together to discuss their subjects, to exchange ideas, offprints and books, and generally to behave as active exponents of the subject they profess.

What was really troubling Stoklund was the way in which ethnology had hitherto developed, or had been practised, with strong emphases on the material and largely pre-industrial aspects of rural society. Rural society, it had been thought, was where the tradition bearers were to be found, where traces of the past in the present remained. Here survivals could be pin-pointed and used as indicators of western man's ascent from a more primitive to a more civilised status. Stoklund, as an ethnologist conscious of changing times, was deeply influenced in what he said by the need to take into account new circumstances. New methods of approach had to be found, more appropriate to an increasingly industrialised and urbanised society. There was also a need to adopt more theoretical approaches, though without being overwhelmed by the dangerous allure and generalising tendencies of the social sciences, which Stoklund saw as his Charybdis.

To put what he said into perspective for Britain—of which Scotland is part—we must look at the background to the development of ethnology. We may begin with eighteenth-century antiquarians, who related the concept of antiquities to 'physical and visual remains and scenes and to the memorials of the great rather than the lowly' (Dorson I (1968 (b)), 1). At the same time, they were also learning to stress the role of tradition, in particular oral tradition. This preserved the superstitious fancies of the common people, 'sharing with material remains the same character of misshapen fragments surviving from a bygone day'. A clergyman like John Brand, who wrote his *Observations on Popular Antiquities* in 1777, might view these with a degree of revulsion as 'pagan-Popish deviltries', though still mindful of Terence's dictum: *Homo* sum, *humani* nihil à me alienum puto (*Ibid*, I, 6, 12). That is a very good motto for an ethnologist.

Let me mention a somewhat unlikely bedfellow, Thomas Carlyle. His knowledge of German literature and thought undoubtedly gives him a claim to be the first systematic British ethnologist, whether he realised it or not. In his only novel, *Sartor Resartus* (1833), he actually developed an approach to a theory of material culture. He described his novel as a 'Satirical Extravaganza on Things in General'. It was allegedly his edited text of a disquisition on clothes by the learned Professor Diogenes Teufelsdröckh, entitled 'Die Kleider ihr Werden und Wirken'. Clothes, whether coverings for the body physical or as enfoldings of the human spirit, are used as a system of symbols to carry Carlyle's thought. He divides the work into two parts, one 'Historical-Descriptive' and the other 'Philosophical-Speculative'. The concept of collection and analysis as a basis for theoretical structure is, of course, not unfamiliar. Carlyle was in no doubt that the two went hand in hand. Theorists may build on theories, but the outcome will be weak if they have not first undergone the harsh discipline of assembling the infinite range of detail of their subject, and letting analysis of that dictate the lines of theory.

Another aspect of Carlyle's remarkable sense of awareness touches on changing fashions of thought, or what our accommodating English language calls Zeitgeist. Homer's Epos remains true, but it is not our Epos, not our truth. Its truth is of a different era. It has to be reinterpreted for succeeding generations (McSweeney and Sabor 1987, 170; Fenton 1990, 178-9). The development of any subject over a long period has to take into account changing fashions in human thought. We may never in reality be able to shake off the accumulated mental detritus of our educational system, or the pervasive influence of upbringing and environment, or the more or less subtle and continuous propaganda from the media. These prevent us from seeing clearly into the minds of people in periods that have passed, though we must always be prepared at least to try. Even if we are going no further back than to the eighteenth century, we can still distinguish three broad phases in the development of ethnology, each conditioned, as it were, by the Zeitgeist.

In summary, the first or antiquarian phase, which saw the coining of the word 'folklore' in 1846 and the foundation of the Folklore Society in London, ran through the materialism of the Victorian period and into the period between the two world wars. Scots did play a role—for example, Andrew Lang, with books like *Custom and Myth* (1901), and Arthur Mitchell, author of *The Past in the Present: What is Civilisation?* (1880)—but the period is generally marked by thinking that was British or even international in character, often deriving from or related to religious beliefs.

A second, more easily identifiable phase, can be labelled as one of national self-consciousness, with an increasing awareness of core-and-periphery interrelationships. It occupied the middle third of the twentieth century, and is marked by active collecting in the peripheries allied to the appearance of folk and open-air museums, academic institutes and 'folk life' societies, all influenced by Scandinavian models, and all seeking to identify the traditional characteristics of the regions they served.

The third phase covers the last two or three decades and has a very different character. There has been a turning away from rural-based pre-industrial concepts of what was 'traditional'. 'Contemporary documentation' is the buzzword, meaning the recording of and research into the lives and surroundings of working people in industrial and urban environments, often using techniques with which the sociologist will be familiar. The impetus, coming to Britain from Sweden, has gained a foothold in our museums, partly through the activities of the Social History Curators' Group and partly because so many local authority museums have lately been run by Labour-dominated local authorities. To this extent ethnology has developed an element of class-relatedness, which it should observe and analyse, without being swallowed up by it. As a working guide to the historiography of ethnology in Britain, we may sum up the three discernible phases as those of man, nation, class, though this is far too simplistic. Each phase runs into and overlaps with the other; and the model does not take account, as it should, of cross-class phenomena deriving from anxiety for our present-day environment.

Obviously, there is much work to do. The University of Edinburgh has given the opportunity by establishing the Chair of Scottish Ethnology. It is now up to me and my colleagues in the School of Scottish Studies to ensure that we breed a new generation of students able to cope with new approaches as well as understanding and using the old. We have to keep in close touch with international best practice. Ethnology, with its historical approach and its interdisciplinarity, is no easy option. It is a subject of infinite variety, with its own parameters. We are beyond the dangers that Professor Bjarne Stoklund envisaged. There is a vastly increasing demand for its services as new or renewed forms of national heritage are sought in Europe, based on accurately researched and not ideologically manipulated data. Ethnology is developing a sense of social purpose far removed from the romanticism of its formative period. As a subject, it has crossed the Rubicon.

REFERENCES

DORSON, RICHARD M.
1968 (a) *The British Folklorists*, London.

DORSON, RICHARD M.
1968 (b) *Peasant Customs and Savage Myths* (2 Vols.). Chicago.

E.E.
1967 *Ethnologia Europæa* 1.4; Introduction.

FENTON, ALEXANDER
1985 'The Scope of Regional Ethnology.' In A. Fenton, *The Shape of the Past 1. Essays in Scottish Ethnology*. Edinburgh.

FENTON, ALEXANDER
1990 'Phases of Ethnology in Britain. With Special Reference to Scotland.' *Ethnologia Europæa* XX 2: 177-188.

J.F.I.
1970 *Journal of the Folklore Institute*, Indiana University, VII, 2/3.

LANG, ANDREW
1901 *Custom and Myth*. London, New York and Bombay.

LYSAGHT, PATRICIA
1990 'Swedish Ethnological Surveys in the Western Isles of Scotland, 1939, 1948; Some Data from Ireland'. *The Review of Scottish Culture* 6; 27-51.

LYSAGHT, PATRICIA
1993 'Don't Go Without a Beaver Hat! Sean ó Sùilleabháin in Sweden in 1935.' *Sinsear. The folklore journal*, No. 7; 49-61.

MCSWEENEY, K. AND SABOR, P.
Ed. Carlyle, Thomas, *Sartor Resartus*, Oxford 1987.

MITCHELL, ARTHUR
1880 *The Past in the Present: What is Civilisation?* Edinburgh.

SANDERSON, STEWART
1991 'A Golden Chain: some Irish Folklore Connections.' *The Importance of Irish Folklore* (External Evaluations by Stewart Sanderson and John MacQueen. Lectures delivered at University College, Dublin, 23 September 1987), Baile Àtha Cliath, 5-18.

SNELL, KEITH D. M.
1989 'Rural History and Folklore Studies: Towards New Forms of Association.' *Folklore* 100/ii; 218-220.

STOKLUND, BJARNE
1971 'Europæisk etnologi mellem Skylla og Charybdis.' *Fortid og nutid,* XXXIV, 6; 659-670.

STOKLUND, BJARNE
1972 'Europäische Ethnologie zwischen Skylla und Charybdis.' *Ethnologia Scandinavica*, 3-14.

WIDDOWSON, JOHN
1990 'English Language and Folklore: A National Resource.' *Folklore* 101/ii; 209-220.

WIEGELMANN, GÜNTHER
1971 'Zur Benennung des Faches (Nachwort).' *dgv Informationen* No. 80. I.

'As Some of Your Own Poets Have Said . . .'

DONALD E. MEEK

[The following is the text of the sermon delivered by Dr (now Professor) Donald Meek at a church service in Greyfriars Tolbooth and Highland Kirk to mark the fortieth anniversary of the School of Scottish Studies in 1991. Because of a number of requests to see it in print, it is included in this volume of *Scottish Studies*.]

We meet this morning to commemorate, and even to celebrate, the fortieth birthday of the School of Scottish Studies. It is often said that life begins at forty, and so, if I am not mistaken, we not only commemorate and celebrate—we also anticipate, and look forward to many more years of the School's activities as an integral, but distinctive, part of the University of Edinburgh.

During these forty years, the School of Scottish Studies has established itself in the Scottish consciousness as a major cultural institution. Its collectors have been active throughout Scotland, from Shetland to Galloway, from Tiree to Arbroath, from Lewis to the Borders—active in the collection of the traditions of the Scottish people in several languages—Scots itself, English, Gaelic and other tongues. Its transcribers have spent hours transferring the spoken word to the written record. Its scholars have shared their insights into the nature of the tradition, its many varied forms and characteristics. The result has been that much that would have been lost for ever has been preserved, and the status of Scottish tradition has been enhanced.

It may appear to some a little incongruous that, although the School of Scottish Studies is not a religious institution, we should commemorate its achievements as we do today, in a religious context. It was not established to record specifically religious material, although it has certainly done that, in its tapes of hymns and Psalms and sermons; it has not sought any accommodation with any church; and its staff probably represent many shades of opinion in these matters. Nevertheless, we are gathered here today, as the School itself would wish, to give thanks to God for those forty years of activity.

It is, in my view, appropriate that we should do so. Whatever our opinion, we will, I trust, accept that there are times when sacred and secular can come together to their mutual advantage, and when both can be strengthened in the process. It is one of the sadder aspects of modern life that we tend to compartmentalise our activities, and, in so doing, separate sacred and secular. We can even construct walls between them, so high that few can climb from one compartment into the other. We who would make an open profession of religion must confess that we have been the builders of such walls, and that we have all too often policed them with vigour.

When we go back to the Scriptures with an open mind, we find some surprising interaction of sacred and secular at various levels. In Acts chapter 17, the Apostle Paul is in that great city of Greek culture, Athens. Here we see the Hebrew of Hebrews, the once-proud teacher of the Jewish law but now the zealous advocate of the resurrected Lord Jesus, crossing a cultural boundary into the philosophy and life of another people. His tactics and approach have much to tell us about his views on the relationship between sacred and secular culture. If we cast the Apostle in our own mould, we may come out with several interpretations, each as different from the other as we ourselves are. But I think that if we are faithful to the New Testament narrative, rather than to our own preconceptions, we will find that the Apostle is showing us very clearly that secular tradition has its own place in the purposes of God, and that it can be used to strengthen the sacred message that we would wish to transmit to others. In short, I would like to suggest to you that true, New Testament Christianity is not the enemy of the secular tradition, nor does it fail to accommodate it and appreciate it where appropriate.

I focus my attention on the remarkable phrase, used by the Apostle, ‘As some of your own poets have said’. As that phrase has reverberated through my mind in the last couple of weeks, I have been very much aware that we in Scotland have a rich heritage of poetry, as well as prose, in our several languages. We have heard the verse read in Gaelic; in Scots it reads, ‘een as some o your ain poets has said’. How appropriate, therefore, to anchor our thoughts in this phrase.

First, let us note that the Apostle was not, in fact, referring to any known Christian poets among the Greeks. He was here drawing on pagan, non-Christian tradition. The first quotation comes from the fourth line of a poem attributed to Epimenedes the Cretan (‘For in thee we live and move and have our being’) and the second from the Cilician poet, Aratus (‘For we are also his offspring’). Both poems had to do with Zeus, perceived as the Supreme Being of Stoic philosophy rather than the head of the Greek pantheon. This revelation may well surprise us, but, if it does, it will demonstrate only how unaccommodating we are in our interpretation of the New Testament. Paul the Apostle would readily confess that he was ‘debtor both to the Jews and to the Greeks’, and his debts to both cultures were extensive.

Let us not lose the significance of the Apostle’s use of Greek poetry. We can conclude that he is aware of the rhetorical force of using quotations which would be meaningful to his audience, and which would reinforce his own arguments that there is an ‘unknown God’ who can be known. But perhaps—and this is more significant—Paul is indicating that these pagan poets, in trying to establish the attributes of Zeus as Supreme Being, have glimpsed into two major aspects of God. The God who was unknown to the Athenians was not necessarily unknown, or at least totally unknown, to their Greek poets. What aspects of God had they perceived? They had perceived His role as the upholder of life—'In him we live and move and have our being'—and as the Father of humanity—'For we are his offspring'. These are the perceptions by which the Apostle is able to find common ground with the Athenians, and to press forward his argument about the Nature of God and the way in which He should be worshipped.

The Apostle's message to the Athenian philosophers is thus one which acknowledges their own rich tradition of poetry and thought. It does not belittle their culture. Paul does not engage in a bout of iconoclasm, destroying their idols by physical force or verbal abuse. Rather, he sees that deep in the hearts and aspirations of those people is a religious motivation. They are very religious. Religious in their own way, of course. They are devout, sincere people, but they have not captured the real fullness of the God who is the creator of the ends of the earth, 'who fainteth not, neither is weary'. Nevertheless, they are on the road to identifying the 'unknown god'—they are searching for him, and in the course of that search their poets have produced insights that are worth preserving and re-using.

Here we encounter a splendid principle of missionary endeavour in the cross-cultural context. It is one of respect for existing structures and existing views; it recognises what is good and re-uses it as a vehicle for portraying the Christian God. In the history of the British Isles, there have been times when missionaries used precisely this principle; they recognised that, even if the Fall had destroyed some of the image of God in His creation, yet glimpses of that image remained and it was possible for God to break through to the minds of men and women who hardly knew Him, but were nevertheless striving to know Him. Indeed, some of our own poets from the period of the early Irish Church operated along these lines, and produced hymns in praise of God which were filled with the images and concepts of the pre-Christian heroic period. They knew that these would resonate and make connections with a web of references from an earlier attempt to find a supreme being.

Of course, down through the ages there have been other views of non-Christian heritage, which have come into force as strong reactions against idolatry and secular paganism. All too often the iconoclasts have made a powerful impact, and have turned the Christian faith into a grim programme for the destruction of pre-existing culture. It is hardly surprising that people find this off-putting, and that the last thing they want to do is to find God, the true God. Seen in this context, the true God is the avowed enemy of their indigenous culture, and the words of His son, Jesus, may sound hollow—'I am come that they might have life, and that they might have it more abundantly'. When Jesus came to earth, he came to show that God could inhabit the most utterly human and distinctive aspect of human culture—the human body, which had been occupied by pagans and non-pagans, by rich and poor, by slave and free, by moral and immoral, by good and bad, across the centuries. When the Word became flesh and dwelt among us, what an investment that was in human culture!

Christian faith, in its real glory and beauty, is not the end of culture, but the beginning of a true appreciation of it. It is the beginning of a new discrimination, a new awareness. Paul knew well that the Athenians were already a discriminating and aware people; they spent their time discussing and debating, and he wanted that debate to go on, until their views were enlarged, and they could see the majesty and glory of the One True God. 'As some of your own poets have said'—ah, that was the way to lay the foundation of the argument, but he went on to show them more on that basis, and to explain the plan of God for the world.

What can we say of Paul that is relevant to ourselves? We can say that here was the Apostle of Christ, but here also the Apostle of the democratic intellect, the teacher who wanted to be relevant to the cultural circumstance. He knew that poetry was one of the great gifts of the Creator, and that the Creator could use it to His glory. It could be a step along the way towards an understanding of the ultimate revelation of God in Christ. Here we see the Christian Apostle open-mindedly taking a step into the pre-Christian world of his Athenian hearers. The question is whether we are as open-minded as he was, but prepared to move in the other direction, as we view the Christian message before us. Are we prepared to entertain even the possibility that God can be known to us?

Paul's readiness to employ the insights of the pagan poets of Greek culture is by no means an isolated example of the manner in which true New Testament Christianity harnessed and enriched the culture of its own day. Briefly, and in conclusion, I would point you to the example of the Lord Jesus Christ himself. As His earliest disciples, He chose some of the fishermen of Galilee, men who would have been filled with the tales and traditions of the fishing community; and as He communicated His messages about the immanence of the Kingdom of God, did He not employ parables and stories which were surely already part of the lore of the people? The Incarnation was intended not to impoverish, but to enrich, the whole of human culture.

Let us then pause this morning as we reflect on the heritage that we have received from those who have gone, that heritage which includes the riches of tales and poetry, of music and song—that heritage which has been transmitted by the ordinary men and women of past days. Is it not consistent with the Christian ethic to preserve it and to cherish it for the next generation, to let it breathe through the blanket of death-dealing snow which is the persistent enemy of our cultural distinctiveness? And is it not valid to see within some parts of it the strivings of the hearts of our own people for a meaningful encounter with God? We have had many poets in Scotland who have been overtly and unashamedly Christian too—our Dugald Buchanans and our Peter Grants and our Horatius Bonars. But there have been other poets also who have made no overtly Christian profession, but who have nevertheless glimpsed the reality of God in the world around them.

I close therefore by reading a poem by one of our own poets—a poet who composed in Gaelic, Scots and English, and who was no less familiar with Arabic and Italian and French and German and with the Scandinavian languages. That poet is the late George Campbell Hay. In this poem, Hay glimpsed the glory of God in creation as he saw a squall coming in from the west, and blotting out temporarily the rocky grandeur of the island of Arran:

THE BATTLEMENTS

Wondrous clouds are heaped aloft,
with a dark flush and a fierce swelling;
strong turrets, towers full of pride,
threatening banners, mist and rage.

Fearful darkness creeps before them,
and down out of them the lightning flashes;
they trail after them the grey rain
like a blinding curtain across the sea.

Yonder are waves and land, their colour lost,
blotted out by the torrent from the skies,
and gapped Arran gone under a cloak—
it is a terrible glory of the glories of God.

As one of our own poets has said, ‘a terrible glory of the glories of God’. Have we lifted up our eyes to see as he saw?

Amen.

ACKNOWLEDGEMENT

The translation of ‘Na Baidealan’ (The Battlements) quoted above is taken from D. MacAulay, ed, *Nua-Bhàrdachd Ghàidhlig: Modern Scottish Gaelic Poems*, Edinburgh 1974, 118-120.

Jewish Cuisine in Edinburgh

SUSAN STORRIER

INTRODUCTION

> 'As in any Jewish household, food was of prime importance. . . . There were the chickens and, of course, the eggs. The birds turned up at the table, meal after meal, but Mother, rather like an alchemist, succeeded in transforming them into all manner of dishes. . . . A special occasion would be the appearance of her marvellous borsch soup, made from beetroots. She used an old Eastern European recipe and I can still recall the taste today' (Denton and Wilson 1991, 18-19).

So writes Howard Denton in his autobiography *The Happy Land*. Denton's reminiscence is typical of many older Jews in the city of Edinburgh today, who look back with nostalgia and warmth on the food of their youth, remembering clearly a cuisine which was all their own and had little to do with the eating habits of the *goyim*, or non-Jews, amongst whom they lived. Things have changed and Jewish meals in Edinburgh can now often look very different to those dished up sixty years ago. Indeed, many other aspects of Jewish life in Scotland have been virtually transformed during the course of this century. It is the aim of this paper to give an overview of twentieth century culinary change and continuity within the Edinburgh Jewish community and to relate this to the general processes of cultural retention, adaptation and acculturation at work within the group.

Cuisine is a word with a considerable range of meanings and connotations. In academic terms, Rozin and Rozin have provided a succinct definition of cuisine as 'a culturally elaborated and transmitted body of food related practices' (1981, 243). Such a food related practice, be it an attitude or a mode of behaviour towards food and its selection, preparation and consumption, has been termed by some writers a foodway (Simoons 1967, 3). The particular pattern of foodways will be unique to any one culture group. Thus the terms 'cuisine' and 'foodways' are interchangeable. The study of a cuisine or set of foodways can produce some very useful insights for those interested in investigating the boundaries and nature of culture groups, and such insights can be used to complement, extend, verify or refute findings from other cultural indicators such as language, dress and belief.

Food, like the term cuisine, can mean different things to different people at different times. Aside from being the means of sustaining life, food can be used to express a vast array of cultural information. Perhaps one of its prime cultural functions is as a means of expressing personal and group identity. Ek-Nilsson claims that attitudes towards certain dishes show where one belongs culturally and socially (1981, 79), and it seems reasonable to suppose that this function of food is especially important if identity is perceived by those concerned as being under threat. Not surprisingly, foodways can often have most significance for members of immigrant and other minority groups. Recording the amount of change in foodways over time has been used to indicate the degree to which immigrant groups have retained or shed their culture of origin, and the extent to which acculturation has taken place (Theophano 1991, 44) and there seems no reason, at first glance at least, why this may not be appropriate in relation to the Edinburgh Jewish community.

Of course it is never advisable to draw conclusions about a culture group on the basis of one indicator alone. A study may seek to focus on foodways but it should not look at them in isolation, for culture groups are complex, multi-faceted phenomena. Rarely are all aspects of their being reflected in just one indicator, even if that indicator is a particularly useful one such as foodways. Bringéus (1970, 45) and Spiro (1955, 1240-1252), among others, claim that foodways are often the last culture trait to remain significant for a group. Although this investigation is in no way exhaustive, and indeed should be regarded as a preliminary study, efforts will be made to try to present culinary findings in the light of other types of cultural evidence and to make use of appropriate comparative material from similar communities in other parts of the world. Much of the information used was given by members of the Edinburgh community itself. To them I express my sincerest thanks for generously and kindly allowing themselves to be interviewed and sharing some of their rich body of knowledge and thought.

The Edinburgh Jewish community seems an ideal group on which to focus a study of both foodways and cultural change. Its small and dwindling numbers have been thought by some to make the community especially vulnerable to acculturation (Berman 1989, 11) and it is also apparent, even to an outsider, that Jewish communities the world over possess a fascinating and unique relationship with their food. Before looking at Edinburgh Jewish cuisine, however, an outline should be given of the history of the Jewish community in Edinburgh and the nature of the general Jewish relationship with food.

THE EDINBURGH JEWISH COMMUNITY

Edinburgh is home to Scotland's oldest Jewish community. In contrast to England, where the first Jewish communities were formed in the twelfth century under William the Conqueror, the first Scottish congregation of Jews or *kehillah* was formed in the capital city in 1816 (Phillips 1979, 1), when twenty or so Jewish families came together to employ a permanent minister, the Rev. Moses Joel of

London, to tend to their spiritual needs (Smith 1986, 20-22). That there was an earlier Jewish presence in Edinburgh is attested in the eighteenth-century burgh records (Daiches 1929, 197) which note a number of Jewish men operating on a temporary basis in the city as merchants and traders, despite being denied full merchant status as a consequence of their religious beliefs. This exclusion from the full commercial life of the city discouraged the domiciling of Jewish families in Edinburgh as did the unsettled economy of the country and the highly developed native mercantile infrastructure (Daiches 1929, 196-7). It was not until Jews were granted the same trading privileges as their native counterparts and the country had grown less turbulent and more tolerant in the nineteenth century that organised Jewish communities were to be found in Scotland.

The members of the early Edinburgh community came to Scotland either from England or, as was more often the case, from Holland, Germany and the Baltic ports. Once trading opportunities were fully granted, Edinburgh became an attractive place in which to establish a Jewish community—it had excellent links via the port of Leith (Fig. 1) with the Continent, and with the Baltic in particular, and had a large, relatively wealthy class of people who needed the services of skilled

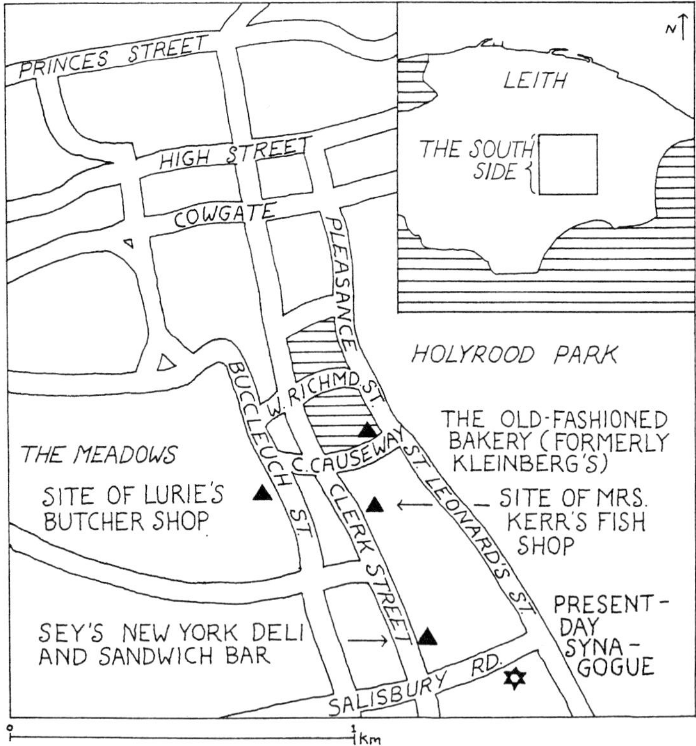

Fig. 1: The South Side of Edinburgh showing the location of the 'Happy Land' (shaded) and present-day synagogue with businesses serving the Jewish community past and present.

craftsmen. Such economic opportunities allowed the Jewish traders and artisans who settled in Edinburgh to achieve a greater degree of economic advancement than that obtainable in either English or continental settings, and this resulted in an early community which was characterised by modest affluence. The geographical focus for the community was the South Side of the city, especially the area known as the Happy Land, centred on the Pleasance and Richmond Street (Fig. 1). Here the community flourished and consolidated its position within wider society whilst remaining small in numbers (until the 1880s there were fewer than twenty Jewish families in Edinburgh). The picture is very much repeated in terms of Scotland's second Jewish community. A congregation of Jews was established in Glasgow in 1823, and although estimates of its size vary, it probably comprised between ten and twenty families. Situated on the north side of the River Clyde in the Garnethill area, this community also experienced a very slow rate of growth and a certain measure of prosperity and stability, coupled with easy relations with, yet cultural isolation from, the wider community. Both Scottish Jewish communities were very much integrated into wider Scottish society in economic terms whilst at the same time fully retaining their own Jewish cultural life. Both were also strictly Orthodox in belief. New forms of Judaism had been finding favour in England and on the Continent from the first decade of the nineteenth century but Scotland's communities were quite untouched by these innovations until the late nineteenth century and have indeed remained largely conservative in outlook to this day.

The Edinburgh and Glasgow communities were by far the largest Jewish communities in Scotland, but there was a number of other, smaller communities founded in Scotland in the period before the 1880s. A small congregation was established in Dundee in 1874 and a tiny community existed in Aberdeen also. However, neither of these flourished and today they have all but ceased to exist.

In the 1880s a new wave of Jewish settlers began to arrive in Scotland. Unlike the members of the early communities, these people often came to Scotland in a state of near destitution. They came from Eastern Europe—from parts of Poland, Lithuania, Latvia and Russia—and were in effect refugees, fleeing from religious persecution, conscription into the Tsar's army, and extreme poverty in their 'homelands' (Sachar 1988, 489-90). The US was seen as the 'Land of Opportunity' and arriving there was for many of these Yiddish-speaking East European Jews the ultimate goal. The cost of passage was high, however, and it was often necessary to stop en route to earn the required sum first. Britain, being relatively near, and prosperous at this time, proved the ideal stopping-off spot for such migrants, and central Scotland was especially attractive as a result of its abundant opportunities for unskilled workers in rapidly expanding industrial towns. Many of those who saw Scotland as a temporary base became permanent settlers, either because they found themselves trapped in a cycle of poverty which prevented them from amassing enough capital to cross the Atlantic, or because they did so well, working for others at first and then setting up their own businesses, that they felt their aspirations of prosperity and financial security fulfilled and saw no reason for uprooting themselves and their families once more to set off for the States.

Not all Yiddish-speaking Jews came to Scotland by default, of course. The country was a desirable enough location in its own right, with ample employment opportunities and pre-existing Jewish communities to provide practical, emotional and spiritual support. Glasgow, the 'Second City of the British Empire', had a manufacturing base and thus attracted many more migrants than did Edinburgh with its administrative and professional slant, but in both cities the Jewish population expanded quite astonishingly at this time, with the Edinburgh community rising in size to over 250 families, and Glasgow becoming home to nearly 16,000 Jews. In Edinburgh the community grew to such an extent that one synagogue was no longer adequate and several new congregations were formed. New Jewish bakers', butchers' and grocers' shops opened up for the community's use, all of them with a distinctly East European flavour.

The South Side of Edinburgh came in the late nineteenth century to house both the pre-existing community and the Yiddish-speaking Jews, and the two groups quickly blended into one cohesive whole. However, the East European flavour dominated and continues to do so to the present day. Indeed, the Pleasance area became something of a Yiddish *ghetto*, operating along the same lines as the original ghettos of Eastern Europe with their strong internal bonds (Roth 1960, 204-5), but without the same element of persecution from the wider community.

Relations between Jews and wider Scottish society have always been on the whole surprisingly harmonious, given that there was little cultural contact between the two groups until the 1930s. In Glasgow the older community in Garnethill also established close links with the new Yiddish-speaking community, situated in the Gorbals area to the south of the River Clyde, and again the East European influence came to dominate in a quiet but pervasive way (Rodgers 1982, 113-21). The degree of harmony and homogeneity of belief and political adherence displayed within Scottish Jewish communities was generally in contrast to the state of affairs within English Jewish communities such as those of Liverpool and London and the large Jewish communities of US cities where infighting and vigorous, often violent, disputes were a common feature of life.

The arrival of large numbers of immigrants in Scotland ceased after the passing of the 1905 Aliens Act, but Scottish Jewish communities continued to grow in size as a result of natural increase until the 1930s. Since then there have been several significant changes in the nature of Scottish Jewry. A continual loss of population from communities is evident as the Scottish economy has weakened and young Jewish Scots, in the same manner as other young Scots, have moved south to England or have gone abroad, especially to North America, to seek employment and educational opportunities. Estimates vary and include only those who attend synagogues, but today it seems the Edinburgh community contains around 400 members and Glasgow 3,000. It may be significant that, as early as 1932, a new synagogue was built at Salisbury Road (Fig. 1) to serve all Jewish religious needs in the city. The synagogue was the idea of Rabbi Salis Daiches, who was concerned with strengthening community cohesion by having all members worship under the same roof. However, it may be possible that dwindling numbers also played some role in prompting the formation of a single congregation. Over the course of the last sixty years the number of Jewish shops and other businesses has decreased considerably in both cities and there has been a continual movement out of the ghetto areas of the South Side and the Gorbals, and a geographical scattering of the communities as members have risen in socio-economic terms and have become more widely involved in tertiary education and in wider society in general. New Jewish institutions have been developed to cater for professionals and many young Jewish Scots are now highly educated, reside in suburban areas and live a life quite removed from that of their grandparents and, in some cases, even their parents.

It would be wrong to give the impression that the last sixty years of Scottish Jewish life have been characterised by nothing but decline, however. The 1930s saw the arrival of a small, third wave of Jewish immigrants in Scotland escaping Nazi persecution on the Continent. Nazism had the effect of clearing much of continental Europe of its large Jewish population and forcing those who were able to flee to the US or, as a second choice, Britain. The majority of those who came to the UK went to large English communities which housed non-Orthodox congregations and which presented healthy employment prospects. Those who did arrive and settle permanently in Scotland (some later moved on to the States) went mainly to Glasgow but a few joined the Edinburgh community, adding a new and quickly integrated dimension to Jewish life in the capital with their more radical views on Judaism.

Until the 1940s the Edinburgh community was almost exclusively Ashkenazi, that is, belonging to the Northern European Jewish tradition (the term 'Ashkenazi' coming from the Hebrew word for 'German'). After that date, however, small numbers of Jews from the other Jewish mainstream tradition, that of Sephardim, and other parts of the world, began to join the Edinburgh community, often attracted to the city by its universities and colleges. The Sephardim ('Sephardi' meaning in Hebrew 'Spanish') belong to a tradition established in the sixth century BC when the first Holy Temple was sacked in Jerusalem by the Babylonians and Jews were forced to flee to what is today Spain (Sephardi Sisterhood 1971, Intro. E). The tradition was subsequently carried to many parts of the Mediterranean, Near East and India after the expulsion of the Jews from Spain and Portugal in the fifteenth century. More recently Sephardi communities have been established in the US and England, and now a number of Sephardi Jews live in Edinburgh along with American and Israeli Jews of various traditions and religious persuasions. It has been estimated by one informant that around eighty members of the present-day community are first-generation migrants and clearly these people together form a substantial minority. However, the dominant flavour of the Edinburgh, and indeed Scottish, Jewry remains Ashkenazi, and East European Ashkenazi at that, despite the fact that Scottish communities now have links with most other types of Jewish community to be found in the world.

JEWISH FOOD AND BELIEF

In most Jewish communities, Ashkenazi or not, there are very close and special links between food, belief, identity and community. It is belief, along with its associated practices, including food practices, which has primarily defined Jewish communities, and food has played a vital role in maintaining Jewish religious and secular identity and community life throughout the centuries. Judaism is very much a family and home-based religion and therefore it is not surprising that great emphasis has been put on that prime home-based activity of food preparation and consumption. Eating and religion are very closely tied together. A series of edicts relating to diet—collectively known as *Kashrut*—have been codified into Jewish Orthodox religious practice. Kashrut can be important in terms of secular identity for it helps Jews to be constantly aware of belonging to a distinct group and helps maintain close relations within the group. Jewish authors have explicitly discussed such matters in their writings. Fishman (1958, 104) claims '. . . the dietary laws . . . distinguish us from other peoples and prevent us from assimilating with them. So they have been vital for preserving the identity and purity of the Jewish race', whilst the authors of the Jewish students' handbook *Keeping Kosher on Campus* (Union J.S. 1991, 2) are of the view that 'somehow an awareness of others who operate within identical and very specific parameters creates a strong bond of kinship and fosters a sense of community'. Adherence to Kashrut is shared by all Orthodox communities. Carr and Oberman state in relation to the dietary laws that they are the foundation on which all Jewish cooking is built irrespective of the country in which the cook is living (1973). Kashrut is the important element, and theoretically speaking at least, other aspects of cuisine do not matter. Jewish cooking is therefore not like any single national cooking style (Carr and Oberman 1973, 6), and the exact configuration of foodways will vary from community to community. Orthodox Jews are free to pick up the traditions of wherever they are living as long as they adapt them to fulfil the requirements of the dietary laws. For that reason one finds that many of the foods traditionally eaten in the Jewish communities or *shtetls* of Poland, Lithuania and Russia were typically East European and were not confined solely to the Jewish community. Over the centuries of the *Diaspora*, or scattering of the Jewish people, Jewish communities have ceased to use Middle Eastern foods and have become accustomed to using instead the foods of their adoptive 'homelands'. This is true not only for the Ashkenazim, as the Sephardim have a long tradition of making dishes from the various areas, such as the Mediterranean, in which they settled. Wherever Diaspora communities have been in the same location for an extended period of time we find the unselfconscious use of local culinary traditions in combination with Kashrut. In Eastern Europe things might not always have been pleasant, or even safe, but at least Jewish communities there were of long standing and were relatively stable and enabled Jewish cuisine to become in many respects almost identical to that of wider society.

The nature of Kashrut requires an albeit brief description if its full significance is to be appreciated. Essentially it comprises a list of prohibited and permitted foods, with instructions for the preparation and consumption of the latter. The laws are based on various edicts in the *Torah*, the first five books of Moses, known to Christians as part of the Old Testament. Much of Kashrut is concerned with meat consumption. The complex rules have been built up around flesh eating in particular because Judaism considers it a moral compromise for man to eat meat, to take the life of another living creature and as such meat consumption should not be an easy, unthinking matter. As is well known, certain mammals may not be consumed—notably the pig—but all other animals which cannot be said to be both cloven hoofed and to chew the cud are also considered unfit for consumption and are termed *trefah* or *treif* (literal meaning 'torn'). Even with those animals which do fulfil the requirements, care must be taken to ensure that they are slaughtered in the correct ritually sound way by a rabbinically trained butcher or *shochet*. An animal which has died of natural causes cannot be eaten. The ritual method of slaughter helps rid the animal's carcass of as much blood as possible, for there is a strong aversion to blood within the Jewish tradition. There are further requirements, such as the removal of certain veins (the process of removing these veins being known as *porging*) and certain types of fat, which must again be carried out under religious supervision. Meat which has been slaughtered in an appropriate way still cannot be eaten until it has been *kashered* or *koshered* (made fit for consumption) by being soaked and salted to remove any blood lingering in the flesh. In the normal course of events, until very recently at least, it was the housewife who undertook the duty of kashering the meat to be consumed in her home. Kashered meat may not be eaten with milk or cooked with any milk product. Fully Orthodox households will have two separate sets of kitchen utensils, crockery and cutlery, and even perhaps separate sinks so that meat and milk never come in contact with each other.

The laws surrounding the consumption of fowl are similar. Their flesh cannot be eaten with milk and only certain domesticated species may be consumed. Fish are a much easier form of flesh to consume as they require no special preparation or means of killing. The single requirement is that only species with fins and proper scales be eaten—for that reason shellfish are not kosher and are avoided with great care in the Orthodox diet. No insects, reptiles or any 'crawling thing' may be consumed. There are few restrictions in connection with eggs, and there are no restrictions on the eating of fruit and vegetables which may be consumed freely at both meat and milk meals. The same generally applies to cereals and distilled alcoholic drinks, although certain types of grain and grain products must be avoided for one week of the year. Wine and grape juice must be made under rabbinical supervision and be declared kosher.

Wine plays a very significant role in Jewish festival, but food is just as important. During certain festivals particular foodstuffs are prohibited, whilst certain others are prescribed either by religious law or by religious tradition, or by secular tradition. In the latter case the exact foodstuffs eaten will vary from community to community. One of the mot important festivals in the Jewish year is the seven- or eight-day-long celebration of *Pesach* or Passover in spring (seven days in Israel, eight in Diaspora communities). This festival celebrates the liberation of the Jewish people from their captivity in Egypt and its fundamental focus is God's love for His people. It is not surprising therefore that Passover has a central role to play in Jewish religion and in Jewish custom and family life. The religious regulations relating to Passover are many and it will only be necessary to outline some of the more important food-related ones here.

The days of Passover see the eating of unleavened bread (a symbol of the haste with which the Jewish people left Egypt) and consequently all leaven must be removed from the homes before the week begins. The prohibition extends to the consumption of foods which might ferment easily, so that wheat and many other types of cereal cannot be eaten during this period.[1] Indeed, all food eaten during this festival should have been produced under rabbinical supervision so that there is no danger of accidental contamination. This obviously poses a great challenge to the women who have until very recently been solely responsible for food preparation in the home. The loss of staples such as bread and flour has been overcome by the substitution of *matzo* meal (a ground-up, unleavened wheat biscuit which because it is pre-baked does not ferment), used throughout the world in a variety of ingenious ways.

The most important event of the Passover week is known as the *Seder*. This is a service conducted at home on the first one (Israel) or two (Diaspora communities) nights of Pesach (Fishman 1958, 65) at which parents narrate the events of the Exodus to their children over a ritual meal of freedom (Daiches 1975, 35). Many of the foods eaten at the Seder meal have been laid down by rabbinical law since time immemorial. Three unbroken pieces of matzo must be laid out on the table alongside a special platter containing a roasted egg, a roasted lamb shank bone, horseradish root (bitter herbs) and chervil, parsley, or lettuce, a small amount of a wine, fruit and nut mixture called *charoset* and a small basin of vinegar or salt water. Each of these foodstuffs helps to remind the gathered family members of the deliverance of their forefathers from slavery. For example, charoset is a reminder of the loam mixed with straw for Pharoah's buildings, or is sometimes interpreted as the mortar used by the Israelites (Bokser 1963, 112). In addition to the foods on the table, wine is present and each person is required to drink four glasses of it during the meal, young children sometimes having grape juice instead.

There are several other important festivals throughout the Jewish year at which the nature of the food eaten is dictated by religious law and custom. *Rosh Hashanah* or Jewish New Year can take place any time between the first week of September and the beginning of October. At this celebration sweet foods such as honey are eaten before the main meal to symbolise hopes for a sweet new year. Fish heads may sometimes be served also to symbolise being on top of life. *Hannukah*, the Festival of Lights, celebrates over an eight-day period, usually in December, an important victory of the Israelites over their oppressors as well as the rededication of the Holy Temple in Jerusalem and the lighting of oil lamps within it (Carr and Oberman 1973, 130; Shapira 1989). The celebratory meal on the last day of the festival includes doughnuts and other fried foods in remembrance of the holy oil used in the temple. *Shavvuoth*, Pentecost, is a two-day festival which takes place seven weeks after the second day of Pesach and sees the serving of milk foods and fruit. It has close associations with the wheat harvest and first fruits.

One of the most important of Jewish festivals takes place not annually, but rather every week. This is *Shabbat* or the Sabbath—a day of rest which begins at nightfall on Friday and ends at nightfall on Saturday. The evening on Friday is the highlight of the week, being a time when the family comes together to share a celebratory meal. A blessing with wine is said and an ample meal is eaten. Two twisted loaves of rich white egg bread (*challah* loaves) are present on the table and play an important part in the ritual aspect of the meal (Plate 1). They symbolise the double portion of manna which on Friday was provided for the Israelites in the wilderness to last them two days (Shulman 1988, 5). The loaves are presented side by side with a napkin over them. The man of the house blesses the bread and will cut off some of it, add salt to it (a reminder of God's statement to Adam—'By the sweat of your brow you shall eat bread') (Shulman 1988, 5) and divide it among the company.

JEWISH FOOD IN EDINBURGH

In the past, all these festivals, plus numerous others, would have been observed in Edinburgh in full accord with Judaic law and tradition. First generation Yiddish-speaking Jews in Scotland would have celebrated festivals to exactly the same extent as they did in their homelands. They would also have celebrated them in an identical manner in terms of secular custom, with the foodstuffs traditonally eaten in, say, Russia or Poland appearing on festive tables in the South Side. The same held true for non-religious celebrations and events such as betrothals, weddings and funerals, and indeed everyday fare was very much akin to that dished up in Eastern

Europe. Jewish life in Edinburgh from the 1880s to the 1930s was very much a reproduction of life in Eastern Europe, and this desire by migrants to recreate an old, familiar environment in as complete a way as possible in new and unfamiliar surrounds can be seen in relation to many other groups. Despite the fact that those living in the ghettos or shtetls of Eastern Europe had always been marginalised and often victimised by wider society, and that the Jewish people as a whole perceived themselves as wanderers still seeking the Promised Land, there was a sense of belonging and of stability in the old communities which made leaving and coming to Britain or the States a very traumatic experience for many. Such an experience no doubt helped to strengthen the notion of an Eastern European homeland and did much to temper people's memories of life there.

Foodways were very much part of the process of making the strange familiar and food in Scotland took on a new significance for Jews. Formerly, observance of Kashrut was instrumental in maintaining Jewish religious identity. In Scotland food continued to play this role for it remained strictly kosher, but in addition food strengthened secular Eastern European Jewish cultural identity by reminding immigrants of the way of life of the shtetl—a way of life they came to see as being as important in defining their own identity as Judaism itself. Indeed the culture of the shtetl came to be a symbol of Jewishness in western consciousness (Daxelmüller 1986, 104). Salomonsson, quoting Borda, states that 'national foods' are a means of identification for people in an alien setting (1984, 38) and this certainly seems to hold true for the Jews in Edinburgh. By their sheer strength of numbers, the customs and traditions of the former shtetl dwellers came to be known, and to a large extent adopted, by virtually all Jews in Scotland in the late nineteenth century. Foods such as pickled herring and ryebread became as much a symbol of Jewishness in Edinburgh as going to the synagogue, or keeping Passover. The symbolic value of eating such foods is attested in David Daiches' autobiography, *Two Worlds*, where he relates how his grandfather, who admittedly was resident in England, would have an aperitif of cognac, sliced pickled herring and dark ryebread before each and every one of his main meals (Daiches 1975, 89).

Much care was taken over food preparation by Jewish housewives in Edinburgh, as indeed in other Jewish communities throughout the world. The creation of a nutritious, inexpensive and interesting menu which was fully observant of Kashrut was a great challenge to the cook's skill and provided many women's main form of creative and religious expression at this time. Women's role in the public religious life of the synagogue was minor in comparison to men's, and their domain was very much within the home. Certainly some women must have found this prescribed role difficult, in conflict with their own desires and personalities, but the central position of Kashrut to Judaism ensured that women were regarded with great respect because of the domestic arena in which they worked. Many older members of the present-day community in particular speak with awe and admiration of their mothers' cooking, which was a focus for family life and participation in religion. Many of the changes which have arisen in recent years in relation to food within the Edinburgh community stem in part from changes in women's roles and their attitudes and aspirations towards their lives, and especially towards their homes and religion.

The greatest culinary effort was made in relation to special meals, and the typical menu of a celebratory meal in Edinburgh at the turn of the century is impressive in its ingenuity. Traditions varied in detail from family to family of course. Evelyn Cowan states, in relation to the Glasgow community, that there was a great rivalry between the Litvak and the Polish Jews in terms of cooking (Cowan 1974, 74), and there seems no reason to believe that this should not have occurred in Edinburgh given the other shared characteristics of the communities. Nevertheless we can make some generalisations. The Pesach Seder would see a meal in which either chopped liver, chicken or fish would be an important element; all three were important in other celebratory meals and, for those wealthy enough to afford them, could also be used as everyday fare. Chopped liver would be akin to paté and chicken was usually served plainly roasted or in the form of soup. Celebratory fish could comprise thinly sliced smoked salmon, or less luxuriously (or for midweek meals), fried white fish. A favourite fish dish for the Seder and also for weddings, betrothals and bar mitvahs—confirmation ceremonies for boys—was *gefilte* fish (like many culinary terms a Yiddish word). This dish of minced fish flesh, vegetables and seasonings shaped into balls and sometimes stuffed back into the fish skin and poached in stock, has clear Eastern European origins and has come to be seen as the classic Ashkenazi dish, popular wherever Ashkenazi Jews now reside, including Israel. Certainly the recipe helps to impart flavour to bland species of fish. Scottish Jewish housewives were forced to substitute haddock and other white salt water fish for the pike or carp of Eastern Europe because such fresh water fish simply was not available in local fish shops. The community had no fish shop of its own to supply the traditional species and instead made do with what was available in Mrs Kerr's fish shop in South Clerk Street in the South Side which was for long heavily dependent on Jewish custom despite the fact that the shop was not owned and run by Jews. Even at this early stage therefore we see the beginnings of localisation of Jewish cuisine in Edinburgh with the substitution of ingredients. This is further borne out by the fact that often the gefilte fish balls were fried in Scottish homes rather than boiled as they would have been in Eastern Europe. Jewish housewives soon picked up on the Scottish love of fried food and incorporated that cooking technique to a greater extent than ever before into their own cusine. Such taking on board of minor aspects of the wider society's cuisine seems to accord with the general level of interaction between the two groups at this time, with contact being present but only at the formal level.

Throughout Pesach, excluding the Seder itself, food would generally comprise a slightly richer version of the everyday diet, with matzo meal and crackers replacing the usual breads and flours, etc. Soups would normally be enriched during Pesach by the addition of thin strips of omelette or noodles termed *lochshen* or *lokshen* (sometimes used in ordinary meals) or by matzo meal balls, and many sweet treats were made with baking sometimes beginning a week before the festival started. Macaroons, sponge cakes, *imbers* (carrot and ginger sweets) and *eingemachts* (a beetroot preserve) would all be manufactured by the housewife at this time (Bullon 1990).

Rosh Hashanah in Edinburgh often saw the consumption of traditional East European honey cake and various apple dishes, such as strudel. At Shavvuoth a rich cheesecake would be served, or cream cheese *blintzes* or *glinches* (pancakes), or cheese tarts. *Teiglach* (nuts in a dough with a thick syrup) were also popular. Hannukah was characterised by the consumption of *latkes* (fried potato cakes).

Friday night saw the housewife pulling out all the stops in culinary terms with the meal comprising several courses. Often a chicken soup was served first or *borsht,* a beetroot soup sometimes served with sour cream if there was no meat included in the meal, and this would be eaten along with the challah loaves. A roast stuffed chicken, cabbage stuffed with meat, matzo meal, vegetables and seasoning (*holishkes*), eggs and onions, or fish in some form might follow. Potato salad was a favourite side dish, as were honeyed carrots (*zimmes*). Dessert would often have to be milk-free and was usually very sweet, with dishes like apricot whip, apple strudel, and almond biscuits being very popular. If one is to observe Shabbat in the full Orthodox manner there should be no lighting of fires from after dark on Friday to dusk on Saturday. This means that Saturday lunch and often the evening meal as well will have to be cold or else, if a hot meal is deemed necessary, a way has to be found round the restrictions. In Eastern Europe during the severe winters cold food, such as cold cuts of salt beef, tongue and chicken or cold fried fish and salads which typified the summer Shabbat menu were not really adequate. A hot meal was essential and one way of obtaining this was to put a slow cooking stew on the back of the stove and leave it there from Friday afternoon to lunchtime on Saturday. The meal was hot but allowed the housewife to avoid having to actually light a fire during the Sabbath. Often such stews were made with beans and cereals alongside a small amount of meat, and were filling fare. The best known of these stews was *cholent,* a hearty stew made most often with onions, carrots, potatoes, seasoning, a little fatty meat and haricot beans or barley (recipes varied from family to family). Sometimes a large dumpling was cooked in with it. Such bean stews were widely eaten in Eastern Europe and not just by Jewish communities, but the very slow cooked version was very much a Jewish speciality and in Edinburgh cholent continued to be a regular feature in the winter menu, despite the milder winters which made the consumption of cold food less of a hardship. The traditional accompaniment to the Shabbat stew was lokshen or noodle kugel—wheat noodles with breadcrumbs, eggs, seasoning and animal fat which again was put on the stove on Friday afternoon and left to cook very gently until Saturday lunch. Dessert would be cold, often along the same lines as the Friday night sweets.

Aside from fish, fruit and vegetables, everyday basic foods (to a greater degree than even festive and celebratory fare) could often only be purchased from the specialist grocer, butcher and baker shops set up by the community to supply its own needs. A considerable number of these outlets existed in early twentieth-century Edinburgh. Until the last decade or so, when the community became too small to support them, several remained in operation, providing the community with East European staples, kosher meats and wines and, almost as importantly, a place where Jews, especially women, could meet informally and exchange news. Kleinberg's the bakers in Crosscauseway in the South Side was a renowned meeting place, where fresh kosher bread, cakes, pastries and biscuits could be purchased and neighbours would meet. The shop was also popular with non-Jews seeking fresh-baked goods on Sunday morning. Joshua 'Joe' Lurie's kosher meat shop in Buccleuch Street was another landmark and focus for informal community activity which sold kosher wines and margarine in addition to meat (it closed in the late 1980s). At the grocers, items such as ryeflour, matzo meal and pickled herring were bought as staples. Weekday foods and dishes included *sauerkraut* (or pickled cabbage) which was regularly consumed, and pickled cucumbers and beetroot as well as bean, cabbage or lochshen soups (often served with *kneidlach*, dumplings). *Chremslach* (matzo meal pancakes) were enjoyed not only during Pesach, and housewives who chose to do so could make their own numerous kinds of delicious homemade cakes and biscuits, as well as plainer but equally appetising *bagels* (parboiled white wheatflour rolls) (Figs 2 & 3). Omelettes and stuffed vegetables were good substitutes for meat dishes during the week. *Kreplach*, egg and flour dumplings filled with meat and onions, were a way of making a little meat go far in true universal peasant fashion. Indeed the relatively low level of meat consumption amongst the Edinburgh Jews is itself an important factor in differentiating the community in culinary terms from the rest of Scotland's urban population, who, even if they could scarcely be accused at the turn of the century of over consumption of meat, especially good quality meat, nevertheless consumed ample quantities of sausages and minced beef unless of the lowest economic means. While most of the wider Edinburgh community were well accustomed to a high fat, and relatively high protein, diet typical of urban areas across Western Europe in the later industrial period, the residents of the 'Happy Land' retained fully their East European peasant-style, time-consuming cuisine with large quantities of carbohydrates used in combination with small amounts of animal protein.

There were, however, a few small moves towards the adoption of the wider community's eating habits in the early years of the Edinburgh Jewry. Although families would generally never have considered 'eating out' in restaurants and cafés,

Fig. 2: *Challah* loaf used during the Friday evening *Shabbat* meal. Such loaves are usually around fifteen inches long and weigh at least two lbs. each. This example came from The Old Fashioned Bakery. (*Photo: Ian MacKenzie*)

Fig 3: *Bagels*. These white wheatflour rolls are becoming increasingly popular with the wider community. On display are (clockwise from top) a plain bagel, poppy-seed bagel, raisin bagel and a sesame seed bagel from Sey's New York Deli and Sandwich Bar. Bagels are usually three to four inches in diameter. (*Photo: Ian MacKenzie*)

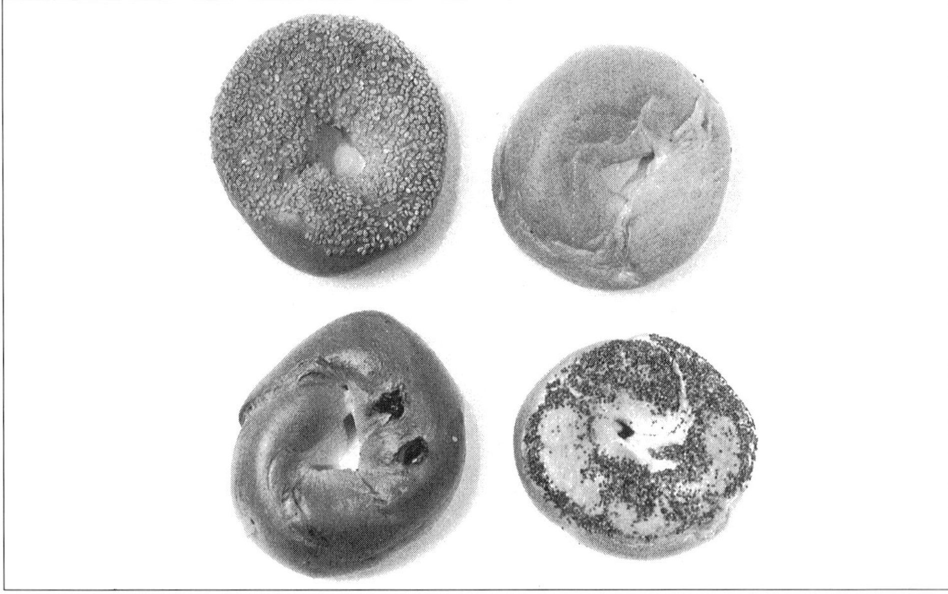

Scottish-style foods did find their way in small quantities into Jewish homes. Kleinberg's the bakers made kosher drop scones and tea breads, as well as the Jewish strudels and honey cakes. David Daiches relates how winter teas in his childhood (in the 1920s) were a mixture of Scottish and Jewish traditions, where scones and jam were served alongside traditional Jewish specialities (Daiches 1975, 169). Daiches' father was the community's rabbi and the family had perhaps more contact with the wider Edinburgh society than did many others (they also lived outwith the Pleasance area), but most Jewish families would have sampled Scottish specialities from time to time, provided of course that they were in accordance with the dietary laws. If eating in the 'Happy Land' was very much determined by tradition this need not imply that housewives and bakers were not interested in experimentation and innovation, on a modest scale at least. The Jewish community in Edinburgh until the 1930s was aware of, and interested in, the wider community's food traditions but the important point to note is that Scottish-style foods were minor in importance at this time and were often seen as treats and fancies whilst the basic diet remained firmly East European.

This situation was to change, of course, and after the 1930s two new emphases were increasingly felt in Jewish cuisine in Edinburgh: the intrusion of non-ethnic foods and a decline in observance of Kashrut.

(1) Intrusion of Non-ethnic Foods

In the sixty years following 1930 the importance of East European food and dishes gradually diminished whilst the wider community's eating habits became less peripheral and versions of the dishes which were popular throughout urban Scotland increasingly found their way into Jewish homes. General Scottish eating habits have, of course, themselves changed dramatically throughout the period from the early 1940s to the present, primarily as a consequence of ease of travel, which has allowed people to sample, much more than ever before, other cultures and their cuisines. Foods and dishes which had come to be seen as traditional in Scottish urban contexts during the industrial period were first augmented in the 1960s and are now almost totally replaced by a form of international cuisine which can be found across Europe and North America. Children of Jewish immigrants in Edinburgh have tended to eat more of the wider community's food than their parents did and have less reliance on Eastern European specialities. More so their grandchildren, today's young adults, who are likely to make use of East European dishes only on occasion, and certainly not as the main component of their daily fare.

Significantly, it is in the realm of everyday diet that the changes have been felt most. Festivals and celebrations still see the consumption of the same dishes made by the first Yiddish-speaking Jews in Edinburgh by their descendants. Great importance is placed on these by older people especially. This using of forebears' recipes for special occasions and times is seen among Jews from different traditions in the community. Sephardi housewives, for example, will make Mediterranean dishes of stuffed vegetables and rice for Friday evenings and for weddings, Pesach and the occasional week-day meal. Even the youngest adults in the present-day community will know about foods such as cholent and gefilte fish from eating these dishes on the Sabbath or during festival and from hearing their parents and grandparents reminiscing about them, although such dishes may not have the same significance for them as they do for their parents. Young people may even eat traditional foods fairly regularly if living with elderly parents or grandparents (older members of the community generally use the old recipes more on an everyday basis and have not taken up the new eating habits. The lunch club at the synagogue, which caters for old folk, serves very traditional foods and dishes such as lochshen pudding). Some young adults will know how to prepare the old dishes in the time-honoured fashion, but few will actually make foods such as chremsach and kreplach on a regular basis to eat on a weekday. Instead they will make dishes very similar to those of the wider community, international in nature and quick and easy to prepare. There is still plenty of knowledge of old Eastern European foods within the younger age-groups of the community but little everday experience of them, although as ever it must be remembered that the situation varies very much from person to person.

We can discern here a progression through the decades of this century, and more importantly through the generations (for one's dietary habits seem, in respect of ethnicity at least, to be often dependent on one's generational distance away from arrival from Eastern Europe and not on how long one has lived outside of Eastern Europe), from a diet almost identical to that of Eastern Europe with just the occasional substitution of ingredients and experimentation with cooking techniques, and infrequent treats of Scottish dishes (generally adopted by those born in Eastern Europe—now very old, if alive at all), through an intermediary stage where everyday cuisine is increasingly similar to that of the wider community but some traditional dishes are still made and festival foods remain very much East European and are valued as such (children and grandchildren of those born in Europe—old and middle-aged people), to the most recent situation whereby the everyday diet is virtually identical to that of the wider community and festival foods, although still traditional, have less significance for the individual (middle-aged and young adults). If one is to project this trend into the future, it does not seem unreasonable to suppose that the children of today's young adults may place even less emphasis on eating traditional foods at festivals, and indeed some may choose in the future to eat completely non-traditional foods on such occasions.

It is tempting to explain the above progression as a manifestation of acculturation; the gradual loss of a group's own cultural traits and the adoption of those belonging to another, usually larger group. It certainly seems to be the case that often immigrant groups lose most of their unique cultural markers, including even foodways, after three generations or so. Each generation feels a greater familiarity with the wider community and a greater sense of social and often economic security, and they are able to identify more and more with the larger group and need rely less on their own group. Language becomes the language of the majority, the physical and mental ghetto ceases to exist, community members are employed in diverse occupations, rates of out-marriage increase and, finally, eating habits become those of the wider community. Significantly, when food does begin to change it is in the arena of the everyday that innovations are first felt while festivals and other special occasions, where group members assemble and the concept of group identity has most significance, retain links with the past for the longest time. The final stage of acculturation is where even festival foods become those of the wider community, and it would seem that the Edinburgh community is nearly at that stage now. Certainly, little Yiddish is spoken, and people live scattered throughout the city, working often in the professions, whilst increasingly marrying non-Jews and occasionally having, as one informant claims, 'purely gastronomic ties to the community', which are often only manifest on special occasions. The small and shrinking size of the community might be thought to make it particularly susceptible to influence from the wider community, and Benski (1981, 307-19) has outlined similar changes in regard to the much larger Glasgow Jewish community and sees these as being symptoms of the process of acculturation.

However, it is apparent to anyone in the least familiar with the Edinburgh Jewish community that the situation at present is exceedingly complicated, and cannot easily be attributed to one process. From discussions with community members, and scrutiny of comparative material, it seems that numerous factors and processes may be at work. A short paper like this cannot hope to investigate all of these factors and processes, but it can highlight a few of the more important ones.

Several points can be noted which help counter the idea of acculturation being the sole process responsible for change in Edinburgh Jewish cuisine and Edinburgh Jewish life in general. For a start, many of the changes which have taken place in the community have been paralleled by change in wider Scottish society. The increased use of Standard English, increased access to tertiary education, greater variety of employment options, increased rates of marriage with people from beyond one's own locale, and new eating habits, often as a result of new roles for women, are all realities for most urban Scots today. What the Jewish community is experiencing therefore may be more a case of modernisation than acculturation.

It must also be remembered that there is a perfectly reasonable precedent for a pattern of transformation within the context of secular Jewish culture, which as stated previously, need not imply any loss of Jewishness nor even indicate modernisation. This is the tendency to adopt the broad aspects of life in the host country whilst at the same time maintaining Jewish religious belief to the full. In terms of food, this means eating the wider society's foods, but adapting them to fulfil Kashrut. It is now quite possible, and indeed natural, for Jews to eat Scottish food and be true to their religious traditions and identity whilst at the same time moving away from an East European secular cultural identity and set of eating habits. Judaism, or Jewish religious identity, was for long characterised by a lack of radical change and was largely independent of the attendant and changeable secular Jewish cultural identity. Such a bipartite sense of identity was simply a response to Diaspora conditions which forced Jews to live in environments where it was impossible to retain a Middle Eastern secular cultural identity, but where it was absolutely vital to maintain religious identity. Jewish foodways have reflected this dualism so that although foodways can experience change in new environments, the fundamental principle on which they are founded, Judaism and Kashrut in particular, remains.

Religion is the stock from which a new Scottish Jewish cultural identity can sprout. If one is able to discern full maintenance of Jewish religious identity in Scotland, and specifically, a trend towards the creation of a Scottish kosher diet, one can further reduce the case for acculturation. What then is the state of present-day dietary law observance in Scotland?

(2) Decline in Observance of Kashrut

The situation in relation to Kashrut in Scotland is far from straightforward at the present time and bears discussion. In broad terms, there has been a decline in the observance of Kashrut. This is not the case in relation to all of the community's members for there are still at least half-a-dozen or so fully observant families in the capital, whilst amongst the rest of the community observance varies in degree from person to person. There is a slight tendency for older members of the community to be more observant of Kashrut, but age is not the most significant factor, nor is generation; rather it is a matter of individual preference, for adults at least. Some people keep a fully kosher home but will eat non-kosher when eating out. Others do not keep a fully kosher home but will not eat meat and milk together, and the products of prohibited animals. Few will go so far as to eat pork and shellfish, but there are some who have no dietary restrictions whatsoever. These changes in the obervance of Kashrut have occurred alongside decline in various other forms of Orthodox religious observance, such as refraining from certain activities on the Sabbath and the keeping of minor festivals. Whilst Pesach and the Friday night meal are still generally observed, regular attendance at synagogue has gone down. Although there is no shame attached to being less fully observant, there is a feeling of regret within the community as a whole that the old ways are passing and that new generations will have little in the way of example to follow.

Does this then prove the case for acculturation? Secular change in Jewish communities as shown above, need not imply acculturation in the strict sense of loss of group identity as long as religious identity remains strong, but it would seem at first glance that even that is crumbling in Edinburgh today. This would leave us no choice but to accept the notion of acculturation. Yet if one looks at Jewish communities throughout the world one gets the sense that *change* in religiosity does not always necessarily equate with a *loss* of religiosity and that, despite declining rates of Orthodox observance, Judaism is generally in a healthy state and Jewish communities although changing are not on the brink of being swallowed up by wider communities. Rather they are in a phase of accelerated evolution with processes larger than acculturation at work.

Ashkenazi Jewish communities throughout the world seem to be experiencing, or have experienced, the same changes in religious observance, including the observance of the dietary laws, that the Edinburgh community has experienced[2] (Sephardi communities have witnessed much less change in religiosity—their form of Judaism has always been fairly flexible anyway) (Brook 1989, 142-6). Indeed, it would appear that Edinburgh Jews have retained full Orthodox observance for longer than many other Jewish communities in the world, including those of Israel. As noted before, British Jewish communities, and especially Scottish ones, have been typified by conservatism (Jakobovits 1981, 33). It does not seem acceptable to say that Ashkenazi communities are experiencing acculturation in religious terms, for although the number of fully observant Orthodox Jews is declining in most communities (and there are a few exceptions in the States where ultra-Orthodox congregations are actually growing) there is little evidence of these people being converted to any other faith, except in rare instances. Rather Orthodox Jews are being won over to other forms of Judaism such as Reform and Liberal Judaism, with some completely abandoning any form of religious belief.

Reform Judaism, as its name implies, is a reformed version of Orthodoxy. Roughly speaking, one can say that Reform Judaism has removed many of the laws which are seen as not having a productive role in the modern context and much of the change has been directed towards Kashrut. It is possible these days to be a devout religious Jew and not keep kosher. Some Reform Jews will, for instance, see it as being acceptable to mix meat and milk. There is undoubtedly a link between the growth of Reform Judaism in this century and the development of the women's movement, as Jewish women have sought to become fully involved in worshipping God in the public sphere and not just in domestic settings. Some congregations have gone further into the realms of Liberal Judaism, where there are borrowings from Christian religious musical tradition and no restrictions on diet. Finally, some Jews have abandoned religion altogether and see Jewish identity primarily in secular terms, with Zionism (the movement for the creation of a Jewish state) and radical politics being important elements in their identity. It is interesting to note that in parts of the States, such as New York, where in addition to large religious Jewish communities there are also substantial numbers of radical or non-religious Jews, the consumption of East European foodstuffs and the use of Yiddish is strongest. Wherever religion is absent from the lives of Jews secular Jewish traditions often seem to have more importance. It is only the religiously secure Jew who can afford to dispense with secular Ashkenazi culture, which says much about the present-day Edinburgh community.

These new forms of Judaism and the new agnosticism practised by some Jews are a response to the modern world, and again we are dealing primarily with modernisation and not, it would seem, with the results of acculturation, although the effect of greater contact on a non-superficial level with wider society has hastened these changes and given them direction. In the pre-industrial ghettos of Eastern Europe Judaism became fossilised in Orthodoxy, a form of the religion essentially medieval in nature. For hundreds of years the natural development of Judaism was arrested by the highly artificial world of the ghetto where misunderstanding and frequent persecution restricted contacts with wider society to the level of the superficial. One might see new foods on sale in the market place and learn new languages so as to be able to discuss business with the native inhabitants, but there would rarely be occasion to discuss religion with them. There could be little questioning of Orthodoxy. Few would have wanted to question it anyway as it had evolved to suit the needs of the people almost perfectly, and vice-versa. There was then neither need nor means for change.

The first seeds of discontent were sown during the early industrial period when some began to perceive the difficulties of Orthodoxy in dealing with the new way of life. The first Reform congregations were set up in early nineteenth-century Germany (Brook 1989, 116). The move to locations in western Europe and North America saw for a while the recreation of the ghetto environment and the clinging to Orthodoxy by settlers yearning for the stability of the past. Many of those Jews who remained in Eastern Europe had no such need to preserve the past and allowed their beliefs to develop in line with contemporary life (Weinreich 1960, 331). When community members in places such as Edinburgh felt secure enough in their new environment they too began to question some aspects of Orthodoxy, and change was given added impetus and direction from closer contact with the wider population and greater understanding of other belief systems (Berman 1989, 11). The pointless horror of the Holocaust and the establishment of the State of Israel, which gave for the first time ever an alternative focus for Jewish identity, affected the position of Orthodoxy, and indeed of Judaism itself in the minds of some Jews. Today the unthinking observance of Orthodoxy is rarely possible or considered desirable. Judaism has been tested and possibly is all the stronger for that. Although the community still values its non-religious members and recognises that for some their Jewishness comes from secular factors, those who maintain religious traditions do so with as much or perhaps even more vigour, although of a different kind, as their forebears did in Eastern Europe. The individual Jew in a community in any part of the world must now judge for himself or herself how relevant inherited religious beliefs and practices are to his or her life. Those who are religious have chosen to follow their faith and there are few who adhere to religion out of habit alone, as sometimes happened in ghetto days. In this respect members of Jewish communities must go through the same process which people everywhere in the Western world, with its mass communications and overwhelming choice of potentially obtainable lifestyles, must go through. Although many Jews still consider Orthodoxy the best way of relating to God, many others clearly have found the old Orthodox form of Judaism, with its numerous edicts and prohibitions created in biblical times and extended in the Middle Ages, largely irrelevant to the modern world. However, the majority of these people still see Judaism as a viable faith and have sought out their own religious path. Brook (1989, 171) claims that there are 'now as many versions of Judaism in Britain as there are Jews', and even more versions of Jewish identity for the Zionist and the Gastronomic Jew also figure significantly in the membership of communities. For those fortunate enough to live in large communities with several congregations it may be possible to find a congregation which suits one's own particular viewpoint. However, in a small community which has only one nominally Orthodox congregation such as Edinburgh, people must be tolerant of each other's views and degrees of observance.

CONCLUSION

It can be argued that the level of Orthodox observance in Edinburgh today seems to be largely a response to the modern world and owes little to the picking up of the ways of the city's wider community. Consequently, the decline in the observance of Kashrut in Edinburgh should not be seen as a product of acculturation except at the broadest level where modern Western culture has impinged on a largely pre-industrial way of life. Likewise the increasing frequency of Scottish-style meals in Edinburgh Jewish homes over the last sixty years may not indicate so much a loss of Jewishness as the continuance of a millennia-old Jewish tradition, and again a response to modern life. Cultural retention and adaptation may be more important processes than acculturation in relation to the changes in Jewish life, and specifically Jewish eating habits, which have taken place in Edinburgh over the last sixty years. One cannot dismiss the notion of acculturation completely out of hand, of course, and Weinreich (1960, 342) has stated, in relation to American Jewish ritual, that cultural change is generally a product of innovations which arise from within the group in combination with those that stem from without. Nevertheless it would be wrong to place too much emphasis on acculturation and to fully equate cultural change within the Jewish community with cultural loss.

This study has focused on foodways which have proved a useful starting point for an investigation of cultural change within the Edinburgh Jewish community. However, the picture presented by cuisine has had to be looked at in the light of other cultural indicators (notably belief with which it has in this context an unusually close relationship) and more importantly in relation to the present situation within other communities. It would be easy to give a one-sided analysis of the material presented in this paper, attributing change to a single process, but comparative material brings to light further processes which must be considered. The importance of the comparative approach cannot be too strongly stressed in relation to the study of culture groups.

As a postscript, what of the future of Orthodoxy in Edinburgh? The real threat to Orthodoxy looks as if it will come from the shrinking size of the community which makes it increasingly difficult for those who wish to maintain full Orthodox observance of Kashrut. Although the kosher bakery (formerly Kleinberg's—now called The Old Fashioned Bakery) is still in operation, serving both members of the Jewish community and Edinburgh's large vegetarian population, other sources of kosher food are few and far between. There simply is not the population to maintain the necessary kosher infrastructure. Some of the big supermarkets operated by US or English companies stock a small kosher selection and it is possible to get kosher meat and even kosher milk (rabbinically guaranteed free from contamination) delivered from either Glasgow or Manchester, although these products are rather expensive. Most people wishing to keep kosher in Edinburgh eat a strictly vegetarian diet and refrain from eating out (there are no kosher restaurants in Edinburgh, although there are now a good few vegetarian eating places run by members of other groups). A new delicatessen was opened up at the community's request from Glasgow—Sey's New York Deli and Sandwich Bar—to sell kosher food. However, this has been little used by the community as, unlike the Glasgow branch of the firm, the shop sells non-kosher food also. It is possible to keep kosher in Edinburgh today, says one Orthodox informant, but it requires effort and forethought. Things are very much easier for those in Glasgow or in English communities, and especially for those in US cities such as New York where kosher food is widely available and many Jewish specialities have entered the everyday diet of the wider community.

The future of Orthodox Judaism in Edinburgh could be said to look bleak, for, as the young leave the community, the provision for Kashrut observance might decline until it becomes virtually impossible to keep kosher (unless one wants to be totally vegetarian) and those wishing to remain fully Orthodox find themselves having to move to another, larger community. Whether Orthodoxy will remain viable in any part of the world remains to be seen. Reform and other new forms of Judaism seem to be continually gaining popularity, although, as previously mentioned, in some parts of the US new, extremely Orthodox communities are springing up as a backlash to the Reform movement. The future of the Edinburgh Jewish community as a whole does not seem too secure as it will have to contend in the future with shrinking numbers and shrinking synagogue attendance. There may come a day when the community is too small to employ a regular minister and may cease to exist as an organised community at all.

However, to draw such a conclusion may be to underestimate the resilience and ingenuity of a remarkable community which, in the last few years, has set up three new groups to look at contemporary Jewish issues (the Edinburgh Jewish Discussion Group, the Jewish Philosophy Group, and the Future Generations Committee), and whose members of the Literary Society recently voted in debate that there *was* a future for Orthodoxy in the capital.

I would like to express my thanks to the following individuals:
Shari Cohn, Professor David Daiches, Vicki Lowrie, Rabbi and Mrs Shapira, Ian Shein, Susan Shenkin, Robin Spark, and the proprietors of The Old Fashioned Bakery and Sey's New York Deli and Sandwich Bar.

NOTES

1 Although traditions vary to some extent in relation to what can and cannot be eaten during Pesach, it is generally the case that five species of grain must be avoided throughout the festival. These are collectively termed *chametz* and comprise barley, wheat, rye, oats, and spelt. See *Introduction to Judaism, op. cit.* 63.

2 See (for US communities) Glazer, L., *American Judaism*, Chicago, 1957; 131. (For US and Israeli communities) Goldscheider, C. and Zuckerman, A. S., *The Transformation of the Jews*, London, 1984; 221-242. (For British communities) Brook, S., *The Club: The Jews of Modern Britain*, London, 1989.

REFERENCES

BENSKI, J.
1981 'Identification, Groups Survival and Inter-Group Relations: The Case of a Middle-Class Jewish Community in Scotland.' *Ethnic and Racial Studies* 4(3).

BERMAN, C.
1989 'Jews who Fled from Fear and Found a Brave New World in Scotland.' *Observer Scotland* 12 Feb.: 11.

BOKSER, B. Z.
1963 *Judaism: Profile of a Faith.* New York.

BRINGÉUS, NILS-ARVID
1970 'Man, Food and Milieu.' *Folk-Life* 8: 45-56.

BULLON, F.
1990 'The Fragrant Old Days.' *Edinburgh Star* 7: September.

CARR, J. AND OBERMAN, P.
1973 *The Gourmet's Guide to Jewish Cooking.* London.

COWAN, EVELYN
1974 *Spring Remembered: A Scottish Jewish Childhood.* Edinburgh.

DAICHES, DAVID
1975 *Was: A Pastime for Time Past.* London.

DAICHES, S.
1929 'The Jew in Scotland.' *Records of the Scottish Church History Society 3.*

DAXELMÜLLER, CHRISTOPH
1986 'Jewish Popular Culture in the Research Perspective of European Ethnology.' *Ethnologia Europæa 56(2)*: 97-116.

DENTON, H. AND WILSON, J. C.
1991 *The Happy Land.* Edinburgh.

EK-NILSSON, KATARINA
1981 'The Social Functions of Festival Food: A Few Thoughts on an Investigation in Northern Sweden.' In Alexander Fenton and Trefor Owen, eds., *Food in Perspective: Proceedings of the Third International Conference on Ethnological Food Research, Cardiff, Wales, 1977.* Edinburgh 77-81.

FISHMAN, I.
1958 *Introduction to Judaism.* London.

JAKOBOVITS, I.
1981 'An Analysis of Religious Versus Secularist Trends in Anglo-Jewry Especially During the Past Fifteen Years.' In S. L. and V. B. Lipman, *Jewish Life in Britain 1962-1977.* New York.

PHILLIPS, ABEL
1979 *A History of the Origins of the First Jewish Community in Scotland: Edinburgh 1816.* Edinburgh.

RODGERS, MURDOCH
1982 'Glasgow Jewry.' In Billy Kay ed., *Odyssey: The Second Collection.* Edinburgh 113-121.

ROTH, L.
1960 *Judaism: A Portrait.* London.

ROZIN, ELIZABETH AND PAUL
1981 'Some Surprisingly Unique Characteristics of Human Food Preferences.' In Alexander Fenton and Trefor Owen, eds., *Food in Perspective: Proceedings of the Third International Conference on Ethnological Food Research, Cardiff, Wales, 1977.* Edinburgh 243-252.

SACHAR, M. M.
1988 *The Course of Modern Jewish History.* London.

SALOMONSSON, ANDERS
1984 'Some Thoughts on the Concept of Revitalisation.' *Ethnologia Scandinavica: a Journal for Nordic Ethnology.* 34-37.

SEPHARDIC SISTERHOOD
1971 *Cooking the Sephardic Way.* Jerusalem and Los Angeles. Introduction E.

SHAPIRA, S.
1989 'Chanukah: A National Festival.' *Edinburgh Star 4*: December.

SHULMAN, L.
1988 *The Shabbat Handbook: Aspects, Explanations, Prayer and Song.* London.

SIMOONS, F. J.
1967 *Eat Not This Flesh: Food Avoidances in the Old World.* Wisconsin.

SMITH, C. J.
1986 *Historic South Edinburgh.* Haddington.

SPIRO, M.
1955 'The Acculturation of American Ethnic Groups.' *American Anthropologist 57*: 1240-1252.

THEOPHANO, J. S.
1991 'I Gave Him a Cake: An Interpretation of Two Italian-American Weddings.' In S. Stern and J. A. Cicala, eds., *Creative Ethnicity: Symbols and Strategies of Contemporary Ethnic Life*. Utah.

U.J.S.
1991 Union of Jewish Students, *Keeping Kosher on Campus*. London.

WEINREICH, B. S.
1960 'The Americanisation of Passover.' In R. Patai, F. L. Utley and D. Noy, eds., *Studies in Biblical and Jewish Folklore*. Indiana.

Scotland's Three Tongues in Australia: Colonial Hamilton in the 1860s and 1870s

KERRY CARDELL and CLIFF CUMMING

> They speak in riddles beyond the Tweed,
> The plain, poor English they can deftly read;
> Yet when without the book they come to speak,
> Their lingo seems half English and half Greek.
>
> (Leighton 1868, 4)[1]

The town of Hamilton, Victoria, is situated inland from Portland, the port through which white settlement of that state commenced in the 1830s. Lying in the centre of a rich pastoral area known as the Western District, Hamilton has long had a reputation as a Scottish settlement with many large grazing leases to the east of it being pioneered by Lowland Scots. Some of the Highland and Island Emigration Society's settlers came ashore at local ports and the first issue in 1857 of the Australian Gaelic-language newspaper, *An Teachdaire Gaidhealach*, notified its readers that circulation agents for the paper had been appointed in Portland and Hamilton, bearing witness to the presence of Gaelic speakers in the district. A local estimate in 1864 claimed that three-quarters of the population of the district came from north of the Tweed.[2] This paper looks at the written legacy of these Scots in the years 1860 to 1875, principally through the pages of the local newspaper, the *Hamilton Spectator*, in the first fifteen years of its life.

It might be expected, in view of the make-up of the population of the area, that the Scottish voice would have coloured much of the day-to-day life of the region. To some extent it is hardly correct to speak of 'Scots' as though they constituted a unified group. Both Highland and Lowland Scots were present, as well as those who arrived in the district after long periods of settlement overseas or in other Australian colonies such as Tasmania. This diversity created the opportunity for a variety of opinions and differing, if not directly conflicting, attitudes towards certain common issues such as religious worship and other aspects of Scottish culture. We have few examples of the day-to-day relationships between English and non-English-speaking

Scots, but the glimpses we do have show the problems relating to inter-communication and the depth of affection held by those from the Gaidhealtachd for their native culture.

In such a context, it is of interest to see how the Scottish voice represented in its three major forms—English, Lowland Scots and Gaelic—through the medium of the popular press. Those Scots whose writings appeared in the local newspaper addressed literary, community and specifically Scottish matters. As all reveal themselves fully literate in standard English and competent in its use, some attempt is made here to examine why the different authors chose, on occasions, to make use of Gaelic and Lowland Scots.

THE LITERARY VOICE

Hamilton Scots employed each of their three tongues in order to address 'Scottish' local issues such as fraternal associations and their own ecclesiastical affairs. They sometimes resorted to Lowland Scots when they sought to inject notes of satire or humour into their discussion of broader community matters such as local and state politics. Another area with which some Scots concerned themselves in the pages of the local newspaper was the writing of original pieces of literature. In this they had at least tacit editorial encouragement, for in deference to the large Scottish component of its readership, the *Hamilton Spectator* ran a number of articles on Scottish culture and history including such items as: a reprint of *Mercurius Caledonius* from 1660-61 (2 Nov. 1872, 4), 'Peculiarities of the Scotch Marriage Law' (6 July 1872, Supplement, 1), 'The Sea Serpent in a Scottish Loch' (2 Nov. 1872, Supplement, 1), and 'The Songs of Scotland' (12 Sept. 1868, Supplement, 1). Verse and song from the motherland was also reprinted, just as this and other newspapers acknowledged the presence of other ethnic groups in the district by carrying very occasional pieces in the language or dialect of these groups.[3] The preponderance of Scottish items appearing would seem to reflect the prevailing demographic realities at the time.

However, care was taken to include humorous pieces among these non-English and dialect offerings. Two examples of such items are the story of the English lady bemused by a Scots maid's offer of a 'pig' to warm her bed, and the tale of the non-comprehending Englishman, whose response to having a simpleton described by his Scots informant as 'wanting tippence like', was to hand the boy a sixpence (25 Sept. 1863, Supplement:ff.7; 10 Sept. 1870, Supplement, 2). Inclusion of such pieces sought to ensure that Scottish cultural material printed in the journal would be read in a tolerant and genial spirit by the general (i.e. the English) readership. One reader who obviously did so was the Englishman and local poet who used the pen name 'Mount Sturgeon'. One of his poems, 'To Mary', is inscribed, 'An English Attempt in Scotland's Vernacular' (24 April 1863, Supplement, 3), and in it he abandons his usual diction to enter into the spirit of all this 'Scottishness'. The first stanza reads:

> O' a' the lasses I hae read,
> In story brave, or dour, or dool;
> What spears ye?—jist cam' in my head,
> But Mary—ance o' Warrnambool.[4]

The editorial hand can sometimes be seen at work, too, ensuring that 'Scottish' matter was read in an appropriate context. The poem, 'What Ails Ye At The Organ, Grannie?' by James Smith (5 July 1873, Supplement, 1), is described as a 'humorous Scotch poem' on a 'subject which just now seems to be giving some of our Presbyterian friends a world of trouble'. As will be seen later, the reference was to local attempts at introducing music into Presbyterian church services. Thus, general readers were alerted before they read them that lines like these related to a particular church controversy which, although an easy target for fun, was a serious enough issue for a certain section of the community.

> Sic hurdy-gurdy trash, Jamie,
> Shall ne'er get my guidwill, my man,
> An sae ye needna fash, Jamie.
>
> Nae drones, wi' dismal twang, Grannie,
> Were heard when David sang, Grannie.

A Scots voice, appropriate for the narrowly Scottish subject, is made instructive and palatable to a wider readership with a modicum of adroit editorialising.

The fact that they originated in Scotland, and were printed for the delectation of a Scottish readership, seems to have been sufficient warrant for the paper to include a number of relatively unadulterated Lowland Scots poems. These included 'Caller Herrin' (11 June 1870, 2) which at least had the advantage of being well known because of its popularity as a song, but there were other pieces, reprinted from Scotland, which may have been quite taxing for the non-Scot. For example, two verses of the unattributed 'My Luggie' (27 July 1864, 4) read:

> Then cam the threshin' jist to please, 'twas exchange for her jaw,
> Poor Tam was cuffed an' clouted sare for keeping nature law;
> Then sent 'quick march' to cripple Bob's for bottle o' his ale—
> On comin' hame the cork flew out, but luggie was his pail:
> The froth puffed up like reeking lowes till luggie was run owre,
> It fizzed an' spart in spite o' Tam jist like an April shower.

Tam threw the empty bottle down,
An' hame wi' luggie fu';
The whole house swore I was a loon,
An' aff to Bob's they flew.

Back to the house wi' vengeance cam, and cudgelled me right sair,
Then pured the ale out luggie's hold, but guidness what a stare
When out came swimmin' sparrows twa, that very morning kittled,
My grannie's specks flew owre her crown, my mither's nerves were nettled;
The swipes were thrown in my face, poor luggie to the door—
'Nae deil was ever born like Tam' the whole house loudly swore.

I owre my waesome sparrows cried,
A bankrupt beggar stood;
Stock gane-by every friend belied,
As ane o' reptile brood.

This is not just pseudo-Lowland Scots, English vocabulary rendered into what was regarded as Scots spelling. There are sufficient genuine Scots terms here which, combined with a certain disjointedness in the narrative, would have rendered these verses quite difficult for the non-Scot. Similarly, the article 'The Scotch Psalms' (8 March 1873, Supplement, 2), with its sample of P. H. Waddell's Scots version of the Psalms must have sent many rushing to the King James text of the 'Old Hundredth'.

1. Skreigh till the Lord, the haile yirth, maun ye:
2. Beck till the Lord wi' blytheheid an' a'; ben afore him, wi a sang o' glee.
3. Ken ye fu' weel, the Lord he's God: himlane, *it was*, made us; oursel *made* na we: his folk are we syne, and eke o' his hirsel the fe.
4. Ben till his yetts wi laud; till his faulds, wi' a lilt saw hie; lilt ye laud till himsel; an' that name o' his ain, bless ye.
5. For gude is the Lord; his gude-will's for ay; an' frae ae life's en' till anither, that truth o' his ain, it *sal be.*

The largest single category of Lowland Scots verse found in the Hamilton newspaper speaks of the homesickness of Scottish emigrants and of their nostalgia for the land of their birth. One of the finest such pieces to appear was 'Farewell to Edinburgh' by Harriet Miller Davidson (4 May 1872, Supplement, 2). The writer was currently a resident of Adelaide and the poem had already appeared in the Scottish press. It depicts Edinburgh as a 'queenly leddy', beloved for her 'bridal veil o' snaw' in winter, for the 'radiant, ruby light' with which her windows shine during the summer sunsets, and for the thousand lamps 'twinkling in every street and square' at night. Departure from the city was painful, and hopes of eventual return were cherished:

Oh, my bonny, bonny leddy!
I'm fain to bide with thee

There's nane o' a' thy mony bairns
Has ever loved thee mair
Than I who now maun leave thee
Wi' weary heart and sair.

Oh, keep some wee bit corner
In thy grand auld heart for me,
Where, when I'm auld and weary,
I may creep back to dee.

Sentiments such as these were common enough in colonial newspapers. The Scots accent employed in this poem was an act of choice directed towards the original readers in Scotland. Though it was also common for Irish and Scots writing nostalgic verses in Australia to write them in accented English, evocation of the voices of 'hame' enriched the memories and pictures so dear to the homesick authors. The paucity of the appearance of such material in this local Hamilton paper thus needs some attempted explanation.

The *Hamilton Spectator* was a commercial enterprise, so it is no surprise that 'Scots' verse, original or reprinted, was the exception rather than the rule and we can consider several reasons for this. Authentic Lowland Scots could be heavy going for the non-Scottish reader and newspaper proprietors had circulation figures to consider. In the period 1861-1875 the actual amount of material in Scots averaged out at one piece per year. Even poems in imitation of Burns such as 'Higho! The Lasses O', by A. McLean (19 June 1869, 1), and the unattributed 'A Girl's a Girl for a' That' (28 August 1869, 1), are written in the standard English poetic diction of the nineteenth century. In this regard, the *Spectator* was not typical of the rest of the state. Original poetry in Lowland Scots was a decided feature of the Melbourne newspapers such as the *Port Phillip Patriot* from their beginnings in the early 1840s, a situation repeated in many other provincial journals. The organ of the Victorian Scottish Union, *The Scot at Hame an' Abroad*, continued to publish verse and prose in Lowland Scots from its origin until its demise in the 1930s. There obviously was no shortage of this kind of writing and what made its way into print would thus only have been a fraction of what was actually submitted. Another reason why the Hamilton press did not publish material in Lowland Scots more frequently may simply have been the enormous popularity of the prevailing (English) poetic diction of the day. Sentimental, nineteenth-century verse style was certainly no less fashionable at this populist level in the provinces than we know it to have been in the more urbane 'literary' circles!

If we turn to a particular Hamiltonian poet we can find another specific reason for the relative local neglect of Lowland Scots as a poetic voice. Ossian Macpherson had twenty-seven poems accepted for publication by the *Hamilton Spectator* between 1861 and his death in 1875. Although he wrote verse in Gaelic (he won prizes for this in Melbourne and Geelong for five consecutive years before moving to the Hamilton district), none of these verses appeared in the paper, and only two of the twenty-seven of his offerings in the Hamilton press were in Lowland Scots. These were his very first piece printed there, and a reprint of his poem 'Shinty', which had been written while in London in 1842. Macpherson confesses to having been an itinerant and no stranger to poverty. Around Hamilton he had tried to make his living as a private tutor and rural schoolmaster, as well as serving as an area correspondent for the newspaper. Anything from his pen expressed in a manner which could be construed as 'vulgar' would have had the potential to harm his professional standing in the eyes of local parents and thus threaten his livelihood.

If this was the case, it makes it difficult to understand why Macpherson chose to announce his arrival in Hamilton in 1861 with a poem strongly marked by Scots vocabulary. This piece, 'To My Mither at Hame' (4 May 1861, 2), consisted of five eight-line stanzas of rhyming couplets. It reminisces about the sorrow of the emigrant's parting, and goes on to become consciously autobiographical. 'I did na' come here, mither,/mindfu' o' wealth,/But to seek once again the sweet blessing of health.' (In another place Macpherson tells us he was in Madeira in 1848, an invalid waiting to die). The lines 'Aft houseless and hameless, wi' travel fit sair,/Pinch'd wi' hunger and thirst', confirm his later prose avowals that he had had first-hand experience of the rigours of the lifestyle of bush swagmen. Readers know, of course, that a narrative persona might bear either a close or a distant relationship to the biography of the poet in question. The author can win praise for inventing a personality; it is not always assumed that he bares his own soul. Thus, when Macpherson's persona says, for example, 'mid poverty's blicht, I am glad and content', or 'An' my heart in its language sae hamely and rude,/Pours forth in its fullness a puir gratitude', the Scots spelling serves to stress the fact that this is the voice of the exile, albeit one who is content with his current lot in life. To the mother overseas, this voice would be reassuring—neither time nor distance has changed her son—while to the poor emigrant in Australia, despairing of ever obtaining land of his own, the vernacular familiarity of the voice would help render palatable the implied moral contentment with one's present position in life.

But such examples are rare in Macpherson's published work. Although he wrote many poems on Scottish themes for the *Hamilton Spectator*, these reveal very little resort to the form of Lowland Scots. Poems describing Highland legends, like 'The Black Captain' (31 August 1861, 3), and Scottish history such as 'Cluny's Lament', which dealt with Cluny Macpherson of the '45: the attainted, long-secreted, and ultimately in-exile chief of Clan Chattan (18 Feb. 1865, 4), and 'Queen Mary's

Murder' (1 Jan. 1870, 1), might seem obvious occasions for the employment of Scots. This approach Macpherson declined to take. The loyalty, courage and dignity of the individuals in these poems is presented entirely through English, perhaps because these are Scots in whose lives and sufferings he saw a universalised significance. The title of the poem 'Queen Mary's Murder' leads us to anticipate a certain historical bias, and this is confirmed in the author's note attached to the poem. This declares that 'the reign of that wretched woman [Queen Elizabeth I, was] a veritable calendar of horrors'. The judgment of history, which he presumes to announce concerning Mary's execution, 'That gory blot on England's name', is presented as though it were more than a simple parochial Scottish judgment, and the deliberate eschewing of a narrowly Scottish voice would seem to reflect this wider purpose:

> And curst shall be, by lips unborn
> The butchery of that winter morn.

The deliberative manner in which Ossian Macpherson selected the tongue most appropriate for ends in the poems discussed thus far continued to be evident in the many other poems he wrote with Australian settings or themes. The local newspaper contains nationalistic poems by him ('Arm Ye Australia', 30 Nov. 1864, 1), sentimental ones ('The Australian Babes in the Woods', 11 Jan. 1865, 2), occasional verse ('On the Attempted Murder of Prince Alfred'[5]), and a large number of poems on the death of people known to him (not the least of which is 'In Memory of Adam Lyndsay Gordon', mourning the death of a well-known colonial poet of Scottish descent, 13 May 1871, Supplement, 1). None of these poems listed, nor the numerous unlisted ones, employs a Scots voice in the use of vocabulary. Possession of three tongues and the developed ability to versify in each meant that Macpherson had considerable flexibility. When writing verse for an English-language newspaper he employed Gaelic not at all, and Lowland Scots sparingly. When he wrote of Australia he felt little need to speak in a specifically Scots voice. The issues he raised, the deaths and tragedies he mourned, the events he celebrated were, or were positioned by his poetry as though they were, matters which touched the lives of the wider citizenry and not just those of his brother Scots.

To argue that English became the literary language of choice for the Scottish-born poets of provincial Hamilton because they fell victim to the all-pervasive fashion for Victorian poetic diction, or to maintain that they opted to write in English so frequently simply because, of the languages at their disposal it was the one most appropriate to the vast majority of the subjects they chose, is to over-work each of these causal factors, important though they were. A smattering of 'braid Scots' certainly would not have been inappropriate in Macpherson's poems. Judiciously used it could have enhanced both the effect and the local colour of works such as the graphic 'The Black Captain' and the angry 'Queen Mary's Murder'. It seems that one other factor was at work in the district which has to be brought into this discussion. Those Scots who penned verse still had Scots available to them as a literary medium, its accents still marked their own everyday speech. But the events and experiences of their Australian environment were beginning to impinge upon the moral and cultural values they had brought from Scotland. As this mingling progressed, Scottish poets in the Hamilton district appear to have opted less frequently for the use of a Scots tongue. A Scottish voice may still be detected in their work, but they tend to move away from narrow linguistic affirmation of 'Scottishness'. Its presence may still be detected, of course, but it takes on other forms.

It has already been noted that the district newspaper ran quite a number of articles and verses dealing with Scottish culture. Obviously, for many Scots, pieces like Robert Buchanan's 'The Lead Melting' (29 April 1871, Supplement, 1), which describes some of the customs by which a future spouse could be foreseen, would have served to keep alive the memory of old traditions:

Twas clear, cold, starry, a silver night,
And the old year was a-dying,
Three pretty girls, with melted lead,
Sat gaily fortune trying.
They dropt the lead in water clear,
With blushing palpitations,
And as it hissed, with fearful hearts,
They sought its revelations.

It is also true that many Scots settlers made active attempts to keep such inherited customs alive in the new land, as Ossian Macpherson found when he visited a neighbouring township, Konong Wootong, at the end of October 1864, and of which he wrote in his poem 'An Australian Halloween' (12 Nov. 1864, 3):

I passed that night at Wootong Halloween

The poet tried his nuts, with anxious gaze,
And picturing one form amid the blaze;
Perhaps he thought the emblems might be true,
Alas,—his nuts were cracked ere half burnt through.
And when blindfold, before each fairy plate,
He wished—his fond desire—for gentle mate,
His hand thrice grasped the platter that was clean!
No wife for him at Wootong Halloween.

At first such transplantation of customs may have strengthened the old values, making over Australia in Scotland's image, as it were:

> Bard of all coming time, immortal Burns,
> Couldst thou have dreamt that ever would have been
> Another Scotland *here* and Halloween. (*Ibid*)

But four years later this same poet's 'A Few Lines for Home' (26 Dec. 1868, 4), although tinged with sadness because of the separation from loved ones at the festive season, values the Australian landscape for what it is, not for the imported culture it nurtures. The poet is comfortable in the Victorian outdoors and expends as many lines on it as he does on 'memory Scotland':

> When snow falls fast, and frost is keen,
> And scarce one verdant spot is seen,—
> When skies look dark, with anger scowl,
> And winds without discordant howl,—
> When Christmas fires, with radient [*sic*] glow,
> Their cozy welcomings bestow—
> And gathered round, the loved and dear,
> Think of us, friends,—think of us here.
>
> While wand'ring mid our fields of bloom,
> While bright the sun, soft the perfume;
> Or gazing on the ocean blue,
> Sparkling in all its summer hue;
> Or 'neath the gum-tree's welcome shade,
> Our forms in lazy comfort laid:
> Our hearts will with you be today—
> We think on you, friends, far away.

We all filter the new through the old, referring immediate and unfamiliar experiences to the value systems and traditions with which we are familiar as we attempt to incorporate and make sense of novelty. It is natural that settlers in the Hamilton district who resorted to names like Sir Robert Bruce, Royal Charlie, and Highland Donald for their farm stallions (18 Dec. 1863, 6) and equally evocative names for their farms and geographical features, would seek to understand strange and new aspects of their Australian environment through appeal to the cultural traditions of their homeland. Thus, to take one example, when the Highland Scot, James Grassie, sought to come to terms with local (and, of course, non-literate) aboriginal civilisation, the understanding he reached clearly owed something to forms and traditions ultimately derived from the vernacular heroic literatures of western Europe. These lines purport to be an aboriginal epitaph and Grassie penned them under this title, 'Translation of an Aboriginal Epitaph' (18 Sept. 1863, 4):

Stay, chieftain stay!—and drop a tear!
Coup Carrip's bones lie sleeping here:—
Coup Carrip, bold, who wedded fame,
And handed down a deathless name
To future years, the white man's foe—
He laid the pale intruders low.
Here in peace his ashes lie;
But his deeds can never die.

In the following decade, district whites were still 'seeing' aboriginal Australia through their own cultural norms. Despite the editorial introduction, which seeks to relate the story to Germanic tradition ('It is somewhat singular that a tribe of savages should have conjured up a superstitious fancy so closely related to the Ellmaid legend of elegant German literature'), this unattributed versification of a local aboriginal legend seems to have been constructed with the Kelpie and other aspects of the Celtic supernatural in mind. The aboriginals' Coorg was a spirit to be found in the bush around a certain water-hole and was incorporated into a poem entitled 'Coorg' (23 April 1870, Supplement, 1):

Hark to the spirits of Scaith—how she screams,
And the bittern responds in fear
And the herdsman starts in his midnight dreams,
And trembles when Coorg is near.

She has lights to lure the swagman bushed
From his path to her grotto lone,
And music to her are the accents wild
Of the bushman's lost and benighted child,
Or its mother's expiring groans.

Oh, traveller, traveller, shun her sands,
And head for the Snizort plain.

As experiences peculiar to Australia became the subject of emigrants' literary productions, Scottishness is to be sought not in the direct narrative voice of a poem, but rather in the perspectives and assumptions which underlie the words spoken by the narrative personae. The Scots of Western Victoria showed considerable panache in selecting from their three languages a tongue and an accent suitable for the immediate purpose they had in mind, were it civic or literary. Whatever the level of vocal dexterity and literary artistry employed in their individual epistolary and literary effusions, we can usually detect the basal voice of Scottish culture underneath the particular tongue or accent employed on a given occasion.

THE PUBLIC VOICE

Gaelic made its first published appearance in a letter to the *Hamilton Spectator* in May 1861. The correspondent was sparing in his employment of the language, using it for his title ('Clann Na Gael, 'An Guilibh Na Cheile'), pen name ('Na Bean Ri Cat Lamhin'—presumably a slightly defective allusion to the Macpherson motto) and to interpolate two phrases within the English text of the letter (11 May 1861, 2). Nevertheless, these traces were enough to attract editorial commentary half as long as the letter itself. The writer declared himself a newcomer to the district, delighted to find such a strong Scottish presence there, but disappointed to learn there was no Caledonian Society in the neighbourhood, a situation which he compared unfavourably with Melbourne and provincial centres such as Geelong, Ballarat and Buninyong. Lowland Scots also made its prose debut in this same letter. The writer declared that his heart 'gaed a loup o' delicht', for example, at finding so many Scots in residence, and he rejoiced in the 'blythesome faces of the many bonnie burdies' daily encountered in Hamilton. Why were these two tongues used to ornament a letter in English, the plain sense of which was evident without them? It is clear that this author was fully literate in English, as were all the others to be considered here. Use of Gaelic or Lowland Scots phraseology or spellings constituted acts of conscious choice, deliberative interpolations placed within letters written primarily in English. Subsequent correspondents provide answers to this question.

This epistle drew a response from another Highlander who first of all chided him for his bad Gaelic spelling, but supported his fraternal aim (18 May 1861, 2). This new correspondent, signed 'Highlander', also used two tongues in his letter. Writing mainly in English, he nevertheless supported the proposal for founding a local Caledonian Society by quoting from a Gaelic poem evocative of the strength of Highland feeling and cultural identity. What Highland heart, asks the writer, can fail to be stirred by the naming of the hero?

Co as t'Albanach nach teid air bhoil,
S' nach teid a' chridhe na chliabh, air ghoil,
Mar bhras, fhairge dol troimhe chaol,
An fuair chluinneas' e' ainm sar ainm an laoch.

The baton was taken up by another correspondent signing himself as a son of

Mull, 'An Gille Muilach' (18 May 1861, 2). He, too, lends his support. 'To us Highlanders', he says, this issue was an important one, and he wrote to stir his brethren to action that the world might know that they were 'Mic Sheann Albainn gun Cul'—true sons of old Scotland. In making the effort to found a society, local Scots would be behaving like true Gaels, 'A bhi gualain ri gualain,/Anns gach cruadal a's gabhadh.'—standing together, shoulder to shoulder, to face the present difficulties.

The writer goes on to ask: 'Is there no influential Gael who will take on himself to call *Clanna na'n Gael ri Cheile?*' He would be delighted, he adds, to see one of the many influential local Gaels stepping forward to call together Highlanders of the area, just as Highlanders were led to outstanding victories on the Slopes of Alma and the Heights of Balaclava:

Sliochd na'n cuirdhan calma,
Nach pilleadh sa gharbhchatch,
Dheanadh slinntrich a's tailmrich,
Car armabh troimh fheoil
Agus braithran na'n Armuin
Choisinn buaidh air uchdach Alma,
Sair airdan Bhalaclabha,
Cha d'fhag iad aon beo.

'Be up and stirring' is the slogan this son of Mull draws from these lines for neighbouring Highlanders. Then, lapsing once more into Gaelic verse, he urges them to gird their loins as though for battle and to take heart in the face of the issue at hand:

Croisabh bhur leasra,
Is treise na'n Gaidheal
Nach gabhadh bonn geilte
Romh fheachdamh a'n namhaid.

He concludes his letter with a poetic exhortation in Gaelic to local Gaels, urging them to raise the Highland standard in the colony, and to continue the traditions which form their birthright:

A Chlanna na'n Gael
Tha 'n tamh ann san tir seo
    Horo togamh an airde!
Bithibh ullamh s ealamh fearal a's fiorghlic
Caranta [?] cruadalach uasal n'ar inntinn,
Gu Comunn na'n Gael;

Theiradh blas do mo chri'sa
Shuidhachadh mar bu dual da
De [?] suaichantas Rioghal,
    Horo togamh an airde!

It is possible to determine the object which the writer of this letter had in view from his English prose alone. However, the importance he attributed to the formation of a Caledonian Society, and the context in which he placed such fraternal association, was revealed only to those who could read Gaelic. In a follow-up letter (8 June 1861, 2), the same correspondent appealed to the spirit of Ossian in his efforts to stir his countrymen into action. He cannot believe that the feelings of those from 'Tir na'm beann na'n Gleann s na'n Gaisgeach'—the land of mountain, glen and heroes—would fail to be stirred when faced with the challenge of establishing a society of Gaels like the brotherhood of heroes of old. Lethargy in regard to this call, he writes, would find the spirit of Ossian, 'King of Gaelic Bards', pointing the finger of reproof at the 'lukewarmness' of his fellow Gaels.

Encouragement came, too, in the other language of the Scot. Ossian Macpherson, the local bard mentioned earlier, competent at composing and translating Gaelic poetry, used his other voice, Lowland Scots, 'to influence a Highland Gathering in Hamilton' (24 Sept. 1864, 3). Drawing on one of his earlier compositions, 'Shinty', the poet sought to evoke the spirit and excitement of Highland sports as a means of commending a Caledonian Society to Scots of the neighbourhood:

Get up, up, ilk Hielan' wight:
The magpie coos, the morn is bright:
Seize the camac: grasp it tight,
An' hasten awa' to shinty.

Then drain the quaich, fill again,
Loudly blaw the martial strain,
An' welcome gie wi' micht an' main,
To guid auld Hielan' shinty.

After relating the details of a keenly fought game, the poem turns to the post-match hospitality, another aspect of Highland culture:

An' now wi' social mirth and glee,
To end the sport we a' agree;
Wi' usquebagh or barley bree,
We'll drink to Hielan' shinty.

Quick, piper, quick: mair loudly blaw!
We'll keep it up, baith great an' sma';
We'll dance it out till morning craw,
'Tis a' for Hielan' shinty.

The individual game, and its consequent festivities, may draw to an end but, as the poet goes on to show, the tradition remains. Each meeting is a renewed pledge to continue the spirit of Highland culture:

But may we a' who now are met,
Till nature claims her final debt:
Be aye resolved ne'er to forget
Our ancient Hielan' shinty.

The use of the three voices available to Scots residents in this part of Victoria proceeded without creating any serious tensions between the various sections of the community. However, on occasions, some disquiet could show itself. It was suggested by another Scottish correspondent that the games, to be an annual feature of the Caledonian Society's activities, could include 'other national sports' as well as those of Scotland. The 'Saxon and the Gael', he continued, 'as members of the same community', would see such a development as 'welcome' (6 July 1861, 2). This suggestion brought to the surface some of the depth of feeling among Gaels towards their own culture. A mixture, as had been suggested, would mean dilution and dilution could destroy the distinctiveness of this aspect of that culture. 'An Gille Muilach', for example, was one who took issue with the idea of incorporating non-Gaelic activities within a Celtic sports day (5 Oct. 1861, 3). It was, he wrote, a recipe for the death of any Gaelic society. He supported his argument by citing the fate of the Australian Gaelic-language newspaper, *An Teachdaire Gaidhealach*, which, he said, had failed after a few months because it was 'a conglomeration of English and Gaelic'.[6] Gaels had refused to support it because of its English content, especially in regard to those matters which would have been dear to them in their own tongue. Had it appeared entirely in the Highlanders' 'own language', he asserted, they would have supported it.

To avoid making the same mistake with a 'proper Comunn na'n Gael, or Caledonian Society', the correspondent proposed keeping it strictly Gaelic. All of its business should be conducted in Gaelic, though English translations of such things as minutes should be supplied, and a separate English-speaking committee could be formed if necessary. Sporting activities 'should consist of all the games peculiar to the Celts' and prizes should be awarded for 'piobrachds [*sic*] and Gaelic poetry'. 'An Gille Muilach' went on to urge the foundation of a Gaelic journal and to declare that while he had life he would 'honour and revere the Gaelic'. He justified his enthusiasm for his 'mother tongue' by quoting the Gaelic verse which hailed the antiquity of the language and which traced its origin to the earliest biblical times:

Do gach iomadh canan,
Bho linn Bhabel fhuair
A'Sliochd sin Adhamh,
Si Ghaelig a thug buaidh.

Such separatist feeling in relation to the sporting programme to be conducted by a Caledonian Society did not, however, become the local norm. The variety of societies which came to be established in and around Hamilton seemed to conduct sports days which reflected a happy combination of Highland games and wider, community-based contests and activities, reflective of the interests of both Celtic and English settlers (15 March 1865, 2). The bard responsible for 'The Caledonian Society's Gathering, 1869',[7] still pictured this event about to take place in a neighbouring town, in the heroic terms evoked by the correspondents who resorted to Gaelic verse and traditions to urge the formation of bodies to conduct such contests, but for him it was to be a communal occasion, not a specifically Highland one:

Children of Scotia! Bold and brave!
Sons of the land beyond the wave,
Awake! and to the field! away!

Children of Erin! gallant band!
Sons of sore and stricken land,
Think upon its wrongs today.

Children of Albion! generous, free,
Join ye the glorious rivalry!

The local popular press was a convenient and regular outlet for Scots writing in a variety of forms. While, as has been shown, some of the published material that made use of Lowland Scots was taken from other journals, there was also a supply of prose and some poetry which originated from local sources. In a variety of voices, Scots were prepared to make comment in satirical, comic or serious vein on community issues. Margaret Auld, or rather the person purporting to be a 'puir auld widow' who wrote under that pen name, regularly used Lowland Scots in 'her' letters of complaint about various local problems. In response to an editorial on the subject of thistles, condemned locally as a nuisance weed, 'Margaret Auld' resorted, in a letter (11 Jan. 1865, 2), to this form of Scots, some humour and a certain amount of cheek, to take the editor to task:

> 'Awhile ago in your leader, "leader?" my certy? why is't caud leader? A ne'er could tell, unless it was that meant to lead folk astray—you spack aboot bad farming, an' said that some o' the fields were nothing but sow-thistles. Weel, mon, since then I looked owre to my neebour's ground and there what shud I see bit the hale lond covered a' owre wi' them: sae I geest spack dacently to Johnson—that's my next neebour's name—so he says to me (and he was verra light in his manner, a thing I canna bear frae ony mon body). I'll take a sythe tomorrow and soon make pigs and whistles o' them.
>
> 'I didna like this mode of talking and trying to put me off. I felt it was not becoming to him; sae I said, "Mr Johnson, if ye think because I'm a lone woman I'm gawn to stan't and see my garden littered wi' yoor sow-thistles yer far wrang. I'll write to the *Spectator* about it". Wi' that, Mr Editor, he turned on his heel and muttered, "Horrid old boar''. Sic an expression set my bristles up. What me! Margaret Auld! to come 16,000 miles frae hame tae be cawd an ald boar! I couldna speak—least I was afeert tae—sae I geest clinched my neeve, gaed in the house, sat down in the spence, and had a good greet tae myself.
>
> 'Mr Editor, help, and keep an old woman frae insult. Your "leader" brought it on!'

In an earlier letter (6 July 1864, 2), the same correspondent, in mock upset at being identified not as an old widow but as one of the townsfolk in disguise, again launched forth at the editor in the same spirit and tongue-in-cheek seriousness:

> 'Noo dinna be feared, I'm no guain tae bother ye wi' ony mare o' my clavers. But really, Mr Eeditor, I canny stan', an a winna, that's mare, to be miscawed, as my O... tells me I hae been (and he's a weel tae do callant, my sister Lissy's bairn he's in one o' yer shops in the toon), syne I wrate ye aboot the birkies after the hoonds. Some say that I, Peggy Auld, am the baker o' baps and cookies, some that I'm Donald that hauds the roupes, and ethers that I'm nae less than our worthy meer. (Losh, man, isn't it aufoo tae caw a Christian man as if he was a powny; what for canny they caw him a provast or the lord provast; man wise I'm shure.) Noo, I like a' three o' them very weel—especially when the het water's handy—but it's no jest right tae the memory o' my paer auld man that's deed and gone this sax years come Candlemass, that I, a lane woman, should be ta'en for a man, just because I write a wheen letters to you.'

But Scots did more than write in this vein in order to provide entertainment. In among the attempts at humour lie some genuine social complaints. That Margaret Auld wrote for a specific purpose is revealed in a letter purporting to be a response to someone who had recognised her as a neighbour from Scotland. As most of the letter is written in standard English, the touch of Lowland Scots demonstrates that a Scots voice was deliberately chosen and used, depending on the situation, to create particular effects. The correspondent met Margaret and asked her why she wrote to the newspaper and Margaret, in another letter (23 July 1864, 2) offered an explanation:

> 'Eh, my wee bairn, I dinna ken,' she replied. . . . 'Wherever I am placed in life I feel it my duty to take an initial interest in the locale of my habitation, and either directly or indirectly do what I can to improve and benefit the place or people. . . . These are the only reasons I can give for my public appearances.'

We can see this form of civic responsibility at work in another of Margaret Auld's letters, written in her form of Lowland Scots (20 July 1864, 2), complaining about the poor state of roads in the town:

> 'As ye ken . . . I'm no very often in your braw toon, but the ether nicht I cam in . . I had a letter to post for my sister Lizzie; so away I went, stapping owre the street, to what I thocht should be the pavement at the Post-office, when sough! in I got, sough! sough! owre the kuits amang the glaure, and the mair I struggled the waure I got, until I was quite demented, and not owre amiable in my feelings, as ye may weel jalouse. Noo, wha's to blame for this? Is it your Toon Council? Is it Parliament? Or is it Mr Rogers [the Postmaster] I dinna care what is to blame, but it's a disgrace to yer toon to hae yer Post-office crossing in sic a state, and the sooner it's mended the better, or I'll no come ony mair to pit my letter to ye. . . .'

Remedial action brought a quick response from her (30 July 1864, 3).

> 'Margaret Auld's complemints to Mr Rogers o' the Post-office, and desires to thank him for the bit brigg he's made o'er the slough. He's a dacent douse body is Mr Rogers, an' a better man than a' the Cooncil, Parlement, or the Government pit thegither.'

A couple of months later Margaret returns to the fray, raising what was a common complaint about public thoroughfares in the early days of town councils i.e. lack of signposts (14 Sept. 1864, 3). After setting out on a journey from Dunkeld to Hamilton, she had ended up in Cavendish, a township situated in quite a different direction:

> 'I ken fu's weel ye maun hae plenty to pit intae the paper frae *men*? and etless gomerals—without my auld wif's clavers, still I canna but think ye'll try to gee a wee nook to the complaints o' a puir auld widow woman like me. Weel, "to mak a long story short", what I have to noo to compleen of is, the awfoo dangerous state of yer bush roads. I dinna mean to sae much aboot there being fu' o' ruts and holes enough to break a' the gigs in the kintry. Gae me an honest Scotch gig, Mr Editor, and no' thae kittle-looking buggies that hae na mare solidity aboot them than the kintry they cam frae—a' poother and smoke, and brag. The danger I mean in yer roads is, that ye never ken whar ye'r gauen! ye gang awa' as ye think straight for yae place, but lo! and behold! after two hours fetching thro' the mud, ye fin' ye'r on the wrang tract, and ye hae gist to gang back again . . . I'm

sure it wu'dna' cost muckle tae pit up a wheen posts, an' hae printed on a boord a notice like this, which I think very explicit: THIS IS NO' THE ROAD TO CAVENDISH, BUT IT IS THE ROAD TO HAMILTON.'

One long continuing problem, especially in the rural areas of the colony, was land tenure. An Act of Parliament came into force in 1865 opening up large areas of crown land for purchase in relatively small lots. Smallholders could pay for their lots in instalments, provided they resided on the land they received and made specified improvements to it within a certain time. There were many problems with this Act, much newspaper space was consumed by discussion of its operation, and several years passed before it began to work in something approaching an equitable way. One of the major problems was that the large-scale graziers ('squatters') who already held much of the land in question under special grazing licences, were able to use 'dummies' to obtain land on their behalf and various other sorts of chicanery to prevent smallholders making selections on their runs. It is this topic which Scot 'Sandy Sneck' addressed in a letter (30 Dec. 1868, 3), using both Lowland Scots and a play on the word 'leasing' in order to make a very serious point[8]:

'I am a plain Scotchman, no muckle acquainted wi' Land Rackets and Land Leasing, although I hae heard about them since I hae been in this country. So, you see, being in Hamilton on my ain business (which is naebody else's business), I went to the house whereon is the sign painted "Office of Crown Lands and Survey". But though the building is said to belang to the Crown of England, it is just a decent kind o' weatherboard building, gude enuch to have a dance in, or ony other kind o' amusement, on a public scale. Weel, there were people there who had ridden far and near to come to this kind o' affair which they call having a sale o' lands open for leasing. Now, the auld Scotch word for telling lies is "leasing". And to the astonishment of everybody, two-thirds o' the lands said to be open for leasing were shut up against everybody, and the names o' the lands crossed out wi' blue ink. If this is no real "leasing" I leave ony body to judge. Some folks had come as far as frae Lake Wallace, and they were clean disappointed: and mony a growl there was at what they called "the sell" . . . there was great grumbling at this roup o' lands open for leasing. There is something wrang, Sir, depend upon it—something wrang! There should be mair public announcement, and as much care as possible should be taken not to bring folks on a gowk's errand.'

Lowland Scots also found its way into local dramatic effusions, another instance of the use of the Scots tongue in the service of satire. In the following skit, one that made its way into print, a local playwright debunks a newly knighted politician ('Sir James Jingle'), who is shown in conversation with Queen Victoria. The sketch, reproduced here, rounds off the wide range of community issues which Scottish settlers, living in and around Hamilton, addressed through the medium of Lowland

Scots. From local chit-chat we moved to town potholes and the absence of signposts, then to the dubious manipulation of land sales in the colony and finally to the politics of Empire (30 April 1870, 3). The issue raised was the contentious one of increased immigration to the colony of Victoria in a bid to rid England of some of her unwanted over-population:

Vic.: Well, Sir James, how do you like the handle to your name?

Sir J.: Oh Brawley! it makes a body think something o' himsel'; and I am verra thankfu' to ye for it.

Vic.: Thanks is but poor payment; but I suspect you will give us a more substantial proof of your gratitude.

Sir J.: Weel, mem, I hae but little siller, and . . .

Vic.: Don't mention money, for poor old Peabody's will keep the wolf from the door for a time; but I'll tell you what—my garden is overcrowded with labourers, and I fear they will be eating each other some of these days, so I intend to draft off a lot for exportation. How many shall I send you?

Sir J.: Oh, I'll tak a wheen o' them, and gar the bodies out here true that they are a' needed.

Vic.: Exactly so; but I pray proceed very cautiously, for I see you have some eye-openers among the canaille in your quarter.

Sir J.: True, mem, true; and fu' weel ken I that some o' our newspaper cattle would be the better o' haein their tongues clippit.

THE 'ELDER VOICE'

Unlike the other areas considered, the area of church life became a focus for serious tension and discord between the several linguistic voices of the Scots. We know from the Scots version of the Psalms mentioned above that some devotional material in this tongue was in circulation in the district. Although Gaelic worship was widely conducted there is no tangible evidence of systematic public worship having been conducted in Lowland Scots. Conflict, when it came, was between Gaelic and English and such disagreement as reached the newspaper concerning the two, was conducted in English.

Presbyterianism, the dominant religious denomination of the Scots, was carried by them to each of the regions in which they settled. Initially, much of the worship conducted was that performed within the home, with the head of the house conducting prayers and Bible readings and leading Psalm singing. The arrival of an itinerant minister marked a special occasion when many people from the visited district would gather for a formal service and, if the need was there, to have children baptised and marriages performed. As communities grew and numbers became sufficient to call a full-time minister, churches were established and a routine of formal sabbath worship instituted. The Hamilton district was no exception to this pattern. First the nucleus of a congregation was established, then, some years later, in 1856, a building was erected to serve as a Gaelic church. The Rev. Angus Macdonald ministered ably to the Highland population in Gaelic until his accidental death in 1868.[9]

The deep attachment of Gaels to the forms and language of the worship of their homeland saw the subsequent erection of a number of other Gaelic-speaking churches in the neighbourhood of Hamilton. However, this same attachment was to bring about a certain amount of tension within Presbyterian congregations. The introduction of a musical instrument into worship services, for example, saw a rift open up within various congregations. A correspondent writing of the Hamilton congregation (18 Dec. 1863, 4), and the response of the Highland section of that church to the offer of a musical instrument, amusingly but without much understanding of the Highland religious temperament, recorded the horror provoked by such a suggestion:

> 'I believe that the "Sassenach" portion of the congregation did not as a body object, but your pure Celt would have "none of it", and I was told as a fact that, during the period when the Episcopal body had use of the Scotch Church and had their instrument there, such was the deep and ineradicable horror entertained by some of the Celtic ancients for that harmless-looking instrument, that numbers abstained from paying their devotions hebdomadally, as was their want, asseverating, with a fervency of spirit that did more credit to their warmth of feeling than their taste, that they would rather see "the Duffil in the kirk than yon masheen".'

The letter continued in this vein, ridiculing the part played by the Gaels in seeking to maintain their traditions, especially as they related to their form of worship.

> 'Our Celtic countrymen are very impressionable and especially open to the "convictions" of music. Why they should prefer the nasal harmony that forms the running accomplishment of "prayers and praise" in a great number of our churches where Gaelic is preached, can only be accounted for on the supposition that they recognise the resemblance it bears to their national pipe, and believe in nothing without a "sough", whether it be the "birr" of the drone, or the more dissonant but characteristic falsetto that governs the higher notes of the "chaunter".'

Thus did 'Civis Romanus' caricature and criticise the Gaelic portion of the congregation for their attitude towards musical instruments in church. In a follow-up letter (25 Dec. 1863, 3), he lauded the innovation introduced by one Presbyterian church in Hamilton whereby the minister had the congregation stand during the singing of the concluding Psalm 'instead of their usual lazy and apathetic mode of sitting or lolling on their seats'.

Tension between the different sections of the congregation was exacerbated when the issue of the availability of Gaelic leadership for worship raised its head. The death of Rev. Angus Macdonald led to a vacant pulpit which, following normal Presbyterian practice, was to be filled by the congregation 'calling' another minister to it. In a letter signed 'Gael' (3 Oct. 1868, 3), following a successful call to a non-Gaelic-speaking minister, the divisions engendered by the Gaelic language issue made themselves public. Writing in standard English, the author challenged the assumption that the settlement of the new minister, Rev. Mr McMillan, rested on the unanimous vote of members:

> 'Permit me to state, as one who was present, that the "unanimity" was all on one side; and that the feeling displayed by a considerable number of the English-speaking portion of the congregation does not reflect much credit on them as professing Christians. It is also stated that Mr McMillan is "to a certain extent, familiar with the Gaelic language". If so it must be to a very limited extent indeed; for during his stay in Hamilton, neither did he on any occasion, in public or private, conduct any religious service in that language—on the contrary he has repeatedly expressed his inability to do so. By this I do not mean to cast any reflection on Mr McMillan, but simply to guard my fellow countrymen from being misled. I feel confident that Mr McMillan is cognizant of the gross injustice that will be inflicted upon the Highlanders if any Minister be elected who cannot preach in their native tongue, he will at once decline to accept the call. The Highlanders very justly contend for their rights, and will not rest satisfied with, nor acquiesce in, the election of any pastor who cannot minister to their wants in Gaelic.'

Support from another Gael, Lachlan Morrison, was soon forthcoming (21 Oct. 1868, 3). He wrote to the newspaper to point out that a statement of 30 March 1857, setting up the church, had declared: 'That as a very large proportion, if not the majority, of the Presbyterians in and around the township of Hamilton are Gaelic-speaking, and prefer to have the ordinances administered to them in their native tongue, it is resolved that no minister be requested to settle in Hamilton but one who can minister to the people both in Gaelic and in the English language'. Morrison went on to announce that in support of the continuance of this original aim, a petition had already been signed by 'about one hundred Gaelic-speaking Highlanders of Hamilton and neighbourhood' and presented to the court of the church. This petition, Morrison wrote, had been ignored. Would the English-speaking portion of the congregation, he asked, like to be told that a minister was to be appointed who was only 'to a certain extent' familiar with that language? The argument, he reasoned, should be seen as 'reciprocally applicable. Only last month the average attendance on [*sic*] the Gaelic service for four consecutive Sabbaths was over one hundred and fifty, showing that nothing has occurred for the last eleven years to justify its discontinuance.' Morrison pointed to the possibility of schism in the church if the situation continued the way it was going and noted, no doubt having in mind the issue of musical instruments in church worship as well as the language issue, that the local Presbyterian church was 'a structure which has of late exhibited unmistakeable symptoms of degeneration and decay'.

An attempt to inject a measure of reasonableness into this argument was made by Rev. James Henderson (4 Nov. 1868, 3). He agreed with Morrison that the 'religious rights' of the Highlanders should be defended. He pointed out, however, that one of the great stumbling blocks to the continuation of Gaelic worship in the district was the difficulty of 'securing a suitably equipped pastor' who would be able to minister in both languages. More significantly, he added that, as the English-speakers now outnumbered the Gaelic residents of the district, it would not be possible to honour the original pledge relating to the appointment of a minister able to discharge his duties both in Gaelic and English. The matter continued to simmer for some time and, eventually, after refusing to join with the Union churches, the Gaelic portion of the congregation established itself as a separate Highland church, just as the congregation of 1856-57 had done.[10]

There is little doubt that the presence of Scotland's three tongues, Gaelic, Lowland Scots and English, has broadened the range of creative expression open to individual Scots, and enriched Scottish literary output over many years. Certainly, all three Scottish tongues were present from the earliest days of the provincial newspaper in the small colonial town of Hamilton, at the other end of the world from Scotland; a strong indication that the linguistic plurality enjoyed by Scots did not cease to operate outwith Scotland. The willingness to publish material from other sources in Scots, and to give space to the foregoing sample of letters and literary endeavours in English, Gaelic and Lowland Scots, bespeaks a measure of editorial liberality on the part of the *Hamilton Spectator,* perhaps even an enlightened notion that publication of such material in the public press could help to foster the development of an integrated community spirit. Consideration of the body of material from Scots published in that journal indicates that Gaelic and Lowland Scots did continue to be everyday voices among the emigrants, as evidenced by their use in print to instruct, amuse, and address the issues of current concern. The pages of the *Hamilton Spectator* go some way, too, to dispelling any surviving residue of that old stereotype—the tongue-tied inarticulate Scot!

NOTES

1 Unless otherwise specified, all subsequent references are to this paper.

2 *HS,* 8 October 1864, 4. More recent historical research has revised this figure down but still estimates that Scots formed something around two-thirds of the settlers. See, for example, Kiddle 1980, 14.

3 For instances of German and Lancastrian pieces see *HS*, 28 Jan. 1865, 4 and 4 Feb. 1865, 4.
4 Warrnambool is a coastal town in the Western District of Victoria, some 80 km from Hamilton. It boasted a large Highland population.
5 This appeared in *CA*, 21 March 1868, 3. Coleraine was a town situated about 32 km west of Hamilton.
6 *An Teachdaire Gaidhealach* was mostly in Gaelic but, while it printed the verse of celebrated Highland poets in Gaelic, it had given the poets' biographies in English.
7 *CA*, 19 March 1869. 4.
8 Lands successfully selected under the Act of 1865 were deemed to be only leased because failure to pay the instalments, or to make the requisite improvements, could lead to a termination of tenure.
9 Local poet, Macpherson, contributed a 'Monody on the Death of Rev. A. Macdonald' to the *Hamilton Spectator* on the death of the minister, 4 April 1868, 4.
10 See, for example, *HS*, 7 August 1863, 2; 2 Sept. 1869, 3; 8 Jan. 1870, 2. See also *BC*, 1979, 5-7.

REFERENCES

BC
1979 *Branxholme Congregation, 1879-1979*. Branxholme, Victoria.
CA
1869 *Coleraine Albion*. Coleraine, Victoria.
HS
1860-1875 *Hamilton Spectator*. Hamilton, Victoria.
KIDDLE, MARGARET
1980 *Men of Yesterday*. Melbourne (revised edition).
LEIGHTON, ROBERT
1868 'Scotch Words.' *HS*, 4.
MACPHERSON, OSSIAN
1868 'Monody on the Death of Rev. A. Macdonald.' *HS*, 4.

An Emigrant's Letter in Arran Gaelic, 1834

RONALD I. M. BLACK

> Reference may also be made to the burden of excessive cost of postage; a letter to Great Britain costing 4s. 10½d. Naturally, few letters were sent or received. In those days, however, letters were long and interesting. Encouraging letters sent home tended to increase emigration from the old sod (McKillop 1902: 64).

Thus wrote the industrious chronicler of the settlers from the island of Arran in Megantic County, Quebec; the truth of his statements is borne out by the letter here edited. Its writer, a young man of about twenty-five called William Hendry (or Henry, both spellings being used indiscriminately), was the eldest of thirteen children of Charles and Margaret Hendry of Penrioch in north-west Arran. Penrioch (*Peighinn Riabhach*, Brindled Pennyland) faces Kintyre across the Kilbrannan Sound; it survives as a farm behind the village of Pirnmill, which grew up along the shore in the early twentieth century. A mile north on the Lochranza road, just feet from the shore, is the tiny Congregationalist burial ground of Lennamore. It contains about 31 graves dated 1794-1898, and five of the eight inscribed stones preserve the memory of a Hendry or of a married woman born a Hendry. The name is of Ayrshire origin and has been Gaelicised simply as *Hendri* (Hendry 1857: 1). It is always spelt Hendry in Arran nowadays, and this is the spelling preferred in the present article.

In 1766 the principal tenant of Penrioch was John Currie. On 5 October 1772 its eight tenants were listed as William, Robert and Charles Hendry, Malcolm, William and Neil Robertson, John Currie and John Brown. Having been surveyed, the farm was promptly divided into three 'so as it may only be let to three tenants in place of eight'. These were to be two Hendrys and Neil Robertson. By next year, 1773, Penrioch had only two tenants, Robert Hendry and Neil Robertson, while Alltgobhlach, the neighbouring farm to the south, was taken by J. Hendry and D. Hendry. A rental for 16 September 1782 lists Robert Hendry at Penrioch, 'William Hendry &c.' at nearby South and Mid Thundergay, and 'Ninian Hendry &c.' at North Thundergay and Craw. Robert Hendry married Margaret Robertson, and they had five sons, Charles, John, Neil, Malcolm and Robert. Charles married Margaret Hendry, daughter of William Hendry, Thundergay. No rentals for succeeding decades are available, but judging from our letter, by 1834 Charles

Hendry was dead, and his eldest son William had gone out to blaze a path for the family in the New World (MacKenzie 1914: 357, 359; Burrel 1982: pt. 1, 198-9, 305, and pt. 2, 16.9.1782).[1]

The reason for William's departure is not far to seek. The division of Penrioch in 1773 was but part of a massive scheme by which the 8th Duke of Hamilton's Estate Commissioner, John Burrel, had sought to abolish communal farming throughout the island in favour of smaller, enclosed units yielding increased rents. By 1829 all of Arran was being farmed in the new way except some unentailed properties in the north and north-west which had formerly belonged to the Montgomeries of Skelmorlie and Eglinton. These properties were the farms of the north end between Sannox and Lochranza, which the Duke had intended to sell in 1783, and those clinging so precariously to the north-west coast between Catacol and Machrie (including Penrioch), which he had tried to sell in 1803, eventually giving them as dowry to Anne Douglas, his illegitimate daughter by the actress Mrs Easton, when she married the Hon. Henry R. Westenra, MP, later Lord Rossmore.

The writing was on the wall, and it seemed to be only a matter of time before the Penrioch community would be decimated by the end of run-rig, or even cleared altogether to make room for sheep, as had happened in Glenree in south Arran in 1825. (There had already been some emigration from the island to Chaleur Bay, New Brunswick.) Although William Hendry was not to know it, Penrioch's fate was to remain largely untouched even when finally re-acquired by the Hamiltons around 1844; his own fate became bound up with that of Sannox, as we will see (MacKenzie 1914: 173-202, 215, 226-7; Storrie 1967: 58; McLellan 1985: 150-63; Burrel 1982: pt. 2).

Hendry does not give his address, and mentions no specific locations in America except Quebec, but other internal evidence makes his new abode clear enough. In 1829 the long-expected blow fell on north Arran when the 10th Duke cleared Glen Sannox for sheep, along with the adjoining farms of Laggantuine, Laggan, Cuithe and the Cock, and in that year seventeen families and five other individuals took advantage of his offer to secure land in Upper Canada (Ontario) from the Government for such of his tenants as wished to settle there. Every head of a household and every man over twenty-one was to have 100 acres of his own, and the Duke was to pay half the passage-money. The first party of emigrants, consisting of twelve families and four other individuals, including a William Hendry (eighty-six people in all, we are told), set sail from Lamlash on the 169-ton brig *Caledonia* on 25 April 1829, arriving at Quebec about 25 June. The skipper of the *Caledonia* was Donald Miller, an Arran man, but the undisputed leader of the party was Archibald MacKillop, 'a chief among men', 'a Saul in stature among his fellows, devout, practical, and commanding', called by his grandson 'a good man . . . something of a great man, morally, mentally and physically'; each Sunday during the voyage, except the first, he conducted a service on deck, indeed he went on to lead the fledgling community in a variety of ways, acting as their first pastor and schoolmaster, and gaining the well-deserved title of Captain.[2] The immigration agent at Quebec, for reasons of his own, advised against their planned destination of Renfrew County, Ontario, recommending instead a part of Megantic County in Lower Canada (Quebec), only fifty miles south of Quebec City itself. 'Captain' MacKillop and three others (Baldie Calum of our letter, William Kelso of our letter, and Alexander Kelso) set off to inspect the territory, and reported back that it was 'well watered and well wooded'. The *Arannaich* decided unanimously that that was where they should settle, thus setting a pattern of emigration from the north of the island that was to remain firm for many years to come, and which was chronicled with minute detail by Captain MacKillop's grandson Dugald McKenzie McKillop (McKillop 1902: 9, 13-14, 17; MacKenzie 1914: 216-22; McLellan 1985: 164-6).

That the community described in Hendry's letter is the *Baile Meadhonach* or 'Scotch Settlement' of Inverness, Megantic Co., Quebec, is not therefore in doubt; what is, unfortunately, in doubt is whether or not we may identify the writer of our letter with that William Hendry who sailed on the *Caledonia*, and whose name duly appears on D. M. McKillop's plan of the post-1831 settlement, holding 100 acres on Range 4 between Donald MacKillop and Widow Margaret MacMillan (McKillop 1902: 25).

The difficulty arises when we consider the question, who exactly is the writer's cousin *Uilleam Ruadh* (Red William) who is named twice in the letter? William Hendry of the *Caledonia* was a carpenter (McKillop 1902: 12), but while *Uilleam Ruadh* is clearly described in the letter as pursuing that trade, the only specific work the writer mentions himself doing is making bricks. While the identity of William Hendry, carpenter, who sailed on the *Caledonia*, suits *Uilleam Ruadh* perfectly, therefore, there is no sure trace in the pages of the *Annals of Megantic* of any other settler from Arran called William in the period 1829-34 who had left his family behind. Of William Wallace, blacksmith, who came from Arran, we are given no further information. William Gordon, born 10 May 1818 at Corrie-Burn, came on the *Albion* in July 1829 with his widowed mother, had no other family, and would have been only sixteen years old in 1834; William Johnston came with his father on the same voyage, leaving the rest of the family to follow two years later, but these Johnstons were from Derry in Ireland and do not sound like relatives of the writer, even though they had been in Scotland and some of them were employed in the mills at Bridge of Weir in Renfrewshire (McKillop 1902: 21-2, 35, 48, 83, 138, 141).

If, however, we accept that the carpenter on the *Caledonia* may have been *Uilleam Ruadh* and ask if the *Annals* offer us another William Hendry who could conceivably have been either *Uilleam Ruadh* or our letter-writer, the answer, curiously enough, is yes. Describing the tiny population of pioneers whom the *Arannaich* found already settled in the district when they arrived in 1829, McKillop says:

> William Henry, about 1828, lived in Lower Ireland. He afterwards moved to the 6th range of Inverness. His wife's name was Margaret McKenzie, and he was an uncle of the late William Mowat (McKillop 1902: 35).

Who was this? If he was an *Arannach* he cannot have been there in 1828, for there is no suggestion whatsoever that the first Arran settlers found any fellow-islanders there before them; but the *Annals* are far from infallible, and he may have come in 1829 or later. His nephew William Mowat arrived from Scotland in 1841 and married a MacKillop, and Samuel Henry[3] of Lower Ireland and Inverness, twice mentioned in the *Annals*, may at a guess have been his son (McKillop 1902: 38, 48, 85, 91); he himself kept a sawmill, as is evident from the following:

> About the year 1846, Dugald McKenzie, Sr., drew a load of lumber from the mill of Wm. Henry (Mowats) to Curries, on the Hamilton Road, and on his return trip through the so-called 'Manse-bush', a spruce tree fell across the road. A dry limb of this tree pierced the back of one of the oxen and caused its death soon afterwards. Mr McKenzie unhitched the other ox, pushed the cart off the road, and went home and borrowed another ox-team to take care of the cart and carcass. At the time the tree fell Mr McKenzie was seated on the cart but a few feet away (McKillop 1902: 79).

In another excellent anecdote a William Henry is once again mentioned, but he is described in a way that seems intended to distinguish him clearly from the above. This, without doubt, is William Hendry of the *Caledonia*:

> William Henry, wheelwright and carpenter, used to tell how two of his customers were happily suited. As Henry plied his trade in the shop that stood near the concession, across the 'Little Brook' from my grandfather's house, he received orders to do the woodwork of two wooden plows. One plow was for James McKinnon, piper, schoolmaster and farmer, but withal, a man somewhat short of stature. The other plow was for big Neil MacMillan, father of Donald MacMillan, JP. Both plows were duly finished, the one for Mr McKinnon having low-set handles, as if for the use of a good-sized boy. There was something of an explosion, however, when the smaller man was shown the implement intended for his use, and he declared he would not put up with a toy plow of that kind. To satisfy his customer, the larger plow was handed over. Soon after this the burly form of Mr MacMillan filled the shop door. In answer to a question as to whether his plow was ready, Mr Henry timidly began to explain that he was afraid the only one he had on hand would not suit. 'Is this the plow?' boomed the big man, as he strode in and took a plow in his powerful grasp, to test the height of the handles. 'Yes,' said the carpenter, 'but you'll find the handles a little low.' 'Not a bit, not a bit! They are first rate,' said customer No. 2, as he bore away his prize (McKillop 1902: 80-1).

It is rather satisfying to visualise one William Henry—the writer of our letter, perhaps—ultimately owning a sawmill, while his cousin of the same name has a carpenter's shop. However, it should be said that this failure to identify the writer with any certainty sounds a note of caution upon the use of *The Annals of Megantic* for such purposes; there are certainly errors, inconsistencies and omissions in the *Annals* (McKillop 1902: 34; cf. McLellan 1985: 172), and the fact that they seldom name the townships in Arran from which families came is a major difficulty, so the identifications attempted in this article are offered with some diffidence. Further information on individual emigrants can no doubt be obtained from the estate papers at Brodick listed in Storrie 1967: 74.

D. M. McKillop calculated that by 1833 the Arran settlement in Megantic consisted of 222 persons, of whom seven were Hendrys. These were: (1) William Hendry; (2) Rev. and (3) Mrs Donald Hendry, see n. 4; (4) our letter-writer's maternal uncle Donald Hendry, see n. 41, with (5) his wife and their daughters (6) Janet and (7) Margaret. Uncle Donald, if I may so call him, arrived in 1831 with his (widowed?) daughter Mrs Kate Cristie. Uncle Donald's wife came the following year on the brig *Margret* with: their daughters Janet and Margaret; their son Donald, who returned to Arran the same year and died in the house of Donald Shaw (for whom see below); and their four-year-old granddaughter Mary A. Cristie, later to become Mrs Joseph McNey. Their other daughter became Mrs Mary Shanks and settled in Windsor Mills, Que., instead of Megantic. Other Hendrys by birth mentioned in the *Annals* are Mrs Flora Shaw, who came to Megantic in 1839 with her husband Donald, and Mrs Mary Kelso, who came in 1848 with her husband John. But there were no Hendrys left in Megantic at all by 1902 (McKillop 1902: 42-3, 45, 48-9, 60).

Our letter was in the possession of William Hendry's youngest brother Charles when the latter died in 1916 aged ninety-four. Charles had married Mary Black, and the letter passed to their daughter Isabella (Bella), who married James Hodge. There had been Hodges in Arran since at least 1837, when Daniel Hodge appears as schoolmaster at Lamlash (MacKenzie 1914: 231). James Hodge was piermaster at Lamlash, and he and Bella lived in the pierhouse. Bella died in 1948, and the letter passed to their son Charles, who had spent most of his working life as a shipping agent in West Africa. He married first Elsie Hume, then (after divorce) Mary Lancester, whose father Ian had been successively owner of Lagg and Lamlash hotels. When Charles Hodge retired he became piermaster at Brodick and Lloyds' agent for the island. He had a translation made of the letter (by whom is not known). It is referred to below as Charles Hodge's translation. Letter and translation passed to his son by his second marriage, Brigadier David H. Hodge, DL, of Durham. After restoration work by the National Library of Scotland in 1987 it was presented by Brigadier Hodge to the Isle of Arran Museum Trust in 1988, and is now kept at their museum in Brodick. The National Library retains a photocopy, Acc. 9479.

The Hendrys remained at Penrioch until the 1940s or 1950s, when James Hendry left to farm at Catacol. He died aged sixty-six on 31 May 1965.

Arran Gaelic is an all but extinct dialect which may be said to lie, linguistically speaking, between Kintyre Gaelic and Manx, and which seems to have struck the northerly ear as outstandingly odd, cf. *Gairm* 40 (summer 1962) 318-9. Our letter is therefore of great linguistic interest; to attempt to assess its importance as a historical record of the dialect, I append a list of as many of the reliques of Arran Gaelic as I have been able to trace.

1697 A charm noted in the records of the Presbytery of Kintyre and Islay, dated at Kilmory, Arran, 11 November 1697 (Carmichael 1928-71: 4, 167).

1705 A charm noted in Gaelic script in Kilbride Session Minutes (MacKenzie 1914: 295).

1778 Rev. William Shaw, *An Analysis of the Gaelic Language* (Edinburgh/London; repr. Menston 1972). Contains Shaw's translation of Pope's *Messiah* into Gaelic verse. Shaw (1749-1831) came from Clachaig, south Arran (MacDonald 1973: 2; MacKenzie 1914: 145-7).

1780 Rev. William Shaw, *A Galic and English Dictionary* (London).

1791 Rev. Dugald Crawford, *Searmoin chuaidh a liobhairt aig an Raft-Swamp* (Fayetteville, N. Car.). Crawford (1752-1821) came from Shiskine (MacKenzie 1914: 144-5; MacLean 1915: 102-3; Cameron 1912: 112-4; Scott 1915-28: 4, 63). The Rev. Prof. Douglas Kelly of the University of Mississippi tells me that some of his Gaelic sermons are extant in manuscript in North Carolina and have been read from the pulpit in recent times, by himself among others.

1791 Rev. Dugald Crawford, *Searmoin A chuaidh a liobhairt aig an Raft-Swamp air an fhicheada' latha don cheud mhios do'n fhoghmnar, 1790* (Fayetteville, N. Car.).

1795 Rev. Dugald Crawford, *Searmoin Do Mhnai' chuaidh a sgriobhadh ann sa Bhliadhna, 1795* (Glasgow).

1853 Rev. Angus MacMillan, *Searmoinean* (Glasgow). MacMillan (1776-1843) came from North Sannox (MacKenzie 1914: 144-5, 247; McLellan 1985: 170; Cameron 1912: 112-4, 123-6).

1853 Archibald MacMillan, *Dearbhadh a' Cridhe—Laoidhean Spioradaille* (Lochranza).

1855 Rev. Donald Hendry, *Laoidhean Spioradail* (1st edn. Canada 1855, 2nd edn. Glasgow 1857). The hymns *Laoidh mu Amaideachd na h-Òige* and *An Soisgeul* were also published separately (Glasgow 1855).[4]

1867 James Hamilton, *Laoidh le Seumas Hamilton aon a Sheanairean na H-Eaglais Saoire 'san Eilean Aranach.*

1867 Rev. Archibald Cook, *Notes of a Gaelic Sermon* (Glasgow). Cook (1788-1865), whose influence on Free Church doctrine is still felt today, came from Achareach, Glenscoradale (Kennedy 1895b: 15; Scott 1915-28: 6, 467; MacLeod 1988).

18— Rev. Archibald Cook, *Searmoin* (Inverness). Sermon on Philippians ii.5.

1868 Rev. Archibald Cook, *An Tiodhlac Do-Labhairt* (1st edn. Glasgow 1868, 2nd edn. Glasgow 1885, 3rd edn. Inverness 1915).

1877 James Hamilton, *Marbh-Roinn* (Glasgow). Elegies on three Arran ministers.

1877 Rev. Peter Davidson, *Poems on Various Religious Subjects.* Includes 127 pp. Gaelic hymns. Davidson (1788-1875) came from Glenrosa, Brodick (MacLean 1915: 106; Cameron 1912: 112, 137-8, 143-4).

1889 Rev. Dr Alexander Cameron, 'Arran Place Names', in *Transactions of the Gaelic Society of Inverness,* 15 (1888-9) 122-139. Repr. Cameron 1894: 561-76.

1893 John Kennedy (ed.), *Gaelic Poems and Letters in English, by the late James Brown, Craw, Arran* (Inverness). Kennedy (1854-1910), a native of Badenoch, was Free Church (later UF) minister of Lennamore, his manse being at Catacol; he is not to be confused with his more celebrated namesake the Free Church minister of Dingwall, to whom he was related (*Transactions of the Gaelic Society of Inverness,* 26: vi; Lamb 1956: 288; Cameron 1912: 135, 145, 156, 159). There is a splendid monument in his memory at Pirnmill.

1894 Rev. Dr Alexander Cameron, 'Arran Place Names', in Cameron 1894: 561-76.

1895 Paper by Rev. John Kennedy, Catacol: see References. Kennedy's notes are in Glasgow University Library (MS Gen. 1090 nos. 68-9).

1895 Verse and prose collected in West Bennan and Druim-a-ghinnir (Carmichael 1928-71: 2, 307, 354-5, 370).

1896 Rev. John Macalister, *Gaelic and English Sermons* (Inverness). Macalister (1789-1844) came from Kilpatrick, Shiskine (Cameron 1912: 135-6).

1897 Paper by Rev. C. Robertson: see References. Robertson's extensive notes on the dialect and place-names of Arran are in the National Library of Scotland, MSS 390-1, 420-2 and 424.

1899 Rev. Archibald Cook, *Everlasting Love* (in Gaelic).

1907 Rev. Archibald Cook, *Sermons, Gaelic and English* (Glasgow).

1908 Ronald Currie, *The Place-Names of Arran* (Glasgow).

1914 Chapters 'Folk Lore' and 'Gaelic Songs of Arran' in MacKenzie 1914: 251-350.

1916 Rev. Archibald Cook, *Searmon* (Inverness). Sermon on Job xxxiii.24.

1916 Rev. Archibald Cook, *Searmoinean Gaelig* (Inverness). 2nd edn. Glasgow 1946.

1957 Holmer's *The Gaelic of Arran,* with texts (collected 1938) at pp. 160-91.

1969 Heinrich Wagner and Colm Ó Baoill, *Linguistic Atlas and Survey of Irish Dialects* 4 (Dublin): Arran material (collected 1961) at pp. 189-211.

1976 *Tocher* no. 21, 189-90: 'A "Tynwald" in Arran?'. Recorded from Donald Craig (Machrie/Pirnmill) by David Clement in 1973. Linguistic Survey of Scotland tape 950. Other Linguistic Survey tapes of Arran material are as follows:

Craig, Donald (Machrie/Pirnmill) 913-6, 931-2, 934-5, 937, 939, 941-6, 951-3, 955, 971, 984, 999, 1069, 1077.
Currie, Dan (Thundergay) with sisters 944a.
Currie, Willie (Machrie) 210d.
Hendry, Janet (Catacol) 56c.
Hendry, Mrs Katie (Alltgobhlach) 56b, d.
Kelso, Ishabel (Lochranza) 52, 53a.
Kerr, John (Lochranza) 932, 934, 951-2.
MacBride, John (Shannochie, South End) 57b.
MacLeod, John (Pirnmill) 210e.
Murchie, James (Shiskine) 54b, 55, 56a.
Murchie, Miss Marion (Lochranza) 995a.
Robertson, John (Kilpatrick) 210b, 1150 (= School of Scottish Studies SA 1965/129); with sister Belle Robertson 210c.
Sillars, Mrs I. (Shiskine) 53b, 54a.

This list could furnish the bulk of the material for any complete diachronic study of Arran Gaelic, or indeed of Arran literature for that matter. It can be seen that our letter comes relatively early, and that its personal, informal character is only otherwise to be sought among the Linguistic Survey tapes, which are quite recent. Much of the list consists of religious material prepared for publication in more or less standardised Gaelic in the second half of the nineteenth century. Even the songs published by MacKenzie in 1914 are largely regularised in spelling, e.g. *Deòcan as Deònaid* in Holmer 1957: 179 is *Seòcan agus Seònaid* in MacKenzie 1914: 331 (see n. 18).

We may assume that Hendry's mother was a monoglot Gaelic speaker, but that her children were bilingual. Their knowledge of written Gaelic was derived from Bible study. Hendry seems to have no trouble spelling scriptural words like *Tighearna* 'Lord', *beannachdan* 'blessings, greetings', *teaghlach* 'family' and relationships like *nighean* 'daughter', *seanmhathair* 'grandmother' and so on, but his spelling of non-scriptural words and names is often quite bizarre and of course has the virtue for us of revealing many dialect features. The emigrants' literacy is thus described in the *Annals*:

> Nearly all the settlers could read both Gaelic and English, and all could speak

> some English, though, of course, Gaelic was the current language, and it was in Gaelic that Mr [Donald] Hendry preached. Each family owned a few books, and the settlers were especially well stocked with Bibles, both English and Gaelic, these having been brought out in considerable quantities, as they were under the impression that in the new country it would be almost impossible to get such books. In some instances the books and baggage of the passengers had been damaged by water on the way over. They also had psalm books, and a few such works as Josephus' Antiquities, Rollo's Ancient History, Peter Grant's Gaelic Poems, and devotional works by Baxter, Bunyan, Dyer and Boston. A few families had quite a number of good quality books (McKillop 1902: 31).

Hendry's letter is written on paper watermarked 1829—did they bring paper out with them too? Writing paper was so scarce in Megantic schoolrooms that scraps of brown wrapping paper were used to write on, and copybooks were used twice, first the right way up and then upside-down using the spaces between the lines (McKillop 1902: 58).

The *Arannaich* had been partly bilingual since at least the time of Martin Martin, who wrote of them that 'they all speak the *Irish* language, yet the *English* Tongue prevails on the *East-side*, and ordinarily the Ministers preach in it, and in *Irish* on the *West-side*'; this ambivalence is well reflected in the saying *Arainn bheag mhiodalach bhreugach, a cùl ri caraid 's a h-aghaidh ri nàmhaid*—'Little fawning lying Arran, her back to friend and her face to foe' (Martin 1716: 225; Cameron 1894: 480; Holmer 1957: 185). Hendry's letter reveals the kind of systematic borrowing (*line, clearadh, swampach*, etc.) which is commonly a feature of such front-line dialects, and which is jeered at by William Ross in the song given in the Appendix, and chuckled at by *Caraid nan Gaidheal*, for Cowal, in his review of the Highland Society's Gaelic Dictionary (MacLeod 1829: 14):

> Feòraich de fhear san àite sin, Ciod an t-àm de 'n latha tha e, is cosmhuil gur e'n fhreagairt a gheibh thu, *WELL, ma ta, cha'neil CERTAINTY agam air A PHARTICULAR sin.*

Holmer's remark that 'the Arran people are always accused by their Argyllshire neighbours of an extraordinary indulgence in what is termed "mixed" language' (Holmer 1957: 2) was probably as true in 1782 or 1834 as in 1938 or 1957; it is often heard nowadays of Lewis speakers. Another of the letter's characteristics is a degree of muddle where lenition is concerned—indeed, one is almost tempted to suspect that mutation in Hendry's Gaelic is following rules quite distinct from those of standard Scottish Gaelic. His most troublesome quirk of all is his habit of writing *g* as in English 'George' for slender *d* or *t*, e.g. *minisgair* for *minisdear* 'minister', *Keggi* for *Ceitidh* 'Katie'. When all is said and done, however, the letter represents a colourful pebble atop a cairn of literary achievement that is remarkably large for such an insignificant corner of Gaeldom; even a hundred years later it was reported that 'Arran is an island of scholars and a great many of the Gaelic speakers can read and write the language' (Holmer 1957: 1).

It remains only to be added that the Megantic Outlaw, so well remembered in Lewis, is nowhere mentioned in *The Annals of Megantic*. Donald Morrison, who received the nickname after killing a man in a gunfight, belonged to the community of Lewis immigrants who settled during 1851-5 in the 'Long Bush' around Sherbrooke and as far east as the shores of Lake Megantic, all of a hundred miles south of Inverness. As the Long Bush was settled and cleared, new counties were created—the Lewis settlement became Scotch County, while Megantic County shrank to the district around Inverness itself. The two communities were far apart in more ways than one. Their Gaelic dialects were mutually almost incomprehensible, while nonconformity and the Disruption (1843) separated them in church matters (McKillop 1902: 5; MacDonald 1978: 167-8; Verity 1987).

TEXT

[Square brackets] indicate missing, illegible or almost illegible text. Lacunae are mainly due to the loss of a portion of the letter (about 4 x 6 cms.) where it was sealed. Semi-legible portions have been examined under ultra-violet light. The letter consists of a single folio sheet = four pages, folded to reveal only the address on the outside.

october the fifteenth 1834

May dear mother brothers and sistes

a mathair greadhich tha me gabhail a cothrom-se air sgriobhadh dar niunsuidh a ligal a chluintinn duibh[5] gu eil sinn ule gu maith sanamsa buidhachas do dhia airson a throcairen dhuinn agus a mhianemig[6] gu biodh e ni ceun agibhse ri ra agus bha duil agum ri litir a chur dar nionsuid toisach en tamaridh[7] ach gholabh mi began uine en e steates tiomull da cheud mile on aite so deic agus tree fichead mile en taobh eile line agus be nobair a bha agam chuid do nuine bhi deanamh[8] clacha craidha[9] agus bha uilliam ruagh mo cusinn lam agus cuigear eile do mhuntir[10] en atie agus thanig sien dhachie ach dhean[11] Peter Hamilton cairid domh fein agus dhiar e ormsa na bighinn a chur in fhios dachie ruibhse[12] dhinseadh da mhuintir gun robh e gu maith agus cha neil e teachd dachie gu cion blianadh ma soirbheas leis Aagus tha agum ra innseadh dhuibh nach beo shoni chui a bha lochraoinsa gholabh e leis en tinnis ann e Quebec gu robh en tighearna uile gar nulamhachadh airson na uair sien. Agus tha nighean do uilliam kiliston[13] a bha air sanagan a tha duil acha[14] gu mheil i en tiniscatie[15] agus nighean eile do bhaldy callum nach eil a faotinn a slainte idir (p. 2) Ach tha en eslaint an sgach atie Aagus tha mo chairden leis e mheil mi a dol ma guairt gach laa Agus tha bhrathair mo mhathair agus a theaghlach gu maith, a mheud dhiu sa tha aig en tigh, ach tha e fein a fainachadh gu mhor agus tha iad teachd air enaaidh[16] gu maith on a tanik iad do d[u]iche[17] so tha achda[14] da bo agus beathin bega tha achda[14] air a blianadh so na deanadh chuidachadh maith do theaghlach na dha a bharrachd orra fein agus tha e agra nach measadh e bhi riamh na bu sona na tha e na biodh a clann leis en so cruinn. tha iad cur moran beannachdan dar nionsuidh agus tha goinag[18] mo chiosin[19] fastage[20] se namsa aig e mhinisgair tha i cur moran beannachdan nionsuidh Agus tha ma cairdean leis em bheil mi cur moran beannachdan dar nionsuidh agus a ghiunsuidh mo shean-mhathair agus un[21] Keggi puithar mathair agus tha mo chairid caoimh uilliam adhfurachi air teachd dachie agus tha e gu maith ca dan e ach ma aon seachduin agus gholabh e risg en de air slighe a dhol don atie n robh e roimh tiamull[22] sae ceud mile se so[23] ghabh iad sea mios teachd e nuas roimh leis en raft gu Qebec agus tha uilliam ruagh mo cusin caoimh gu maith tha e uairean ag obair air en taoirsneachd agus a chuid eile saoirachadh ferrain agus tha chuid a dhuil agie gun thig a chuid eile don theaghlach a mach ach cha neil fhios agie agus tha mi creudsinn gu maith gu biod iad na bhear en so na tha iad (p. 3) agus moran a thullie orra ach cha neil mi toirt misneach do dhuine air bith teachd air en uairs oir tha moran tigheachd nach eil toilite don atie so agus cha neil mi fein ra tholite don atie so fathest ach faodidh e bhi gle maith air a hon sin ach tha fhios agam gu biodh mi gu mor na bu tailiteacha na biodh sibh fein se chuid eile don theaghlach en so agus a chuid mor a thainig don atie so en toiseachd.[24] thaink iad re iomad sarachadh [ ][25] en deigh doibh teachd [ ] a mhuintir a tha teachd a nịos e faotinn agus ch[ ] teachd en toiseach en atie so tha toilite deagh [ ] toir achda[14] le oibrachadh[26] gle goirt uairen air a[ ] a dheanas[27] daoine en so cha bhi egal orra gun toirear [ ] Cha druin mise in e[28] clearadh air mo lot fal[a] gad gaineadh tha e go[29] fada o margadh snach biodh mo[r] ann domh ach na biodh duil agum ri sibhse e teachd en so thoisachin air ulamhachadh air air son en so se gholabhain blianadh em o cosnadh a chuidachadh leibh teachd a mach cha neil fhios agum cocu[30] a tha mi deanadh gu maith dar taoibhse a bhi fantuinn en so sna nach eil ach se bhi a bhear lam tha sibhse ligal fhacin air curam dhiomsa gach uair tha sibh faotnn cothrom air agus cha bo choir do[mhsa bhi ro]churamach tiomull oirbhse tha fadail orm go[29] fada se tha mi gun air facinn fein agus mo chairden caoimh uile tha en sin ach tha dochas agum gu faic mi sibh en so air no en sin en uine gun a bhi anabar fada ma se sin toil en tighearna tha en tatie so gu maith fadailach a bhi ann air uairen cha naik snn read[31] se bith [tiomull ach][25] oirn ach e caoile agus ne speran os air cion tha en gheameradh[32] enso dirach fada agus fuar tha sneachd aguin ma namse (p. 4) agus cha nainith domh aon do mo chairdean en sin le a chuidachadh nach feudeadh geainead gle maith en so na biodh iad aon uair bhos tha chuid don fearun dirach maith agus chuid gle surrach tha chuid dheagh[33] swampach clachach creagach ach tha chuid mor dheagh[33] maith airson feum dhaoine tha mi a cur moran beannachden dar nionsuidh fein agus thiunsuidh mo sheanmhathair agus un[21] gach brathair athair se brathair mhathair tha agum agus un[21] gach puthar mhathair es athair agum agus un[21] gach chairid es banchairid tha agum gad nach urrad mi nainmsachadh[34] en draist

Ulliam Hendry

Mrs Charls Henry
Penrioch
Island of Arran
Scotland

TRANSLATION

October the fifteenth 1834.

My dear mother, brothers and sisters.

Dear mother, I am taking this chance to write to you to let you hear that we are all well at present, thanks be to God for His mercies to us, and that we would wish[6] that you should have the same to say; and I had expected to send you a letter at the beginning of the summer, but I went for a short while to the States (about two hundred miles from this place, seventy miles the other side of the Line),[35] and the work I had for part of the time was making bricks, and my cousin Uilleam Ruadh was with me and another five lads[10] from the place; and we came home, but Peter Hamilton (a friend of mine) stayed, and he asked me, if I were sending word home to you, to tell his people that he was well, and he isn't coming home for a year if he gets on all right.[36] And I have to tell you that Johnnie from Cuithe that used to be in Lochranza is dead. He died of sickness in Quebec.[37] May the Lord prepare us all for that time. And there's a daughter of William Kelso's from Sannox[38] that they think is in a consumptive sickness and another daughter of Baldie Calum's[39] that isn't getting her health at all.

(p. 2) But then there's no place without illness, and my friends[40] with whom I go around every day and my mother's brother and his family[41] are in good health, those of them as are at home,[42] but he himself is failing very much; and they have got on well since they came to this country. They have two cows and small beasts. This year they have as much as would be a considerable help to one or two families in addition to themselves, and he says that he would consider himself never to have been happier than he is now if he had his children gathered around with him. They send many greetings to you. And my cousin Janet[18] is in the Minister's[4] service at present; she sends you many greetings. And my friends[40] that I am with send many greetings to you and to my grandmother and to my father's sister Katie.[43] And my dear kinsman William Murchie[44] has come home and he is well. He only stayed about one week and set off again yesterday on the way to the place he was in before, about six hundred miles from here.[45] Before that they took six months coming down by raft to Quebec. And my dear cousin Uilleam Ruadh is well, he is sometimes employed as a carpenter and works the land the rest of the time, and he has some hopes that the rest of the family will come out, but he does not know, and I can well believe that they would be better here than where they are, (p. 3) and many other people besides, but I am not encouraging anybody to come at the moment, for many are coming who are not pleased with this place, and I'm none too pleased with this place myself as yet, but it may be very good for all that. But I know I would be far happier if yourself and the rest of the family were here and also the large number that came to this place at first. They came through many a trial after arriving that the folk who are coming now [are not] getting[46] and [ ] coming first to this place who are pleased [ ] good [ ] many of them by very hard work, sometimes [ ] people stay here they are not afraid that [ ] will be taken [ ]. I have not done any clearing on my [empty(?)] lot [ ] doing(?) it(?) it is so far from a market that it would not be [much use(?)] to me, but if I were expecting you to be coming here I would start preparing for you here and I would go away and earn for a year to help you come out. I don't know whether I am doing well by you to be staying here or not but it's (here) I'd prefer to be. You are showing your concern for me every time you get the chance to and [I] ought not [to be too] concerned about you. I am distressed that it has been so long since I have seen yourself and all my dear kinsfolk who are there, but I hope that I will see you either here or there before too long, if that is the Lord's will. This place is pretty tedious to be in sometimes, we can see nothing around us but the forest and the skies above.[47] The winter here is just long and cold. We are having snow at the moment.

(p. 4) And I don't know any of my kinsfolk there who might not with His(?) help do very well here once they were over. Some of the land is just fine and some pretty useless, some is very swampy, stony and rocky but a lot of it is very good for people's needs.[48]

I send many greetings to yourself and to my grandmother and to all of my paternal and maternal uncles and to all my maternal and paternal aunts and to all my male and female kin though I can't mention them just now.

William Hendry

Mrs Charles Henry
Penrioch
Island of Arran
Scotland

APPENDIX: WILLIAM ROSS'S LAMPOON ON ARRAN GAELIC

The following poem contains numerous Arran Gaelic features (e.g. see nn. 18, 22); as a one-time travelling packman, although born in Skye of a Ross-shire mother, Ross (1762-?91) had visited many parts of the Highlands and islands, and knew his dialects. On a public level it may be a satire on some of the Clyde fishermen who had begun to pursue the herring into the northern Minch in the 1780s, but on a private level its target is undoubtedly Samuel Clough (1757-1815).

Clough was captain of a twenty-gun privateer which, some time during the winter of 1781-2, was bound out of Liverpool for Jamaica. Caught by a gale, he ran before the wind and made the safety of Stornoway harbour. It was probably on this visit that he met Mór Ros, one of the beauties of the town, whom the poet idolised. He set sail again when the wind dropped, but soon returned. He sounds a romantic figure, and was indeed a reasonably wealthy young man, thanks no doubt to the vulnerability of the French merchant fleet—he had assets in both Liverpool and Jamaica. Suffice it to say, he and Mór were married at the beginning of February 1782, by the parish minister of Stornoway, John Downie, who privately remarked: 'Far fowls have fair feathers.' He made a generous settlement on his bride and a will in which he left her everything; then, perhaps a month after the marriage, he finally left for Jamaica. Mór remained in Stornoway, and was still there on 6 December 1782, as a letter of her father's shows; some time afterwards, however, Clough came back and took her to her new home in Liverpool. The rest is folklore, and our poem is but one of a series of cathartic songs made by Ross on the event, each one very different from the rest, culminating in the great *Òran Eile* (MacMhathain 1955: 340-2; Black 1968: 7-8, 43, 121).

Published in John Mackenzie (ed.), *Orain Ghae'lach, le Uilleam Ros* (Inverness, 1830), 95-8; 2nd edn. (Glasgow, 1834), 151-5; 3rd edn. (Edinburgh, 1868, repr. 1870, 1874, 1877), 78-80. I have regularised spelling and punctuation to some extent. In the few instances where the second and third editions differ substantially from the first I follow the former in the text, giving readings from the latter in the Notes. Title in all editions: *Òran a rinn am bàrd, mar gun deanadh seòladair deasach e, air dha bhi ann an taigh-dannsaidh, anns an taobh-tuath.—Tha 'm bàrd air deanamh an òrain do rèir Gaelig an t-seòladair féin.* (A song that the poet made, as a southron sailor would have made it, after he had been in a dancing-house, in the north.—The poet has made the song in accordance with the sailor's own Gaelic.)

1. Bha mi 'n-raoir 'san taigh-dhannsaidh,
Bha iad *tranga* gu leòr—
Bha na h-ìonagan glan ann,
'S iad cho cannach 's bu chòir;
Cha robh srad air a' ghealbhan
O'n a dh'fhalbh sinn o bhòrd
Ach gràine beag luaithre
Bha fo sguadradh nam bròg.

2. Bha na Màireagan uil' ann
Is iad air tionnal gach taobh,
Ged nach d' éirich a' ghealach
Cha robh maill' air a h-aon;
B' fheàrr sud na bhi 'm breislich
Cur a' *cheti* fa-sgaol
Na bhi *pumpadh* na *Deònaid*
Air a' mhór-chuan re gaoith.

3. Chan eil beath' ann as bòidhche
Na th' aig seòladair féin—
Seach gum bi e 'na mharaich'
Bidh na cailean á dhéidh;
Bidh na h-ìonagan cannach
'Ga leantainn gu léir
Toirt am mionnan gu *sure* iad
Nach bi *trùsair* gun fheum!

4. An tug thu 'n air' a Rob Tàileir
'S a chuid Màireagan féin
Agus déidh aig na h-òighean
Air a phògadh gu léir?
Bidh esan da ruagadh
'S da'm buaireadh le 'bheul—
Tha e soireanta sò-ghradh't
Mar gum pòsadh e ceud.

5. A fac' thu 'n Sgiobair bha làimh ris
'S a Mhàireag r'a thaobh,
A làmh thar a muineal
'S i bulach 'na ghaol?
Re'ag i leis thar Caol Mhula
Agus tiumal a' Mhaol
Gu bhith *lòradh* a *phica*
Nuair as dripeal a' ghaoth.

6. ‘Chan eil *doubt*,’ arsa Màireag,
‘Nach *overhàlig* mi ball!’
(Ach gille gramail bhith shìos orr’
Nach toir fiaradh g’ a ceann);
Ged a thigeadh na *sgualaichean*
Cruaidh on a’ ghleann,
Cha bhi ’n Sgiobair fo mhì-ghean
Gus an dìobair a chrann.[49]

7. Tha iasgach an sgadain
Ro bheag againn ’san àm,
O’n ’se ’n t-*ounair* tha *cost* oirn
Cha bhi ’m *brot* oirn air chall;
Bithidh *grog* againn daonnan
’S cha bhi aon fhear gun dram,
’S gheobh sinn nìonagan bòcha
Gu ar pògadh is taing.

8. Gheobh sinn nìonagan bòcha
Is mnathan òga gu réidh—
’Se mo raoghainn-s’ an nìonag
O’n a bhios mi ri beud;
Thàinig còmhlan dhiu tharais
Air an chala so ’n dé
’S bha sinn mar riu a’ dannsadh
Fad ’s a shanntaich sinn féin.

9. Chan eil *shig* ’s na puirt Fhrangach
Nach danns iad air uair,
No car an Dun-Éidin
Gun aig té ’san taobh-tuath;
Miann-sùil bhi ’ga léirsinn[50]
’S iad a’ leumnaich mun cuairt
Mar ri balaich chinn-fhìdhleach[51]
’S sgal pìoba[52] ’nan cluais.

1. I was in the dancing-house last night,
They were hard at it—
There were grand lassies there,
As pretty as need be;
Not a spark was in the fire
Since we left the ship
But a tiny grain of ashes
Squashed under the shoes.

2. The Popsies were all there
Gathered from each airt,
Though the moon hadn't risen
None of them were loth;
Better that than confounded
Clearing the jetty
Or pumping the *Janet*
On high seas in a gale.

3. There's no finer life
Than a sailor has—
Because he's a mariner
The girls pursue him;
The pretty lassies
Follow him as one,
Swearing they're sure
Trousers won't be worthless!

4. Did you notice Rob Tailor
With his own group of Popsies
And all the young virgins
Dying to kiss him?
He goes hunting them down
And tempts them with his mouth—
He's gleg and charming enough
To marry a hundred.

5. Did you see the Skipper close by him
With his Popsy at his side,
His arm round her shoulders
And she completely besotted?
She'd go through the Sound of Mull with him
And round the Mull of Kintyre
To be lowering his peak
When the wind's at its height.

6. 'Without a doubt,' said Popsy,
'I'll overhaul some tackle!'
(As long's a thrawn lad's down on her
That won't give her head leeway);
Even should squalls come
Wild from the glen,
The Skipper won't worry
Till he loses his mast.[49]

7. For fishing the herring
We don't give a fig now,
Since it's the owner that's paying for us
We won't lack for broth;
We'll always have grog
While no man lacks a dram,
And we'll get lovely lassies
To kiss us with thanks.

8. We'll get lovely lassies
And young women easy—
My choice is the lassie
Since I'm up to no good;
A bunch of them came over
By this harbour yesterday
And with them we danced
As long as we craved.

9. There's no jigs or French tunes
That they won't dance as required,
Or movement in Edinburgh
That some lass in the north can't do;
They're a sight for sore eyes
As they caper about
With the fiddle-head boys,[51]
Sound of pipe[52] in their ears.

NOTES

1 The genealogical information on the Hendrys in this article was obtained from Mr Alastair Hendry through Mr Alastair Sillars. It was noted on 13 November 1949 from Mr Stewart Robertson, son of Jessie Hendry, daughter of Charles Hendry and Mary Black.

2 He was captain and then major of a company of volunteers raised at the time of the rebellion of 1837. Afterwards he was promoted to colonel. Already an unpaid inspector of schools, he became a Commissioner of the Peace. He died in 1867 (McKillop 1902: 9, 11-17, 25, 47, 145, 166-7; MacKenzie 1914: 219-26).

3 The name of Samuel Henry's daughter is cited as one of the oddest in the county—Jemima Kezia Karen-happuk Henry (McKillop 1902: 85). Donald Meek has pointed out to me, however, that these are the three daughters of Job (Job xlii:14), and that it is common practice in evangelical circles to name children after such biblical heroes or heroines; he himself has known a family with two daughters called Jemima and Kezia.

4 Rev. Donald Hendry, a Congregationalist. A cousin of William's grandfather Robert Hendry, he was born at Alltgobhlach in 1774 and was known as *An t-Iasgair Arannach* (The Arran Fisherman). His hymn *An t-Iasgair* begins:

Tha m' inntinn tric fo smuairean
'S mi seòladh measg nan cuantan

(My mind is often melancholy/As I sail amongst the oceans). However, it ends:

Is fàgaidh mis' am bàta
'S na lìontan le taing.

(And I shall leave the boat/And the nets with thanks), for he was eventually employed by the Independents (Congregationalists) as an itinerant preacher in the Western Isles and North Kintyre. His work seems to have been supported by the congregation at Sannox, and Mrs Janet MacKay, wife of the influential Sannox pastor the Rev. Alexander MacKay, sent him her good wishes in eight lines of Gaelic verse beginning *Mo bheannachd chum an iasgair a-nis o'n fhuair thu t' iarrtas*, 'My blessing to the fisherman now that you've got your request' (Hendry 1857: 2, 14, 16; Meek 1987: 24). Mrs MacKay was a sister of Duncan MacMillan, great-grandfather of Prime Minister Harold Macmillan (cf. n. 39); her husband accompanied the departing members of his flock to Lamlash in 1829, and preached a farewell sermon from the deck of the *Caledonia* on the text 'Casting all your care upon Him; for He careth for you' (1 Peter v.7). Donald Hendry went out as missionary to the Megantic colonists, many of whom were ex-fishermen like himself, on the *Foundling* in 1831 with his wife Elizabeth Kelso. They had no children. Known in Canada as Elder Hendry, he was not ordained until after the arrival in 1844 of his successor as pastor to the community, the Rev. William Anderson, a Lowlander from Airdrie. Although not licensed to conduct marriages in either Scotland or Canada (cf. n. 37), he did in fact marry one couple in the settlement. A dogmatic Calvinist, he was very able and pious but reserved. He settled on a 100-acre bush farm on the outskirts of Inverness. Worked largely for him by the people, this provided his main source of support. The community was mainly Congregationalist and he was certainly its first minister, but his first meeting-house, built of round logs in 1832, was inter-denominational. About 28 feet long, it was roofed (like the settlers' houses) with bark, with a lean-to at the end for his horse, and had one window, subsequently two. The door was at one end, the fire at the other, with nothing but a hole overhead to let out the smoke. Such an arrangement was, of course, quite normal in Arran, but the result in Canada was that it was so cold in winter that groups of worshippers had to take turns in occupying the bench nearest the fire. Hendry's pulpit was built well above the floor, so in summer he had an excellent view of the congregation, but in winter, when the pine logs were spluttering and scattering smoke far and wide, he was up in the thickest of it. Eventually, by making a collection of bushels of wheat, the congregation raised enough to buy a stove for the building, which largely solved the problem. Hendry preached two- to three-hour sermons, in Gaelic only—twice on Sundays, but only once in the short days of winter, and also every Thursday evening in his own house. Once while preaching he noticed that some members of the congregation were asleep, so he suddenly stopped speaking. The unwonted silence woke the slumberers. 'Aha,' said Hendry, 'I have got the way of you now,' and he rebuked them severely. He died, deeply respected, of 'a lingering and painful trouble' in spring 1847, and many years afterwards a monument was erected to his memory in the cemetery of the new Congregational Chapel which had been built in 1840. His hymns were very popular in Argyll when they appeared in 1857 (Hendry 1857: 2; McKillop 1902: 12, 25-6, 31-3, 40, 42, 46, 51-3, 109, 112, 147, 159; MacKenzie 1914: 218-9; MacLean 1915: 151; McLellan 1985: 165; Meek 1988).

5 It would appear that throughout the letter Hendry is addressing the entire family and not merely his mother. This is a pity, as it prevents us learning anything of his use of second person for single individuals. Robertson found that in Arran, as in Ireland, 'the use of *thu* or *sibh* is determined solely by number, and never by age or rank, except that old people say *sibh* to a minister'; the standard Scottish Gaelic practice, in line with French, is to use *sibh* more generally to show respect, and certainly to one's mother; while Holmer, in stark contrast to Robertson, found that even in the 1930s, in line with English, *thu* was gradually giving way in Arran to *sibh* except as a mode of address by the old to the young (Robertson 1897: 256; Holmer 1957: 123).

6 'In Arran, *tha e a mhiann* = he wishes to, as, *tha e a mhiann a dheanamh*, he wishes to do it' (Dwelly 1949: 650, following Robertson 1897: 254). This phrase suggests confusion between *a mhiann* 'wishing' and *gum miannamaid* 'that we would wish', see n. 18 below.

7 I.e. *t-samhraidh*. This would generally be pronounced [tãvri] in Arran, but this evidence, taken together with *gheameradh* (n. 32) suggests the development of an epenthetic vowel and the delenition of *mh*: [tàməri]. Holmer noted an isolated instance of such delenition, *ag amharc* [ə gɛmərk] 'looking', at Carradale, just across the Kilbrannan Sound from Penrioch, while Linguistic Survey informant Donald Craig (see p.70) had [m] in *tamhail(t)* 'a ghost'. This might be cited in support of Robertson's statement that the speech of north Arran was closer to Kintyre Gaelic than that of the rest of the island, a point about which Holmer could come to no definite conclusion, although he accepted that there may at one time have been recognisable divergences in the dialect of the various parts of the island (Robertson 1897: 229-30; Holmer 1957: 2, 25, 36, 44; Holmer 1962: 34).

8 *adh* is written in above *-amh* to represent actual pronunciation [d'ɛnək] (Robertson 1897: 238; Holmer 1957: 62, 69, 156).

9 I.e. *crèadha*, gs. of *crèadh*, pronounced [kr'a:] in Arran (Robertson 1897: 234; Holmer 1957: 19, 47, 78).

10 *gillean* (lads) is written in above *mhuntir* (folk).

11 I.e. *dh'fhan*.

12 Cf. *nach pill thu rium?* 'will you not return to me?' (Holmer 1957: 1).

13 *Kiliston* = *Caolisten* = the common north Arran surname Kelso (an Ayrshire name of Borders origin). Note that *ao* is pronounced *é* in Arran, and compare the standard development of Morrison ⇝ *Moireasdan*, Robertson ⇝ *Robasdan*, Ferguson ⇝ *Fearghasdan*, Finlayson ⇝ *Fionnlasdan* (MacKenzie 1914: 81, 117; Black 1946: 391).

14 I.e. *aca*, regularly [axkə] in Arran Gaelic, as this confirms, despite the general absence of pre-aspiration from the dialect (Holmer 1957 : 125).

15 I.e. *tinneas-caithte*, in which *caithte* is genitive singular of *caitheamh* 'wasting, consumption'. That this is the Arran name for the disease is confirmed by Dwelly 1949: 951.

16 I.e. *an aghaidh*, cf. Robertson 1897: 243; Holmer 1957: 50, 74.

17 *Dùthaich* 'country' is in Arran *dùiche* (Robertson 1897: 242; Holmer 1957: 59, 80, 106, 108).

18 *Goineag* ('Stinger') is a name for one of the winds of spring:

Trì latha Gearraig,	Three days of Cutter,
Trì latha Goineig,	Three days of Stinger,
Trì latha Sguabaig,	Three days of Sweeper,
Trì latha Faoiltich fhuair,	Three days of cold Wolftime,
Suas an t-earrach.	The spring is over (Smith 1964: 28).

However, such a nickname is unlikely to be in question here, and the probability is that *Goinag* is simply Hendry's attempt at spelling a name of the type *Johnag* (Joan, usually *Seonag* in Gaelic orthography) or *Jeanag* (Jeannie, usually *Sìneag*) or Janet (usually *Seònaid*). The last seems particularly likely, as it generally took the form *Deònaid* in Arran. The chorus of an Arran song goes:

Deòcan is Deònaid,
'Se Deòcan a rinn a' bhanais,
'Se Deòcan is Deònaid a rinn a' bhanais ainmeil.

(Jockie and Janet,/It's Jockie that made the wedding,/It's Jockie and Janet that made the famous wedding.) William Ross, too, uses the name in stanza 2 of his lampoon on Arran Gaelic. Hendry uses *g* for [d'] or [t'] in *mhianemig* = *mhiannamaid* above, and in *fastage* = *fasdaid*, *mhinisgair* = *mhinisdear*, *Keggi* = *Ceitidh*, *risg* = *rithisd* and *geainead* = *dèanamh* [d'ɛnək] below. Perhaps the practice is stimulated by the Arran habit of pronouncing non-initial *sg* as *sd*, e.g. *Latha na Càisde* for *Latha na Càisge* 'Easter Day', cf. Manx *Sostyn* for *Sasgann* 'England', *sushtal* for *soisgeul* 'gospel', etc.; note also south Arran *cuideal* for *cuigeal* 'distaff', *caidil* for *caigil* 'smoor', and conversely *cliug* for *cliut* 'a cuff with the fingers'. Janet was one of the commonest girl's names among the Megantic settlers, but there need be no doubt that the Janet in question here is William Hendry's first cousin of that name, see n. 41 (Robertson 1897: 243; Holmer 1957: 17, 178-9, 195).

19 For *ciosan* 'a cousin' see Holmer 1957: 115.

20 '*Fasdaid*, adjective. Fee'd, as at market—Arran' (Dwelly 1949: 418, following Kennedy 1895: 131).

21 This usage supports Robertson 1897: 252 as against Holmer 1957: 100 that Arran *un* (*chun, thun*) can occur independently of the definite article.

22 *u* is written in above *-a-*. Given as *tiomall* at Shiskine, *tiumall* in south Arran (Robertson 1897: 235; Holmer 1957: 80). *Tiomall/tiumall* is the characteristic form of *timcheall* ('around') in the most southerly dialects of Scottish Gaelic. William Ross mimics it in stanza 5 of his lampoon on Arran Gaelic.

23 I.e. *ás a-seo* ('from here')? In any event, *on atie so* ('from this place') is written in above by way of clarification.

24 Cf. Robertson 1897: 247; Holmer 1957: 70.

25 Ink rubbed when still wet to remove text.

26 ?Altered from *oiber*.

27 I.e. *dh'fhanas*.

28 I.e. *aona* [inə], used as in Irish. *Chan eil aon duine an siud* = Northern [Scottish Gaelic] *Chan eil duine an siud,* "there is no one there". *Aon*, which is not emphasised in such uses, is thus used frequently [in Arran] not as an intensive but as if a step had been taken towards supplying Gaelic with an indefinite article' (Robertson 1897: 256; for pronunciation see Holmer 1957: 93).

29 I.e. *co* 'so', see Robertson 1897: 246 and Holmer 1957: 118.

30 I.e. *có 'ca* = *có aca* = *co-dhiùbh.*

31 *Read* ('a thing') corresponds to Irish *réad,* Manx *red,* rather than to the more general Scottish Gaelic *rud,* cf. Robertson 1897: 234; Holmer 1957: 57, 112.

32 I.e. *geamhradh*—generally [g'avrək] in Arran (Robertson 1897: 229; Holmer 1957: 44), but this evidence suggests epenthesis and delenition of *mh*: [g'amərək]. See n. 7.

33 The use of *dheagh* for *glé* is interesting, cf. Scots *gey*.

34 Cf. *ainmiosachadh*, Robertson 1897: 245.

35 'Walking through the "Long Bush" was an experience of some of the settlers. Young men, at times walked through to Vermont, earned what they could in the summer, and walked back in the fall' (McKillop 1902: 45). Assuming that the distances given are miles of walking and not as the crow flies, and that the figure of 200 miles is the total, they would point to Montpelier, the state capital of Vermont. The *Annals* cite an instance of a MacKillop settler bringing his sister on foot from Inverness to Montpelier for medical treatment. If on the other hand the total intended is 270 miles, the distances given might perhaps point to Manchester, NH, which is about 250 miles from Inverness as the crow flies and is the only specific location mentioned in the *Annals* where a young settler found work on the other side of the Long Bush, albeit in 1848 (McKillop 1902: 45, 136).

36 Peter Hamilton had come from Arran in 1831. He subsequently married Ann MacCurdie and settled down in Inverness. He was still alive in 1900, aged ninety, so he was twenty-four in 1834. His wanderlust seems to have been inherited by his son Donald, who was thought to be dead for eleven years until discovered in Lillooet, BC, in the 1890s by Ronald Currie from Inverness (McKillop 1902: 42, 80, 162).

37 *Seonaidh* was the regular form of Johnnie in Arran, as elsewhere (Holmer 1957: 178-9). The township of Cuithe is three miles over the hill from Lochranza, at the northern tip of Arran. The impression given is that *Seonaidh Chuithe* had been a well-known character in Lochranza—a fisherman, perhaps? Charles Hodge's translation gives his name as Cook; this may be no more than a misinterpretation of *chui* (Cook in Arran Gaelic was *(M)acCùca*), but the Cuithe people were among the emigrants on the *Caledonia,* while one of the four unattached men of the party was a John Cook, the others being Robert and Donald Stewart and William Hendry. John Cook married Mary MacKillop in September 1830. They were the first of the Arran settlers to be married in the new country, and had to walk the 40 miles to Quebec to find a minister (McKillop 1902: 12, 45; McKerrell 1987: 155).

38 A John Kelso was tenant of Mid Sannox in 1766, and of the new East Farm of North Sannox in 1773; a Robert Kelso was tenant of the new South Farm of Mid Sannox in 1773. William Kelso and his wife Mary MacKillop, with their children Mary, Alexander, Catherine, James, Margaret and three-week-

old William, were on the *Caledonia* in 1829; of the children, James lived to 1898 and William to 1892, but none ever married (McKillop 1902: 11, 25, 43, 60; MacKenzie 1914: 357, 359).

39 'Baldie Calum' is the patronymic of Archibald MacKillop, perhaps a son of Malcolm MacKillop who became tenant of the new Mid Farm of North Sannox in 1773; in Megantic the abbreviation Baldie seems to have been applied almost exclusively to him to distinguish him from others of the same name, particularly Captain—ultimately Colonel—Archibald MacKillop (n. 2). In Arran Gaelic, Archibald is *Gilleasbai*', vocative '*Leasbai*'. The parenthesis '(.... Auchie)', placed after the name in Charles Hodge's translation, may be a misreading of '[Malcolm's] Archie', but seems more likely to be the place-name Achadh, otherwise anglicised Achag. The Achag was one of the three divisions made in 1773 of the original farm of Corrie, just south of Sannox, and one of the three houses there about 1801 was occupied from 1793 to 1816 by Duncan MacMillan, great-grandfather of Harold Macmillan (cf. n. 4). Baldie Calum was married to a Janet MacMillan, and their children were Donald, Mary, Malcolm, Angus and Archibald; two of them are referred to in the *Annals* with their patronymic Valdie (Bhaldie), i.e. Donald Valdie, Mary Valdie. The latter is presumably the girl suffering ill-health in 1834, but even so, she survived to marry Peter MacKenzie (arrived 1843), with whom she migrated to Missouri, subsequently becoming Mrs H. Thurber; this may have been Harley Thurber, son of a family already long settled in Megantic when the first *Arannaich* arrived in 1829 (Robertson 1897: 243; McKillop 1902: 11, 40, 43, 60; MacKenzie 1914: 359; McLellan 1985: 172). It may be of interest to note that the only other Baldie mentioned in the *Annals* was yet another Archibald MacKillop, who arrived with his widowed mother in 1831. Called Baldie 'Vaischer' (*Mhaighstir*), he took over from 'Captain' MacKillop as the community's first official teacher. He shared Donald Hendry's 'Old Log Meeting House' (n. 4) until a schoolhouse was built about 1835. He was very badly paid, but a good scholar, and applied to the authorities for reimbursement for the extra burden of teaching Gaelic, which was turned down—'the refusal of the Quebec authorities to sanction the teaching of Gaelic was not unnatural,' remarks D. M. McKillop laconically, 'being but a step in the direction of allowing the Gaelic language to die out'. Not surprisingly, *Baldie Mhaighstir* was one of the first to leave the new settlement for good, a trend perhaps foreshadowed in our letter—he migrated to Ontario about 1836 (McKillop 1902: 55).

40 Or kinsfolk.

41 Mr and Mrs Donald Hendry, their daughters Kate, Janet and Margaret, and Kate's daughter Mary A., now aged six. (As stated above, their other children, Donald and Mary, did not settle in Megantic.) Janet married James Kerr in 1836, the couple walking 15 miles to the settlement of Leeds to be wed by the Church of England minister there and walking back the same day (McKillop 1902: 39, 42, 45).

42 The young men would sometimes go to Quebec City to work as stevedores, etc., or to the lumber camps on the Ottawa River. Many of the unmarried women went into service with families in adjacent settlements (McKillop 1902: 36-7).

43 MS. *Keggi* = *Ceitidh* = Katie, cf. n. 18.

44 In the letter the second part of the name is written *adhfuachi* with *r* added above the *u*, while Charles Hodge's translation has 'William .... (Duncan's Wm)'. I suspect that 'Duncan' may be nothing more than a misinterpretation of *adhfurachi* as *Dhonnchaidh*, reading *n* for *r;* there need be little doubt that it actually represents the surname *MacMhurchaidh* (Murchie), which was pronounced *AcUrchaidh* in south Arran and *AcFurchaidh* at Shiskine on the west side (Robertson 1897: 230, 238). Judging from our letter, the pronunciation ten miles further north again at Penrioch was the same—[ak furəxi]. In Arran Gaelic pre-aspiration is almost unknown (but see n. 14) and non-initial velar *dh* has the same [k] sound as unvoiced *g*; note that Hendry writes *go* for *co*. William Murchie, son of John Murchie and Margaret Hendry, was born at Achadh Mór, less than a mile north of Penrioch, on 22 April 1805. He came to Canada with the Rev. Donald Hendry and a few others on the *Foundling* in 1831. On 20 December 1838 he was married in Lower Ireland to Elizabeth Sillers, who had come from Arran with her parents, brothers and sisters on the *Newfoundland* in July 1829, and they raised a family of eleven. On one occasion their house was burned while they were at a meeting. 'The fire was first considered as accidental, but after a time, some articles of clothing that had a remarkable resemblance to those supposed to have been burned, were seen being worn by the

members of a neighbouring family, who have long since moved away from Inverness.' William Murchie died 17 September 1877; his wife was still alive, aged eighty-four, in 1900 (McKillop 1902: 22, 42, 70, 147, 161-2).

45 As the crow flies this would suggest Cleveland, Ohio, and by any permutation somewhere on Lake Erie, from where the descent could have been made by raft (with a portage at the Niagara Falls) to Lake Ontario and thence by the St Lawrence River to Quebec.

46 While accepting that 'though the hardships and privations of the early settlers were severe . . . in a few years plenty and peace was the general portion', the *Annals* add the rider that 'in some respects the first years were not the hardest, the greatest pinch coming after the first supplies of clothing had been worn out and the utensils, etc., that had been brought out had become useless or damaged' (McKillop 1902: 34, 67). But the letter certainly seems to confirm the view that 'in the year 1831 . . . thirteen families arrived, to find things rather easier for them than they had been for the pioneers' (MacKenzie 1914: 225), for there were not many new arrivals between then and 1834.

47 The pioneers of 1829 were faced with 'a solid block of woods' (McKillop 1902: 18).

48 This confirms exactly the description of the land in McKillop 1902: 24, 26. The settlers' greatest disappointment, perhaps, was that the more they cleared and cultivated, the more rocks and stones appeared—a phenomenon also encountered in other parts of Canada, such as Cape Breton. Cf. MacKenzie 1914: 225.

49 1830 edn. has *Cha bhi 'n Sgiobair fo mhì-ghean/Ach gun dìobair a chrann,* 'The Skipper's only worry will be/That he'll lose his mast'.

50 1830 edn. has *feuchadh* for *léirsinn*, same meaning.

51 Characteristically of the author, a pun is intended between the contemptuous *chinn-fhìdhleach* 'fiddle-head', referring to the ornament at a ship's bow consisting of a scroll turning aft or inward, and the more heroic *chinn-Ìleach* 'Islay-hilt' (same pronunciation), referring to a sword.

52 1830 edn. has *pìobain*, perhaps implying a small pipe such as used by sailors.

REFERENCES

BLACK, GEORGE F.
1946 *The Surnames of Scotland.* New York.

BLACK, RONALD
1968 'The Poetry of William Ross.' Unpublished MA dissertation, Department of Celtic, University of Glasgow.

BURREL, JOHN
1982 *Arran Journal 1 (1766-73) and 2 (1776-82).* Brodick. (Facsimile.)

CAMERON, REV. DR ALEXANDER
1894 *Reliquiae Celticae,* vol. 2. Inverness.

CAMERON, REV. J. KENNEDY
1912 *The Church in Arran.* Edinburgh.

CARMICHAEL, ALEXANDER
1928-71 *Carmina Gadelica.* 6 vols. Edinburgh.

DWELLY, EDWARD
1949 *The Illustrated Gaelic-English Dictionary.* 5th edn. Glasgow.

FERGUSON, MARY AND MATHESON, ANN
1984 *Scottish Gaelic Union Catalogue.* Edinburgh.

HENDRY, REV. DONALD
1857 *Laoidhean Spioradail.* 2nd edn. Glasgow.

HOLMER, NILS
1957 *The Gaelic of Arran.* Dublin.
1962 *The Gaelic of Kintyre.* Dublin.

HUGHES, THOMAS

1882 *Memoir of Daniel MacMillan.* London.

KENNEDY, REV. JOHN

1895a 'Arran Gaelic Dialect'. *Transactions of the Gaelic Society of Inverness* 20 (1894-6): 126-41.

1895b *Memoir and Letters of Rev. Finlay Cook and of Rev. Archibald Cook.* Inverness.

LAMB, J. A.

1956 *The Fasti of the United Free Church of Scotland 1900-1929.* Edinburgh.

MACDONALD, KENNETH

1973 'The Rev. William Shaw—Pioneer Gaelic Lexicographer'. *Transactions of the Gaelic Society of Inverness* 50 (1976-8): 1-19.

MACDONALD, DONALD

1978 *Lewis: A History of the Island.* Edinburgh.

MACKENZIE, W. M.

1914 *The Book of Arran,* vol. 2. Glasgow. (Repr. Brodick 1982.)

MCKERRELL, CHRISTINE

1987 'Life at Cock Farm'. *The Scots Magazine,* New Series, 127, no. 2 (May 1987): 155-61.

MCKILLOP, D. M.

1902 *Annals of Megantic County, Quebec.* Lynn, Mass. (Repr. Inverness, Quebec, 1981.)

MACLEAN, DONALD

1915 *Typographia Scoto-Gadelica.* Edinburgh.

MCLELLAN, ROBERT

1985 *The Isle of Arran.* 3rd edn. Newton Abbot.

MACLEOD, DONALD

1988 'Religion and Mental Illness'. *The Stornoway Gazette,* 23 January.

MACLEOD, NORMAN

1829 'Am Focalair Gaelic'. *An Teachdaire Gaelach* 1 (Glasgow): 13-15.

MACMHATHAIN, UILLEAM

1955 'Mór Ros'. *Gairm* 12 (Glasgow): 339-42.

MARTIN, MARTIN

1716 *A Description of the Western Islands of Scotland.* 2nd edn. London. (Repr. Edinburgh, 1981.)

MEEK, DONALD E.

1987 'Evangelical Missionaries in the Early Nineteenth-Century Highlands'. *Scottish Studies* 28: 1-34.

1988 'Evangelicalism and Emigration: Aspects of the Role of Dissenting Evangelicalism in Highland Emigration to Canada'. Gordon W. MacLennan (ed.), *Proceedings of the First North American Congress of Celtic Studies*: 15-35. Ottawa.

ROBERTSON, CHARLES

1897 'The Gaelic Dialect of Arran'. *Transactions of the Gaelic Society of Inverness* 21 (1896-7): 229-65.

SCOTT, HEW

1915-28 *Fasti Ecclesiae Scoticanae.* New edn. Edinburgh.

SMITH, J. A., CONVENER

1964 *Aithris is Oideas: Traditional Gaelic Rhymes and Games.* London.

STORRIE, MARGARET C.

1967 'Landholdings and Population in Arran from the Late Eighteenth Century'. *Scottish Studies* 11: 48-74.

VERITY, BARBARA

1987 'Gaelic Country'. *The Gazette,* Montreal, 14 Nov. Repr. *Stornoway Gazette,* 26 Feb. 1988.

ACKNOWLEDGEMENTS

I am grateful to my colleagues Professor Donald Meek of the Department of Celtic, Aberdeen, and Mr David Clement of the School of Scottish Studies, who read and commented on a draft of this article, and to the following for much additional help and information: Brigadier David H. Hodge, DL, Durham; Mr John Macdonald, Whiting Bay; Mrs Evelyn Robson, Lochranza; Mr Alastair Sillars, Lamlash; and Mr Alastair Hendry, Glen Rosa. My particular thanks are due to Brigadier Hodge and the Isle of Arran Museum Trust for the loan of the letter and permission to reproduce the text.

Miss Catherine McKinnon's 'Russian Fortune'

JOHN W. SHEETS

> 'I quite agree with you that steps must be taken now to recover this "Russian fortune" that I have heard spoken of since my infancy or let the matter be forever buried in oblivion.'
>
> (8 April 1876, Archibald McKinnon, Guelph, Ontario, to his cousin Donald McKinnon, Edinburgh)

Miss Catherine McKinnon left Edinburgh bound for Russia in the company of 'two English ladies'.[1] She eventually became a nursery governess in the Imperial household of the Czars Alexander I and Nicholas I of Russia, with specific charge of young Alexander II, the future Czar-Liberator of the serfs. The Imperial family held fond memories of their Highland nurse. Alexander II credited his fluency in English to her[2] and in 1892 his son Alexander III ordered a tweed suit spun at her native village on the Ross of Mull. Before the Crimean War, Catherine McKinnon left Russia with a princess of the Imperial family. The princess had borrowed money from Catherine, but promised to repay her with interest plus give her another sum equal to the original loan. After the Crimean War Catherine McKinnon wrote to her Scottish relatives promising they would receive some money. But this never happened: her money was in the hands of a bankrupt Russian colonel when she died in Florence, Italy, in 1858. After false heirs made claims to it, her Scottish descendants (including the future Celtic Professor at Edinburgh University, Donald Mackinnon) contacted their Canadian kin to make a joint claim. Years later, on 29 August 1885, the *Oban Times* published the story of Catherine McKinnon and her 'Russian fortune'.[3] The article concluded: 'There it has been for many a day; and how much longer it is to remain there is a question some would like answered.' Now a private collection of McKinnon papers from Toronto elucidates the story of 'Grand-aunt' Catherine's legacy, her descendants' efforts to recover it, and why they could not succeed.[4]

FROM MULL TO RUSSIA AND TO ITALY

Catherine McKinnon, *Catriona Bheag* or Little Catherine, was born *circa* 1778 in Uisken on the Ross of Mull in Argyll. Her mother was 'a MacDonald' and her father, John McKinnon, was called *Gobha fada,* the 'tall smith', a cattle dealer and blacksmith in the Gribun area of Mull. She was the oldest of four known children, followed by her brother Colin and sisters Janet and Ann. Professor Mackinnon, born in 1839 on Colonsay and a grandson of Janet, 'as a boy had seen several letters written by Catherine which displayed that she had had a good education'.[5] Through her relative Malcolm MacDonald, the tacksman in Ulva, Catherine went to Edinburgh and lived with a McKinnon aunt from Gribun, 'Mrs Smith'. There she met an English 'lady of rank' whose husband held an official appointment in St Petersburg. This lady persuaded Catherine to return to Russia with her as the family's governess. When 26-year-old Catherine left her aunt's Edinburgh house in May 1804, a divinity student from Morvern lodging with Mrs Smith 'helped to pack the girl's box on the occasion'.[6] He was the future Dr Norman Macleod of St Columba Church, Glasgow, known to Highlanders as *Caraid nan Gaidheal.*

Catherine came to a Russia only three years ruled by Czar Alexander I. It was a nation at war—with Persia then Turkey over the annexation of Georgia, with Sweden over Finnish annexation, and with France in 1805 as a prelude to Napoleon's invasion in 1812. Her diplomatic employer introduced her to the Czar's family; later she entered the Imperial household as a 'governess to the younger branches of the family'.[7] She served from the last part of Alexander I's reign (1801-25) into the first part of Nicholas I's reign (1825-55), with years of duty to the young Alexander II, born in 1818.[8]

Catherine McKinnon accrued a substantial savings during her loyal service to the Imperial household. In a will dated 24 June 1836 from Odessa, the Princess Natalie Akazatoff Corsine granted Catherine an annual annuity of 2,000 roubles, should Catherine survive her. Five years later, on 15 November 1841, the Princess borrowed 20,000 roubles at 6 per cent interest from Catherine and guaranteed her a second and equal amount, should Catherine survive the Princess. Colonel Michael Kiriakoff, of the Emperor's Guard at St Petersburg and a landowner near Odessa, received the money from the Princess and became her sole heir and legatee; Catherine McKinnon received two Bills of Exchange of 20,000 roubles each in his name. Catherine left Russia around 1847 with the Princess. On 18 April 1848 Catherine gave power-of-attorney in Russia to collect the debt owed her by Colonel Kiriakoff.[9] However, Russia had changed from when she arrived over forty years earlier. The Russian population had increased and moved into the cities near the factories and trades. The landowners and gentry in the countryside declined in wealth and power. The revolutions of 1848 engulfed Europe; Russia was drifting towards the Crimean War.

Near the end of her life Catherine McKinnon lived in Florence with a 'Madame Stianti', the lady Elena Maybanury who was the widow of Mr Francis Stianti.[10] In October 1856, Catherine wrote from Italy to her grand-nephew John McCormick in Iona about Kiriakoff's debt: 'Now that the [Crimean] war is finished & that my law suit of long 12 years is settled in my favour with all the loss and disasters that the war has made there may be a delay in the payment of it but no danger.'[11] After the war Kiriakoff's estate near Odessa and his assets were mortgaged to the Rural Bank there. When she died in Florence in February 1858, 80-year-old Catherine McKinnon had not received the Russian money owed to her by a legatee of the Czarist family. Upon her death, the two Bills of Exchange against Colonel Kiriakoff were transmitted to the Italian Consul General in Odessa.

TRUE AND FALSE HEIRS

On 21 December 1860 the fisherman Malcolm Mackinnon in Colonsay, the oldest brother of Professor Mackinnon, wrote to his uncle Lachlan McKinnon in Wellington County, Ontario, Canada; Malcolm was Catherine's grand-nephew and Lachlan was her nephew, both through her sister Janet. After describing his new wife of just one week, brother Donald in his first teaching position at Lochinver in Sutherland, and the Baptist revivals on Islay,[12] he ended the letter: 'I don't hear any thing now at all about the Russian affairs. I do not think that people will ever recover a penny of it.' But others laid claim to it. Madame Stianti produced a codicil to any will, neither signed nor attested by Catherine McKinnon, leaving all to her. She notified Catherine's executors in Mull, including Archibald McKinnon from Torrans. He sent papers to the solicitors Martin & McLean, WS, in Edinburgh, then promptly 'sent a claim to Russia that he was the sole inheritor'.[13]

In 1865 the British government investigated the Russian estate of the late Catherine McKinnon. They discovered that Colonel Kiriakoff was living beyond his means: the Rural Bank 'undertook the gradual liquidation of his debts but as he failed in some engagement to it a commission was named to administer the property for the benefit of the creditors who are numerous'.[14] One family heir of Catherine McKinnon in Scotland who followed these events was her grand-nephew John McCormick from Iona. They had corresponded in the mid-1850s when he married, started a family, and worked as a merchant in the Ross of Mull. After Archibald McKinnon in Mull made his claim, McCormick suspected that 'Martin W.S. was acting in concert with McKinnon and his heirs'. Hence, he sought Edinburgh counsel but with a personal touch: 'I called on Arch[ibald] McNeill W.S. of Colonsay & gave him the documents to proceed with [and] he was to recover it at once.' Five years passed with no results: McNeill died on 2 June 1870.[15] On 8 March 1871 John McCormick wrote to his Canadian cousin John Munn of Orangeville in Wellington County. He summarised the facts about their grand-aunt's Russian estate and his efforts to recover it, then complained that Archibald McNeill 'never made anything of it . . . I would advise you to have little to do with lawyers as they are a cursed set of men although they must be employed'. He wrote again on 6 July 1871, saying Colonel Kiriakoff would not consider any payment until Archibald

McKinnon's heirs withdrew their claim and true heirs were confirmed; he urged his Canadian cousins 'to act with me—on your getting the cash collected advise me at once how to act and send the mandate'.

John Munn shared John McCormick's letters with another cousin, Angus McKinnon of Osprings in Wellington County. Ten years earlier, Angus's father Lachlan had received letters from Malcolm and Donald Mackinnon in Colonsay. During the mid-1860s their sister Janet, with her husband and family, had left Colonsay for Bruce County, Ontario, approximately 75 miles north-west of Angus and the other McKinnons. Angus obtained Donald's Edinburgh address from Janet and wrote to him on 7 July 1871. About cousin Donald, Angus 'heard very pleasing news regarding your success at College'. Indeed, in 1869 Donald Mackinnon received the MA with First Class Honours in Mental Philosophy from Edinburgh University and 'won the Hamilton Fellowship in that subject—one of the highest distinctions the University has to offer'.[16] Based upon John McCormick's information ('. . . of his letters one would infer that only an effort was required to recover the whole . . .'), Angus assumed that Donald Mackinnon in Edinburgh would 'no doubt be quite familiar with the full details' of their grand-aunt's Russian estate. 'I cannot think of asking anything more than a reply to this hasty letter,' concluded Angus McKinnon to his cousin Donald.

In the summer of 1871 Donald Mackinnon worked as the Clerk to the Church of Scotland's Educational System at 22 Queen Street, Edinburgh. He received Angus McKinnon's letter 'while away in a distant part of the country inspecting schools'.[17] When he returned to Edinburgh in September he 'made various efforts to secure the information'[18] without success until 20 November when John McCormick came to Edinburgh. They went to the nearby office of McNeill & Sime at 8 Hill Street where they met the surviving partner, Mr Sime. Donald Mackinnon was confident that another Colonsay man like Archibald McNeill would 'exert himself in the matter more than one unknown to any of the beneficiaries'.[19] He confessed to Angus McKinnon on 22 November that: 'Mr Sime knew nothing at all of the matter till we saw him and when he turned up the papers he found no enquiry was made by Mr McNeill. The matter rests therefore as it was in 1865.' Nevertheless, to his cousin Angus in Canada Donald Mackinnon summarised the evidence about Catherine McKinnon's estate—an estimate of the debt owed by Kiriakoff, the unsigned will or codicil, and the claims from Mull and Florence—and remained optimistic that Mr Sime, 'a thoroughly respectable agent and an energetic man', could lead them to the money. Mr Sime recommended that a foreign solicitor be hired to investigate Kiriakoff's finances; this required a cash advance, which Donald paid, and Sime would represent them *gratis* until the extended family of Scottish and Canadian heirs could raise funds. Donald Mackinnon believes that '. . . if the debtor is worth pursuing . . . I do not see what prevents the recovery of the money'.

Angus McKinnon's youngest brother, Archibald, was a third-year law student then 'articled to a Law-firm in Guelph'.[20] After Angus wrote to Edinburgh in July, on 23 August 1871 Archibald wrote to the British Consulate General in Odessa about Catherine McKinnon's estate. The Consulate replied on 30 September with detailed information. They verified Kiriakoff's mismanagement of his debts (despite obvious under-mortgaging of his land), his usual residence in St Petersburg (where any claim should be made), the tenuous state of Russian courts ('tedious tribunals'), and the complicated Russian laws of descent (e.g. 1/14 to each daughter, 1/7 to the widow, the remainder among sons). Of utmost importance, the Consulate confirmed that documents critical to any claim were at the Chancery of the Italian Consulate in Odessa: Princess Natalie's acknowledgments in 1841 of her loan from and guarantee to Catherine McKinnon, Catherine's 1848 power-of-attorney, and the Bills of Exchange against Kiriakoff. The Consulate also advised Archibald McKinnon that his grand-aunt's money was expressed in roubles *assignat*, which 'is not the present rouble of Russia' but one-fourth the value of the silver rouble. Archibald wrote a summary memorandum about the estate then, as advised, wrote the British Consulate in St Petersburg on 4 December 1871. He admitted 'the claim is much less than I expected'. He still asked if Colonel Kiriakoff 'would be likely to recognise the claim if formally made and whether that Gentleman understood English or not'.

MORE TIME AND MORE EFFORT

On 22 November 1875, exactly four years after Donald Mackinnon wrote a confident letter from Edinburgh to his Canadian cousins, McNeill & Sime wrote G. E. Stanley, HMB Consul General at Odessa. Mr Stanley replied on 10 February 1876 with both old and new information. He had 'at last seen Mr Kiriakoff who still states his perfect willingness to pay the money due to the estate of the late Miss Catherine McKinnon'. Kiriakoff wanted some consideration because his 'man of business' received Madame Stianti who showed him Catherine's codicil in her favour, then his agent promptly 'paid Mrs Stianti a few thousand roubles'. Stanley asked the colonel 'why Mrs Stianti if legatee under a will did not produce it before a Court and claim the whole' but Kiriakoff 'did not answer'. Stanley also noted 'that action in the matter has been taken at different times in 1864, 1867, 1871, and communicated to Mr Kiriakoff'; as a diplomat, he could 'not understand why it should have been dropped'. Stanley would write to the Consulate in Florence about any will by Catherine McKinnon and he advised Mr Sime about 'preparing all the proofs of heirship and obtaining the legal opinion of a Russian lawyer'.

In Edinburgh Sime gave the Consul's letter to Donald Mackinnon, now the Secretary to the Edinburgh School Board, author and reviewer for a new journal, *An Gaidheal*, husband of a Colonsay woman, and father of two children. He wrote to John Munn in Ontario on 1 March 1876, quoted from Stanley's letter, estimated

Catherine's estate at £10,000, and thought it 'a pity if an effort will not be made by you and other beneficiaries of means in Canada'. In Glasgow, John McCormick also read Stanley's letter; on 9 March he too wrote John Munn imploring their Canadian cousins to send Mr Sime at least £100 'without any delay as they want to bring the matter to a close'. For his part, McCormick had 'written to Mull to get all the proof that is required and have left with their [McNeill & Sime's] agents two letters from the deceased to me date [18]54 & [18]56 to send out to the Consul to overthrow any thing that Madame Stianti may put forward in the case'.

Their cousin Archibald McKinnon, a Guelph solicitor of two years, responded to Donald Mackinnon on 8 April. He explained 'about thee years ago I wrote to the British Consular Agent at Odessa and also to the British Consular Agent at St Petersburg . . . I at that time came to the conclusion that the money could be obtained but that a considerable sum of money would have to be expended in obtaining the same and that the share of each of the heirs would not amount to much . . . The great difficulty in this case will be to serve the different heirs of whom I think it will be hard to find . . .' Despite this sober assessment, he asked Donald Mackinnon to have Mr Sime send him 'a synopsis of the information they have', while he promised 'to remit the necessary funds without much further delay'. To raise this money in Canada, on 10 May nine grandsons of Catherine McKinnon's sister Janet met at Orangeville. They had collected pledges of £170 under eighteen signatures, payable to the elected treasurer 'on or before 1 June 1876'.

The exact number of Catherine McKinnon's heirs in Scotland and in Canada posed a problem as difficult as Kiriakoff's debts, the Stianti claim, or Russian and Italian laws. By 1876 only Janet McKinnon's descendants comprised the trans-Atlantic alliance in pursuit of her sister Catherine's money. Bound by law and by conscience, they searched for the other branches of the family. In Scotland Sime hired a Glasgow solicitor to compile a limited 'Table of Representatives and Next of Kin of Miss McKinnon' based upon a list of 'Miss Catherine McKinnons Heirs'. In Ontario the extended family compiled a genealogy of 'Representatives of Catherine McKinnon residing in Canada' but it only listed descendants of her sister Janet, approximately thirty-five people with known addresses. John Munn and his cousin Donald C. McKinnon, also of Orangeville, ran this advertisement in the Toronto *Globe*:

> Personal—All parties interested in the estate of the late Catherine McKinnon who died in Florence, Italy, in the year 1858 possibly may hear of something to their advantage by communicating with John Munn or D. McKinnon, Box 53, Orangeville.[21]

The Orangeville cousins quickly heard from other descendants who sent all kinds of advice, which they passed on to Archibald McKinnon in Guelph. These comments ranged from personal ('let me know if there is anything in favour of me'[22]), the insistent ('send any information you may possess'[23]), and the supportive ('We will do what is right and fair to assist you'[24]), to the more impoverished ('I cannot subscribe at present owing to the scarcity of funds'[25]) or the detached ('nothing ventured nothing gained'[26]). Some writers revived the name of an Edinburgh solicitor: 'The first I heard of it was from my brother when he came over here three years ago . . . at the time he left the will was in the hands of a solicitor named Martin, Edinburgh.'[27] When John Munn invited John Beaton, Catherine's sister Ann's son, to Orangeville for the 10 May meeting, he declined because 'I have established my claim sometime ago'.[28] After the meeting he informed John Munn that he had given 'power of attorney to Mr Martin in Edinburgh' who 'would send me all the papers belonging to the estate . . . I expect an answer soon'.[29]

Some relatives were more contentious, but forgivable. On 29 May an Ontario friend of Hugh McKinnon of Prince Edward Island sent him a copy of the *Globe*'s notice. The next day Hugh wrote John Munn to declare 'it is useless for me to remind you that I am one who is deeply concerned'. When Archibald McKinnon replied to him on 12 July, Hugh McKinnon 'sent his letter away with a gentleman to Scotland' who would call on McNeill & Sime; he would not contribute any money 'until I hear from Scotland' nor divulge his family's history because 'it is not customary to engage a man and perform the work oneself'. Very patiently, Archibald wrote again on 11 August to which a contrite Hugh McKinnon furnished 'the required information' and was 'much obliged to you for entering so fully into all particulars about the case'. Hugh McKinnon was not a descendant of Catherine McKinnon; his deceased wife Catherine was the daughter of Colin McKinnon, Catherine's brother from Mull. He was 'getting advanced in years'. His belligerence came from his location, his vocation, and his commitments: '. . . money with the farmer is very scarce especially in this island where we are for so many months shut up from the outside world . . . I have a large family to support . . . This winter so far has been very severe.'[30]

ADVERSE OPINION, WAR AND PERSEVERANCE

During the months from April 1876 to August 1877 Archibald McKinnon served as secretary, solicitor, and *de facto* leader of Catherine McKinnon's heirs in Canada. He wrote, received, and responded to letters, notes, memoranda and other documents from siblings, cousins, distant relatives, diplomats, and other solicitors. Within this mass and maze of paper, his correspondence with McNeill & Sime determined a climax to the quest for Catherine McKinnon's 'Russian fortune'. By May 1876 Archibald had not heard from cousin Donald Mackinnon or Mr Sime in Edinburgh. He had a copy of the 10 February letter from Consul Stanley in Odessa to Mr Sime and compared it to his 30 September 1871 letter from a previous Consul in Odessa. He wrote to Sime on 26 May for clarification and communication. He judged the two letters 'much to the same effect' yet insisted 'that the money can be recovered . . . by suit' despite the exaggerated value of the estate. He asked Sime if 'the English or the Russian Law of descent [will] govern this case'. If the English law applied, the number of heirs would be required and Archibald shared with Sime his information about Catherine's descendants through her three siblings.

On 22 June Sime replied with copies of letters and other documents; one item was a translation of the 20 August 1857 codicil to Catherine's will in favour of Madame Stianti. According to Sime, 'the English nor Russian Law of Succession will govern this case, but the law of the country where the deceased was domiciled at the date of death', either Italy or Scotland. About the heirs, Sime sent a copy of the 'Table of Representatives' to correct and expand Archibald's information. He further requested 'the precise date of death of each of Miss McKinnon's nephews and nieces as are in Canada or Prince Edward Isle, and the names of the surviving'. About the codicil, on 19 May Sime had corresponded with D. E. Colnaghi, British Consul at Florence, posing two questions about Catherine McKinnon's estate: (1) 'Whether the document [Codicil] you sent us . . . is a valid document according to the Law of Italy' and (2) 'If valid and competent to carry property, what is the amount thereby conveyed?' Sime feared the codicil 'might appear capable of the constructing contended for by Madame Stianti that by it the 40,000 roubles which appear to comprehend the estate of the deceased are all made over to her'. Through the Consul in Florence, he also requested the opinion of an Italian solicitor about the codicil.

Nearly six months later, on 6 November, Sime transmitted a copy of the lengthy legal 'Opinion by Advocate T. Corsi, Florence, as to M. McKinnon's Estate'. The opinion was adverse to the hopes of Catherine's heirs: 'I) . . . the laws that regulate the efficiency of her Disposition are those that were in force in Tuscany then an Independent state [at her death in 1858] . . . the validity of a Codicil is independent of the existence of any Will preceding or subsequent . . . The Codicil therefore of M. McKinnon is in this respect valid . . . II) By the original two distinct legacies are left to the Signora Stianti . . .' Sime argued 'that there would be claimable by the heirs one sum of 20,000 roubles . . . and also the interest at legal rates upon the other sum of 20,000 roubles'. The Edinburgh solicitor also included his bill for £100 to the Canadians.

On 16 February 1877 Sime wrote Archibald McKinnon 'to remind you of our letter to you of 6th November last, and shall be glad to have a reply'. On 12 May Archibald replied; he had 'commenced soliciting subscriptions from those in this country interested in the estate . . . Now however since Russia has declared war against Turkey [on 24 April] some of those who have contributed think that it would be useless to pursue the investigation any further.' Again, as in the Crimea twenty years earlier, international politics and war interrupted the pursuit of the money. Archibald McKinnon wrote Sime on 29 June, to which Sime promised on 1

August to consult 'with Her Majesty's Consul at Florence regarding the advisability in consequence of the war'. Apparently, Archibald McKinnon in Canada lost his enthusiasm for Grand-aunt Catherine's 'Russian fortune'.

Other descendants maintained the quest, though without success. In 1880 John McCormick and Donald Mackinnon went to a Glasgow solicitor and 'spent a good deal of money in connection with the case'.[31] In 1881 a representative of John Beaton in Ontario demanded from Archibald McKinnon the return of 'a copy of [the] will of the late Catherine McKinnon of Florence, Italy, which Mr John Munn says is in your possession . . .'.[32] On 7 March 1885 another group of six Canadian heirs signed a subscription statement 'for the purpose of forming a fund to defray necessary expenses in endeavouring to recover the estate of the late Catherine McKinnon'. One of the last attempts came from the United States. Czar Alexander III received world headlines in 1892 when he ordered tweed spun for a suit at Uisken on the Ross of Mull, in honour of his father's Highland nurse.[33] In Pendleton, Oregon, Mr Robert Bruce, husband of John McCormick's sister Catherine, read this in the newspapers; on 29 July he sent a letter to the Czar through his 'US Senator J. H. Mitchell'. He thought 'the Czar would see justice done to his father's old nurse'. On 13 August Bruce wrote his wife's cousin, Professor Donald Mackinnon of Edinburgh University, to 'put yourself in communication with me in case the Czar's reply is encouraging for I will have to refer the matter to you having more knowledge of the matter than any body'. We may never know the Czar's or the professor's reply, if any, to Mr Bruce of America.

DISCOURSE AND CONCLUSION

The 'Russian fortune' of Miss Catherine McKinnon from Mull shows how an inheritance can generate both co-operation and conflict among the hopeful inheritors. During five decades of the nineteenth century Miss McKinnon's heirs in Scotland and in Canada expected some return for their efforts. True to the prophecy of Colonsay's Malcolm Mackinnon in 1860, they received no money. Was there ever a chance to realise this legacy, or were the obstacles truly insurmountable? A crucial point is the problematic existence of a valid will by Catherine. On 8 March 1871 her Scottish grand-nephew John McCormick told his Canadian cousins 'there was no will'; on 22 November he and his cousin Donald Mackinnon assumed 'a copy of Miss McKinnon's will was sent to this country after her death in 1859 (*sic*) but being unsigned is of no value'. In late 1875 or early 1876 Colonel Kiriakoff stated to Consul Stanley at Odessa 'that some years ago Madame Stianti claimed under a will to inherit from the late Miss McKinnon' but 'he admitted he had never seen the Will'.[34] In April 1876 an alleged heir in Canada claimed his brother knew the will was with the solicitor Martin in Edinburgh. The solicitors of McNeill & Sime could have asked their Edinburgh colleague about any will. This may be a moot point because the Florentine solicitor Corsi judged the codicil to any will in favour of Madame Stianti.

Two inseparable issues were the actual value of Catherine McKinnon's estate and the actual number of heirs in Scotland and in Canada. In March 1876 Donald Mackinnon of Edinburgh insisted 'by my calculations it cannot be now much short of £10,000'.[35] His Canadian cousin and solicitor Archibald McKinnon had learned five years earlier 'the claim is much less than I expected',[36] just over £2,000. The Canadian relatives identified at least forty claimants to a part of the estate. The number of potential heirs, including those in Scotland, exceeded fifty people, and many of them would divide their portion with extended kin. After the legal fees from Canada, Scotland, Italy, or Russia, a successful heir to an equal share of Catherine McKinnon's 'Russian fortune' might have received the equal to his or her original subscription.

The exertions by Catherine's heirs constituted an international drama with action in Canada, Scotland, Italy, and Russia. Then, as now, legal claims across national borders are affected by the climate of diplomacy between rival states; or, the fates of mere individuals exist in sheer coincidence with international events. In this regard, Catherine McKinnon and her heirs were very unlucky. One biographer of Alexander II contends that 'from the time of the Crimean War until 1874 . . . England remained hostile to Russia'.[37] One must add that Russia returned this spirit in kind and 1874 was only a pause before another war started. In 1854 and in 1856 Catherine McKinnon believed her estate would be settled 'in her favour'. In those few years, though, Russia changed its leadership and lost its power. During the Crimean War 37-year-old Alexander II succeeded to the throne when his father Nicholas I died on 2 March 1855. The war for Russia ended on 30 March 1856 with the Treaty of Paris and anglophobia spread throughout Russia.[38]

John McCormick revived the question of his grand-aunt's estate in 1865 after the British government had criticised the Czar's suppression of the 1863 Polish revolt; moreover, Russia was four years into the liberation of the serfs. When McCormick and Donald Mackinnon recruited their Canadian cousins to a joint claim in 1871, Russia had supported Bismarck in the Franco-Prussian War of 1870. On 23 January 1874, at the Winter Palace in St Petersburg, Alfred, Duke of Edinburgh and second son of Queen Victoria, married Czar Alexander's only daughter, Princess Marie; in May Alexander visited her and Queen Victoria at Windsor. For the moment, England and Russia exuded the spirit of their inter-married royalty.[39] But it would not last in the face of a chronic 'Eastern Question'. Balkan insurrections against the Turks commenced in 1875, then Orthodox Christians in Serbia and Montenegro declared war in June 1876. The English expected the Czar's neutrality in compliance with the Treaty of Paris. Under these conditions, a professional soldier like Colonel Kiriakoff might not have been receptive to a British claim on his mortgaged estate near Odessa. On 24 April 1877 Russia, with Austria-Hungary, declared war on Turkey, a fact immediately understood by the solicitors McKinnon in Guelph and Sime in Edinburgh as calamitous to their common cause of inheritance. The sincere and sustained efforts by Catherine McKinnon's heirs in 1876-77 coincided with a renewed hostility between England and Russia.

The concatenation of dubious documents, an overvalued estate, too many heirs, and international conflict doomed any success for the heirs of Miss Catherine McKinnon. Her descendants discovered one another during their 'fortune hunt' and used this information over their next generations.[40] Rather than identify with an heir's empty pocket, perhaps we should picture the Catherine McKinnon, *Catriona Bheag*, who never returned to her native Mull. One of the family letters of 1876 draws a picture of her dream, her patience, and her generosity: 'During her life time she wrote to my father stating [that] she was about to retire from Russia and come home to Britain but on account of the unsettled state of the Russian war and as some of her money was in the hands of the Emperor of Russia she was detained. She mentioned in the letter that she would not forget him in her will.'[41]

The research was supported by Grant FE-25439-91 from the National Endowment of the Humanities and by Central Missouri State University (College of Arts and Sciences Research Professorship in 1990 and Faculty Research grants in 1990 and 1991). I appreciated the comments by, and encouragement from, Professor Gillies, Dr Margaret Mackay, Dr Mairi MacArthur, Mr Kevin Byrne, Mrs Kathleen Cory, Mr David Dykes, and Mrs Berniece Craig.

NOTES

1 *Oban Times*, 29 August 1885, 2. I thank Murdo MacDonald, Archivist of the Argyll and Bute District Council, for this reference.

2 '. . . it was stated in the *Times* that he owed the good acquaintance which it was known he possessed with the language and traditions of Scotland to the early instructions of "an old Scotch nurse",' *Ibid*; '. . . he sometimes surprised Scotsmen by addressing them in the language and accent of an "auld nurse"', to whom he had been much attached in his childhood . . .' C. Lowe, *Alexander III of Russia*, 1895: 17-8.

3 Catherine McKinnon's story also appeared in the *Oban Times*, 17 Nov. 1894; Rev. D. D. MacKinnon, *Memoirs of Clan Fingon*, 1899: 184-5; *Gairm* 30, 1959; *Scotsman*, 8 August 1987 by Ronald Black. I thank Iain Thornber, Morvern, for the *Oban Times*, *Gairm* and *Scotsman* references.

4 Unless otherwise noted, the dated information about Catherine McKinnon and her heirs derives from the private papers of Mr Robert McKinnon, Toronto; I acknowledge his co-operation and courtesy in this research.

5 Professor Donald Mackinnon (1839-1914) quoted in 'Descendants of John McKinnon of Gribun, Mull . . .' by Robert Lachlan McKinnon (1872-1954) of Guelph, Ontario.

6 *Ibid.*

7 *Oban Times*, 1885, *op cit.*

8 Catherine McKinnon was not the first Scotswoman to work for the Imperial family of Russia. Catherine the Great provided her grandson Nicholas with Miss Jane Lyon, 'the daughter of a Scottish artist'; Czar Nicholas I mourned the death of 'his lioness' in 1842, W. B. Lincoln, *Nicolas I*, 1978, 50-2. Two problems plague the historiography of Alexander II: '. . . . his governesses left no written record' and '. . . soon after his succession [in 1881], the Emperor Alexander III ordered most of his father's private papers to be destroyed . . .'. M. E. Almedingen, *The Emperor Alexander II*, 1962: 8, 10.

9 30 September 1871, Britain Consulate General, Odessa, to Archibald McKinnon, Guelph; Memo re Estate of Catherine McKinnon Deaceased by Archibald McKinnon.

10 22 June 1876, Translation of Codicil, by Madam McKinnon.

11 8 March and 6 July 1871, John McCormick, Iona, Scotland, to John Munn, Orangeville, Ontario.

12 'She is not a tall woman but she is good looking . . . There is a great change in him since he began teaching . . . where there is a great deal of good done by the Lord pouring down of his spirit among the people . . .'

13 8 March 1871, *op cit.*

14 30 September 1871, British Consulate General at Odessa, *op vit.*

15 8 March 1871, *op cit.*; Register of Deaths, St Andrew District, Edinburgh, 6852/330, 1870, New Register House, Edinburgh.

16 L. Mackinnon, *Prose Writings of Donald Mackinnon*, 1956: xiv; 28 Nov. 1871, John McCormick described his cousin Donald Mackinnon as 'a young man of high standing in Scotland, being one of the greatest scholars of the day . . .'.

17 22 Nov. 1871, Donald Mackinnon, Edinburgh, to Angus McKinnon, Osprings, Ontario.

18 *Ibid.*

19 *Ibid.*

20 7 July 1871, Angus McKinnon, Osprings, Ontario, to Donald Mackinnon, Edinburgh.

21 Toronto *Globe* quoted in 30 May 1876, Hugh McKinnon, Prince Edward Island, to John Munn, Orangeville, Ontario.

22 5 May 1876, Mary McKillop, Chester, Ontario, to John Munn, Orangeville, Ontario.

23 8 May 1876, Ann McLean, Manitoulin Island, Ontario, to Donald C. McKinnon, Orangeville, Ontario.

24 15 May 1876, Margaret Smith, Paisley, Ontario to Donald McKinnon, Orangeville, Ontario.

25 18 May 1876, Ann (?)Ewing, Strutsville, Ontario, to Ann McKinnon, Guelph, Ontario.

26 15 May 1876, *op cit.*

27 29 April 1876, Alexander McKinnon, Lindsay, Ontario, to John Munn, Orangeville, Ontario.

28 27 April 1876, John Beaton, Hopeville, Ontario, to John Munn, Orangeville, Ontario.

29 13 May 1876, John Beaton, Hopeville, Ontario, to John Munn, Orangeville, Ontario.

30 23 January 1877, Hugh McKinnon, Prince Edward Island, to Archibald McKinnon, Guelph, Ontario.

31 15 March 1898, Duncan MacKinnon, Glasgow, who also stated 'it's an impossibility to get anything out of the hands of the Russian Gov't.' (from a copy-letter by 'A. J. McLean, 1936').

32 7 Feb. 1881, A. G. Hunter, Dundalk, Ontario, to Archibald McKinnon, Guelph, Ontario.

33 '. . . The order, we understand, had been received by a Mull gentleman through the Duke of Edinburgh, and has been executed by James Lamont, weaver, Ardtun, near Bunessan. The cloth is of the usual Highland kind—a homely-looking tartan, in which the prevailing colours are lichen and indigo. The old gentleman, a good specimen of the modern Highlander, does not seem to take the least pride in the Royal patronage. In any case, whether or not he knows who or what the "Czar of Russia" is, he thinks so little of the matter that he does not take the trouble of mentioning it to his friends.' *Oban Times*, 9 April 1892: 3.

34 10 February 1876, G. E. Stanley, HM Britannic Consulate General, Odessa, to McNeill & Sime, WS, Edinburgh.

35 1 March 1876, Donald Mackinnon, Edinburgh, to John Munn, Orangeville, Ontario.

36 4 December 1871, Archibald McKinnon, Guelph, Ontario, to the British Consul, St Petersburg (draft-copy).

37 S. Graham, *A Life of Alexander II,* 1935: 161.

38 *Ibid.* Chapter Eleven—Russia and England, 161-78.

39 The City of Edinburgh was an exception. 'Several English towns returned Crimean guns to Russia as a token that all enmity had disappeared . . . Edinburgh itself did not do that. The Duke of Edinburgh might marry a Russian, but Edinburgh would not relinquish its war trophies and the captured Crimean guns remain on the Calton Hill to this day . . .' *Ibid.* 169.

40 Professor Donald Mackinnon and his family maintained a correspondence with Canadian relatives into World War I; his daughters Katherine and Mary revived these contacts in the 1930s, then corresponded to Canada through World War II.

41 29 April 1876, *op cit. Catriona Bheag* remains in the oral traditions of Mull: '. . . about the woman who went to Russia . . . Catherine McKinnon, she did not come back, no, she was buried there. They sang a Gaelic song . . . that is what they sang at her graveside . . . she was in Russia at the time of the Crimea and she said the only thing she feared was that they would take Scots prisoners and treat them badly . . .'. Translated from a Gaelic conversation with John Campbell, Taoslan, Ross of Mull, February 1992, courtesy of Dr Mairi MacArthur, Iona/Inverness.

Archaeology and Ethnohistory of Cave Dwelling in Scotland

ROGER LEITCH and CHRISTOPHER SMITH

INTRODUCTION

In the popular imagination cave dwelling is considered to belong to the remote past. Few people realise that habitual cave residence was commonplace in many parts of Europe until quite recent times. In Scotland, the practice only ceased to be widespread around the time of the First World War.

One of us (RL), an ethnologist, has since 1982 been collecting documentary and oral material bearing on cave dwelling throughout Scotland as part of a study of the use of temporary dwellings. Some of this work has already been published (Leitch 1987, 15-20) while Angus Martin has also treated this subject in a study of Kintyre (1986, 123-4). The other author (CS), an archaeologist, has since 1985 been studying the archaeological traces of occupation in a group of caves and rock shelters in Mid Argyll. The majority of cave and rock shelters in the area exhibit some traces of recent use, while all excavated sites were occupied in medieval and post-medieval times as well as during far earlier periods. In our view, this activity may have something important to tell us about the attitude of people in Western Scotland to natural shelters, both in prehistoric and more recent times.

For example, at the most basic level the requirements of shelter, warmth and light were the same for cave dwellers sixty years ago as they were 6,000 years ago. Similarly, caves very rarely change shape and the same constraints of space were imposed on all occupants. Also, caves never move, and if their use at one time articulated with subsistence patterns and the extraction of locally available resources, this may well have been the case at other times as well. Consideration of these general issues led to consultation between the authors and this paper brings together some of the preliminary results of their combined research into cave dwelling in Scotland.

CAVE USE IN SCOTLAND: THE ETHNOHISTORICAL EVIDENCE

The ethnology and ethnohistory of Western Scotland are rich in records of cave use spanning more than three centuries. We are dealing not only with the accounts of travellers such as Martin Martin who journeyed through the Hebrides in the 1690s (Martin 1703), or rather later Thomas Pennant (Pennant 1772), but also records of cave use and cave dwelling feature in official government papers such as the Statistical Accounts and the Census Returns, while a series of government studies of travelling people each draw attention to the continued use of natural shelters (Gentleman and Swift 1971; *Report* 1918). Poor Law Returns and local newspapers are further important sources of evidence, but the most important of all, and the most difficult to gain access to, is the surviving oral tradition.

Research must amount to more than the mere collection of anecdotes and we have tried to approach the material in a systematic way. Firstly, it is necessary to categorise the kinds of evidence available. It is convenient to use four broad categories:

(i) *Myth and Legend*: Tales of legendary or mythological cavemen are numerous throughout Scotland and range from the almost ubiquitous lost piper to Sawney Bean, the cave-dwelling cannibal (Homes 1985), and the 'kerwachs', said to be naked wild men who lived in caves (Campbell 1860-62, 49), and who possibly represent a distant folk memory of a prehistoric cave-dwelling population.

(ii) *Tradition:* There are also many traditional accounts of cave dwelling by individuals, particularly hermits and holy men such as Ciaran in Kintyre or Columba in Knapdale; fugitives such as Bruce, Wallace and Prince Charles Edward Stuart (Forbes 1895, 321-54; 1896, 375-83). Less specific, there are numerous traditions of fugitive Jacobites, criminals on the run and smugglers and 'poachers' (Campbell and Sandeman 1964, 7 (no. 23))

(iii) *Documented accounts:* The main documentary sources have already been mentioned briefly but the following examples illustrate the kind of evidence available.

(a) The *First Statistical Account* for the Oban area[1] records that in 1690 a local cave was used to detain the crew of a ship who, having come ashore, were found to be infested with a pestilence.

(b) In 1772 Pennant (1772, 195-6) recorded that St Ciaran's Cave was in his day used by sailors who landed in order to 'dress (cook) their victuals beneath the shelter' . . . while an 'ancient pair' had not long before made the cave their home.

(c) The Census Returns for 1881[2] record that the Keil Cave in Kintyre was the home of John McFee, aged twenty-two, a tinsmith, Margaret his wife, aged twenty-one, and their one-year-old son Andrew. They shared the cave with John McFee's cousin Alex McCallum, aged forty-five, a basket-maker, Mary his wife and Bella their daughter.

(d) In 1885 the *Campbeltown Courier* (Martin 1986, 122-3) printed an obituary to Esther Houston, described as an agricultural outworker, fisherwoman and 'wilk-gatherer' who had lived in a cave at Southend, Mull of Kintyre, with her natural son.

(e) In March 1915, under the Defence of the Realm Act, cave dwelling was declared strictly prohibited and a warning was issued by the Chief Constable of Argyll to persons 'dwelling in or using as an habitual abode caves or hollows along the shore'—presumably because cave fires might have attracted enemy submarines. The newspaper reported that as cave dwellers were still numerous in Argyll many families were rendered homeless (Martin 1986, 125).

(f) In 1917 an attempt was made to carry out a census of travelling people in Scotland. Of those recorded 2 per cent, or fifty-five individuals, were still living in caves (*Report* 1918).

(g) In the Minutes of Evidence of the 1917 Royal Commission Report on Housing (*Report* 1917), reference is made by Dr George Dick to a Caithness cave that provided accommodation for twenty-five to thirty persons. These were separate families of tinkers, and under cross-examination Dr Dick provided some surprising answers:

> Would you concur in the opinion of the Local Government Board Inspector, who considers that the caves he visited were infinitely more superior from the sanitary point of view to many of the houses to which the vagrants had been driven?
> *Dr Dick:* Yes; certainly.
> Do they keep their caves in a sanitary state?
> *Dr Dick:* That cave was much cleaner than any house I have ever seen occupied by tinkers.
> How is that?
> *Dr Dick:* It is a residence in common and I expect that if anyone commits a nuisance the others look after him (*Report* 1917; Minutes of Evidence 630 [16, 157-9]).

The cave in question was most likely the one on the south side of Wick Bay, opposite the Old Man of Wick. It extended fully 30 feet in depth with a subsequent tapering off in height. Although the cave mouth was left open to the sea, the several different families had their own portioned-off areas within the cave, much the same as a tenement property.

(h) This same cave and others in the Wick area feature in a number of individual accounts (e.g. Mitchell 1880, 73). In August 1866 Arthur Mitchell, along with two friends, visited 'the great cave at the south side of Wick Bay'. Mitchell noted that very high tides with north-easterlies meant that the front of the cave had to be vacated for a position at the rear, which was at a higher level than the cave mouth. Exceptionally high seas meant that the cave had to be evacuated[3] and it is remembered locally that on one occasion, while a party of eleven and their donkey were ascending the treacherous cliff-side path, a woman fell and drowned.[4] At the time of Mitchell's visit in 1866 there were twenty-four 'inmates' in residence, comprising four families and their 'numerous and vicious dogs'.

> The beds on which we found these people lying, consisted of straw, grass and bracken, spread upon rock or shingle, and each was supplied with one or two dirty, ragged blankets or pieces of matting. Two of the beds were near the peat fires which were still burning, but the others were further back in the cave where they were better sheltered (Mitchell 1880, 74).

(iv) *Oral tradition:* Oral evidence has helped keep alive tradition surrounding the use of a sea-cave at Slains near Collieston in Aberdeenshire. Recorded in July 1954, Dr Hamish Henderson's informant alleged that he spent the first year of his childhood in the cave at Slains. Up to four families occupied this cave and each family had a different fireplace. No attempt was made to close off the cave mouth or hang sacking for shelter. The original cave dwellers used to help smugglers from Holland unload their kegs of gin, but around 1890 a battle took place for occupancy of the cave and the original occupants were driven out by 'interlopers'. Prior to the cave being 'condemned' around the time the railway reached Cruden Bay in 1902, the cave dwellers are said to have existed by a strict set of rules with a high priority attached to sanitary arrangements.[5]

Known locally as 'The Coves', the Caiplie Caves lie midway between the fishing burghs of Cellardyke and Crail in the East Neuk of Fife, and were another troglodytes' base with their own particular lore. Most of those who inhabited these caves were solitaries, although in the inter-war period the occupants at times comprised parties of travelling folk.[6] St Adrian and his followers reputedly stayed in these caves but the most famous occupant of recent times was a recluse known as Cove Jimmy. For thirteen years he was to make his abode the Mortuary Cave. With a high, narrow entrance, the Mortuary Cave lies furthest back from the sea, being protected on the west and east by a flange of rock. From the fisher homes of Cellardyke he accumulated odd bits of carpet and linoleum, a table, sideboard, chairs and even a bed. He also installed a pillar-like stove whose flue ran up one wall, across the roof, and out through the top of the cave entrance. Bore-holes in the cave's entrance wall and the remnant of a wooden wedge can be seen to this day. Such was Cove Jimmy's standing that he became akin to a landlord of the caves, regulating the use of the larger Chapel Cave.

At times there existed a self-contained group of tramps and travellers who made light of their surroundings with music and stories. Fresh water was obtained from a spring called the Hermit's Well situated some fifty or sixty yards away on the west side. It was even claimed that one occupant rigged up a primitive shower which consisted of an old bucket with a perforated base.

Other parts of the Scottish coast also had their local celebrities. Near Ardwell, on the western seaboard of the Rhinns of Galloway, William Purves, a former itinerant circus clown, occupied a cave which he equipped with a door and some articles of furniture (*Gallov.* 1909, 63). This second generation clown used to perform in local smiddies before retiring to the life of a pedlar selling small wares and picture postcards of himself.

Indeed packmen and pedlars were a distinctive group of individuals who regularly made use of caves in the seaboard areas of the Western Highlands. In *Ring of Bright Water,* Gavin Maxwell describes a cave-dwelling pedlar named Joe Wilson and his 'cave consort Jeannie'. Wilson, a deserter from the army, had at one time been a professional jockey. According to local oral tradition, Wilson was a well-known character in the Glenelg area:

> He used to come round here collecting rabbit skins, sold onions and things like that. His wife was called Jean, a big heavy woman who sold children's clothes, laces and all these things to women. Joe used to live in a cave right down by the shore, at a place called the Market Stance, where they used to hold the old cattle sales or fairs away back in the early 1900s. It didn't please them so they shifted to a cave further along the coast, quite close to this place called Camusfearna in Gavin Maxwell's book. He lived there for years and used to gather whelks when the tide was suitable.[7]

CAVE USE IN SCOTLAND: A TENTATIVE MODEL

This substantial body of material deals with two broad categories of cave and rock shelter use, one of which may be called 'fugitive lairs'. In point of fact, material of this kind is of little use to the student of cave use in general in that the fugitives in question, for understandable reasons, preferred their lairs to be in remote, inaccessible places. While remoteness is something of a relative concept, accessibility was an important consideration for habitual cave users, and it is records of such use that are of most interest to the student of cave dwelling in general. The ethnohistory of cave use in Scotland provides evidence on a number of themes of interest to the archaeologist and prehistorian of cave dwelling.

Firstly, we can gain some insights into the importance of cave use in the annual subsistence cycle; whether occupation was year round or seasonal, and if seasonal which seasons? Many caves appear to have been used on a regular, but intermittent basis by travelling people down to about the time of the restrictions imposed during the First World War. Before the widespread advent of motorised transport, travellers tended to confine their movements to traditional, or ancestral areas, and within these, natural shelters were used on a regular basis, particular caves becoming associated with individual families or clans. Cave dwelling was for a few months at a time, and part of the year was also spent in tents. Caves could be used at any season, though one first-hand account refers to their use as a specifically summer activity, tents being preferred in the winter. Permanent occupation always seems to have been something of an exception and usually involved elderly people or loners not part of a regular band. Cave dwelling was not confined to the travelling population; groups, conventionally regarded as 'settled', the so-called 'flatties', also became temporary troglodytes from time to time. For example, fishermen from Colonsay are recorded as having regularly stayed in caves on the west coast of Jura while fishing the inshore waters there and the same is reported of parties going from neighbouring islands to hunt deer (Mercer 1974, 76).

Secondly, we can learn something about the range of uses to which these natural shelters were put which appear to have included both residence and storage, while some were used as workshops. Residence is the most common use, though since many travellers were also itinerant craftsmen, especially tinsmiths and basket-makers, many caves were workshops as well as homes.

Thirdly, we can gain some understanding of the way in which the space available was used and how carefully this was organised. In 1956 Stewart Sanderson recorded the facilities established in a cave in Moidart by a travelling packman (Sanderson 1957, 243-5), consisting of a rudimentary bed, chair and table beside a hearth, and sheltered by a low stone wall. Elements of this level of spatial organisation are a commonplace occurrence and there are frequent references in the ethnohistorical record to rudimentary furnishings, bedding, screens and windbreaks. Hearths are of course ubiquitous. One informant records that a hearth should be near the entrance but to the right so as to light the access to the shelter but, presumably, not impede it. Sanitary arrangements were not provided but no cave dweller would foul the group's living quarters.

Lastly, the ethnohistorical record can allow us to glimpse the kind of social organisation that developed among cave users as a way of minimising conflict over the use of restricted facilities. Some caves were large enough to accommodate several families and curiously enough a figure that recurs is four families or about twenty people, all usually of the same kin such as McPhees, McNeills, or Williamsons, and a leader or cave 'chief' was appointed to enforce compliance with the unwritten code of cave conduct. Each family had its own hearth and an analogy with a tenement house is made more than once. Families seemed to have had an accepted traditional right to use particular caves but there was a degree of flexibility in that a small group could be expected to give way to a larger band, usually without duress.

CONCLUSION

In this short paper we have drawn attention to the wealth of ethnohistorical information bearing on the topic of cave dwelling in Scotland. We have cited a range of examples which we consider to be representative of the kind of material available. We have also attempted to show ways in which this material can shed light on problems frequently faced by archaeologists who excavate in caves and who are interested in how and why people throughout time have often sought shelter in what, to the modern perception, are such uninviting places.

ACKNOWLEDGEMENTS

The authors would like to thank Angus Martin for allowing us to use unpublished material collected by him and for helpful correspondence during the course of our research. Carol Goodfellow of Inverness Library kindly agreed to the reproduction of the postcard of the Tinker's Cave at Wick. Professor Alexander Fenton, Angus Martin and Dave Kear read the paper in draft and made a number of helpful suggestions as to ways in which it could be improved. Debts of gratitude are also due to the RIBA, the Prehistoric Society, the Society of Antiquaries of Scotland and the Committee for Excavation and Field Work of the University of Newcastle for assisting with finance towards the research carried out here.

NOTES

1 Notes made available by Margaret Kay on the Oban entry in the *First Statistical Account* 1794.

2 Notes made available by Angus Martin.

3 Letter from Mrs Elizabeth Jack, Halkirk, Caithness, dated 29 April 1982.

4 Letter from Mrs Isobel Salmon, Stanmore, Middlesex, dated 24 April 1982.

5 School of Scottish Studies Sound Archive *SA 1955/155*, Davy Hutchison recorded by Hamish Henderson at Aberdeen in July 1954.

6 *RWL 15* Eugene D'Espremenil recorded by Roger Leitch at Cellardyke on 12 September 1982.

7 *RWL 13* John MacAskill (born 1900), recorded by Roger Leitch at Glenelg, Inverness-shire, on 24 May 1982.

REFERENCES

CAMPBELL, JOHN FRANCIS

1860-62 *Popular Tales of the West Highlands*, Vol. 3: 49. Edinburgh.

CAMPBELL, MARION and SANDEMAN, MARY L. S.

1964 'Mid Argyll: A Field Survey of the Historic and Prehistoric Monuments.' *Proceedings of the Society of Antiquaries of Scotland* (1961-62), xcv: 1-125.

FORBES, R. (ed.)

1895 *The Lyon in Mourning* (Scottish History Society xx), I: 321-54.

FORBES, R. (ed.)

1896 *The Lyon in Mourning* (Scottish History Society xxii), III: 375-83.

GALLOV.

1909 *The Gallovidian* xi.

GENTLEMAN, HUGH and SWIFT, SUSAN

1971 *Report on Scotland's Travelling People.*

HOMES, RONALD

1985 *The Cannibal Family of Sawney Bean and other Galloway Stories.* Midlothian.

LEITCH, ROGER

1987 'Green Bottle Howffs: A Pilot Study of Inhabited Caves.' *Vernacular Building* II: 15-20.

MARTIN, ANGUS

1986 *Kintyre: The Hidden Past.* Edinburgh.

MARTIN, MARTIN

1703 *A Description of the Western Islands of Scotland.* Stirling.

MERCER, JOHN

1974 *Hebridean Islands: Colonsay, Gigha, Jura.* Glasgow and London.

MITCHELL, ARTHUR

1880 *The Past in the Present.* Edinburgh.

PENNANT, THOMAS

1772 *A Tour in Scotland and Voyage in the Hebrides.* Chester.

REPORT

1917 *Report of the Royal Commission on the Housing of the Industrial Population of Scotland, Rural and Urban.* HMSO, Edinburgh.

REPORT

1918 *Report of the Departmental Committee on the Tinkers of Scotland.* HMSO, Edinburgh.

SANDERSON, STEWART

1957 'A Packman's Bivvy in Moidart.' *Scottish Studies* 1, 2: 243-5.

Crogans and Barvas Ware: Handmade Pottery in the Hebrides

HUGH CHEAPE

Certain types of pottery from the Outer and Inner Hebrides and areas of the adjacent mainland have been classified over the last hundred years or so as 'crogans' or 'craggans' and 'Barvas Ware'. These terms serve to indicate not only two distinct classes of ceramic material but also that there is a distinction between an old, indigenous tradition of pottery-making and a relatively modern, exotic tradition.

Crogan is a colloquial Gaelic word with a long pedigree; it is used to refer to ancient or modern earthenware jars, unglazed, more or less spherical, handthrown without the use of the potter's wheel and fired in the domestic hearth (Fig. 1). The word is cognate with the English 'crock', found in Old English sources in the form *crocca* (cf. Old Norse *krukka* with the same meaning). *Crogan* is found in Old and Middle Irish texts in the form *croccán,* frequently qualified as *croccán chriadh,* 'clay pot'. The variant *cragan,* also used in some areas, particularly in Lewis, was the term recorded for this pottery, both ancient and modern, by some archaeologists and ceramics collectors in the second half of the nineteenth century (e.g. Smith 1875: 206). Since then, 'craggan' has also been the term commonly used in museum catalogues. The second term, 'Barvas Ware', has been adopted as a generic name for the modern, that is late nineteenth-century and twentieth-century, similarly unglazed, handthrown, domestically fired pottery made presumably in imitation of contemporary, commercially produced pottery, especially cups and saucers, jugs, teapots and sugar basins (Fig. 2).

The production of this imitation ware came to be identified with the township of Barvas on the west coast of Lewis where it was first 'discovered' and publicised by visitors to the island in the 1860s. The survival of handmade pottery techniques in parts of the Hebrides has created considerable interest amongst scholars of the past hundred years, especially when it was first noticed. The prehistoric-looking pots or *crogain* (plural), which were found not only in use but also still being made by some local families, have been brought to people's attention in one or two publications in which, however, their coverage was only superficial. A closer study is needed of this pottery from the Hebrides and especially of the crogan ware, and the purpose of

Fig. 1: Crogan (22 cm high) made in Lewis in the second half of the nineteenth century, showing rounded base and turned-out rim. (Photo: *National Museums of Scotland.*)

Fig. 2: Teaset of Barvas Ware bought in Lewis by a collector *c.* 1910, probably made in imitation of one of the Scottish commercial wares of the period. (Photo: *National Museums of Scotland*, by courtesy of Mrs Thelma Aitken, Lanark.)

Figs. 3 and 4: Two crogans from Callanish, Lewis. The crogan on the left (19 cm high) has simple scratch-mark decoration and fragments of *imideal* (skin cover) and *iall* (thong) round the neck. That on the right (17.5 cm high), strengthened at the shoulder and neck, was referred to as a 'potato pot' when collected in the 1930s. (Photo: *National Museums of Scotland.)*

this paper is to examine them in the context of available background historical information, both printed and oral. Hebridean pottery of the crogan type may throw light on prehistoric pottery sequences as well as on the economy of island life in the past: they are pieces of evidence of material culture too important to be ignored or left unexplained.

The characteristics of surviving examples of crogans are remarkably consistent and faithful to type, which suggests that they represent a practical response to requirements and have been evolved over generations, if not centuries, of manufacture and use. The globular body of the pot is sometimes shouldered: the technique of throwing this shape without a potter's wheel is more difficult, and the quality of the clay and its impurities may often have limited the possibilities of shaping in this way. The height of the pot is generally the same as the diameter: surviving examples are between 10 cm and 36 cm in height. The neck and mouth are narrow and the rim is everted to suit the storing of food: it was said that the narrow opening would take a woman's hand but not a cow's or a calf's muzzle. In use as a storage vessel, a sheepskin covering was stretched over the rim and tied in round the neck with a thong or cord. This type of skin-covering has been variously termed *imideal, craicionn* and *fùileach*. In the Islands, *imideal* appears to be the standard term for the skin-covering over the top of a jar or pail. *Snàthan imideil* has been recently recorded in Lewis for the relatively modern string used to tie on the skin-covering. *Iall* was an earlier term implying a thong made of leather. Such words as *imideal* and *snàthan* or *snàithlean* with their specific meanings would undoubtedly once have been widespread but it is in Lewis that they seem to have survived actively, where the shieling system also happened to survive longest (cf. Carmichael 1941: 83). *Fùileach* occurs more rarely. It has been recorded in Mull with the specific meaning of a sheepskin covering, a term which may now be impossible to corroborate (Campbell 1902: 12).

Of the surviving examples of crogan ware in museum collections, some are ornamented and some are plain. Ornamentation, when it occurs, is simple, often haphazard, consisting of a series of incised lines either in parallel or converging and diverging (Fig. 3). Raised ornamentation is rare on crogans although an example of one from Callanish, Lewis, now in the National Museums of Scotland, has a horizontal raised band between the shoulder and the neck of the pot; this, however, may represent simply an attempt to strengthen the wall of the jar in the area on which pressure is applied (Fig. 4). Raised ornamentation on Barvas Ware is common but in no way functional and was presumably a device to beautify the pottery for sale.

The base of the crogan is generally rounded, recalling the shape of Neolithic pottery, and emphasising the spherical appearance of the pot. Some have a semi-rounded base which makes them more stable, although when in use in the fire for cooking the fully rounded shape would have been more efficient. To many Gaelic speakers, the proverb *Seasadh gach soitheach air a mhàs fhéin,* 'Let every vessel stand on its own bottom' (Nicolson 1881: 345), must have seemed ironic, or even paradoxical, since their most familiar vessels could not stand on their own without support. But if the vessel was placed in the peat fire, or in the fine peat ash moved to one side for the purpose, the pot would stand upright in it and the heat would be distributed evenly through the walls of the vessel. Another Gaelic proverb alludes to this: *Ardan na poite bige, cha tig e seach an luath,* 'The pride of the wee pot won't go beyond the ashes' (Nicolson 1881: 45).

Crogans and Barvas Ware have attracted the attention from time to time of topographical writers, museum curators and archaeologists, ceramics collectors and a few of the general public. The earliest specific literary references to crogans in the late seventeenth century describe their manufacture and use in just those places where we know that they were last made and used. This is hardly an accident of history but rather a testimony to the suitability of the local clays and the long-term localisation of the traditions of pottery production. For most people in the Hebrides, of course, the pottery was an unremarkable and commonplace aspect of everyday life, as early writers on Hebridean life convey. By the early nineteenth century, references to it suggest that it might have seemed unusual by mainland standards. By the late nineteenth century, crogans and Barvas Ware had become well established in the public notice and from the range of written contemporary comment, attitudes to the pottery ranged from amused scorn to genuine interest, from regarding it as a crude oddity to judging it to be a rare and fascinating local variant of Scottish material culture (e.g. Fig. 5).

The early scholarly interest of the 1860s was not followed up, and both the archaeological and the historical potential of this material have consequently never been realised. Our comparative wealth of surviving Hebridean pottery has therefore received scant attention, probably because it is neither archaeology nor history: it is too recent to be considered an archaeological source and in most instances it is not old enough to be obviously historical. Although the National Museums have a good collection of this material, it has rarely been displayed. Perhaps also the scholar has been deterred because much of the supporting evidence and explanation of the pottery is part of an oral tradition in a language other than English.

Whether recovered through excavation or 'thrown up' by the erosion of settlement sites, pottery is archaeology's most common detritus in the Hebrides, as elsewhere. For the many sherds and fragments of handthrown unglazed ware, fired to a red or brown finish at relatively low temperatures, proper identification and dating is difficult, if not impossible. This applies particularly to much that is already stored in our museums. Other than for such distinctive material as the Late Neolithic 'grooved ware' and 'beakers', Roman wares or medieval green- and brown-glazed, conventionally decorated, wheel-turned pottery, interpretation from the primary evidence of site or stratum is fraught with difficulties. Most of these types of pottery have been found in the form of sherds in the Hebrides, but otherwise much of the mass of pottery fragments found in the Hebrides has been laid aside as more or less unrecognisable and unclassifiable (e.g. Anderson 1890: 138-9).

Generally, the archaeologist labels the 'undiagnostic' sherds as, say, 'Bronze Age' or 'Iron Age'—the periods which have enjoyed most attention—or as recent 'craggan' material. Effectively, this tends to produce a notional gap of anything up to fifteen hundred years for which no interpretation or explanation can be offered. The pages of our archaeological journals bristle with such unanswered problems.Evidence now emerging suggests nonetheless that a well-developed pottery tradition did exist in the Hebrides during the Iron Age and probably in later periods, and also—both from historical evidence and from the knowledge of generations still living—that simple functional pottery was being produced from the sixteenth or even fifteenth centuries into the twentieth.

The reorganisation of available historical data and the retrieval of oral information must have potential, therefore, for the explanation of at least some archaeological problems. If such information can be brought together, it might be possible to show some continuity between prehistoric times and the twentieth century. One example of the questions raised by discoveries of excavated pottery material in the Hebrides will suffice. Excavations on the so-called 'Pygmies Isle' site at the Butt of Lewis were reported in the *Proceedings of the Society of Antiquaries of Scotland* in 1904 by the Highland historian, William Cook MacKenzie. Investigators (his own term) had dug up the floor of the ruined building and had found, apart from bones and peatash, some pieces of handmade unglazed pottery which were lying in the same stratum 'between the upper layer of loam and the lower of sea-sand'. He described some of this pottery as being of a style and colour 'somewhat resembling the old croggans' (MacKenzie 1904-5: 252). Dr Robert Stevenson, reviewing these pottery finds in the *Proceedings* in 1945, pointed out that one of the decorated sherds was a very good example of Neolithic ware, that three of the other sherds had similar Neolithic style of decoration, but that the piece of slightly flattened base mentioned in the original account was of a quite different, and more recent, fabric (Stevenson 1945-6: 141). Given the proper analysis of crogan material, it should be possible to fix this pottery more precisely in time and space, to discover when the piece was made and where and perhaps even by whom.

More recent excavation-reporting has shown a sharper awareness of the chronological hiatus. In an excavation on Barra, for example, 'craggan' pottery material in a dun site of Iron Age date was assigned tentatively but realistically to a recent period, in this instance to the seventeenth or early eighteenth centuries (Young 1955-6: 296). Decorated pottery of a crude type which might have been assumed to be of Iron Age date has been excavated in a medieval and post-medieval castle site at Breachacha, Coll, stratified with imported glazed, wheel-turned ware

(Turner and Dunbar 1969-70: 182-5). The castle developed from a fifteenth-century tower-house, and continued in occupation in different phases into the nineteenth century. Crogan pottery was present in all deposits over the period of four centuries. Its close association with imported wheel-turned pottery at Breachacha seems to point to its being used in that particular social milieu, as well as in more modest circumstances as might be inferred from Hugh Miller's lyrical account of the discovery of the pieces of crogan in 'The Cave of Francis', *Uamh Fhraing,* where the population of Eigg was massacred by the MacLeods in the sixteenth century (Miller 1874: 24).

After the 'discovery' of Hebridean (crogans and Barvas Ware) pottery in the 1860s, some accounts of it were published up to the time of the First World War. With one or two exceptions, the descriptions concentrate on its distinctly odd appearance by generally accepted standards, and also on the nature of its manufacture. They seem to sound a note of curiosity or sometimes condescension, typical of the self-confident late Victorian age that delighted in discovering colonies of primitive peoples who might be considered as worthy of patronage, philanthropy, charity or firm evangelisation and missionary zeal. That curiosity was, of course, heightened when the objects of charity or mission were located not in the South Seas but within a day's journey of Britain's centres of civilisation.

From the middle of the nineteenth century improved communications by sea and rail brought tourists in increasing numbers to the Hebrides. Scholars and archaeologists mingled with the sportsmen and the curious among the new moneyed classes. The formation of the MacBrayne company after 1851 made the Hebrides accessible from the Clyde, and as the railway network expanded, steamer services linked up the railhead ports of Oban, Mallaig and Kyle of Lochalsh with the Long Island. Many of the new types of visitor found much to interest them in the way of prehistoric remains, and 'Notes' and 'Comments' articles on these began to appear in the press and archaeological journals. Some of these articles were given a new dimension, consciously or unconsciously, through the influence of developing disciplines such as Folklore Studies and Anthropology. The new breed of scholars in the field in the late nineteenth century studied and collected material culture of indigenous and aboriginal people, whose tools and techniques seemed to differ little from those used by Mesolithic and Neolithic man as revealed by his archaeological remains (e.g. Mitchell 1897-8b: 182).

The survival of 'the past in the present' in nineteenth-century Scotland inspired a book by that name and also laid the foundations of the ethnological collections of the National Museums. The author and architect of this work, Dr, later Sir, Arthur Mitchell, travelled widely in the Northern and Western Isles in his capacity as Deputy Commissioner in Lunacy in Scotland. Mitchell went into the field and identified, described, drew, measured and published what he regarded as primitive survivals. In Lewis, Mitchell travelled with Captain Frederick William Leopold

Fig. 5: Crogan (20 cm high) from Barvas, early nineteenth century, collected by Dr (later Sir) Arthur Mitchell in 1860, as illustrated in his book, *The Past in the Present* (1880). The style of the engraving might have been suggestive of the primitive and exotic, to the Victorian mind.

Fig 6: Teapot (14cm high) made in Barvas *c.* 1860 and bought by Dr Arthur Mitchell as illustrated in *The Past in the Present* (1880). It was described there as imitating Staffordshire pottery, but was probably influenced, rather, by lowland Scottish wares.

Fig 7: Barvas Ware teapots newly fired in peat on a central hearth, in Barvas, Lewis, 1907. On the dresser behind the figure, two more teapots can be seen together with factory-made pottery. Above the fire, the *slabhruidh* (pot links and hook) can be seen. (Photo: *Mrs E. C. Quiggin, by courtesy of Edinburgh Central Library, I. F. Grant Collection.*)

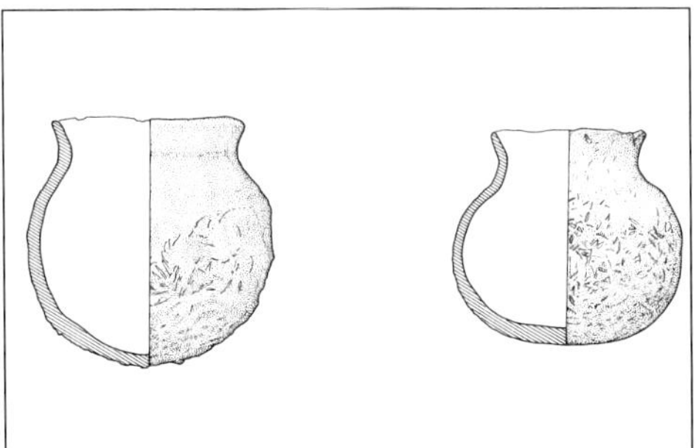

Figs. 8 and 9: Two small crogans. That on the left (11 cm high) contained the seventeenth-century coin-hoard found near Stornoway. That on the right (9 cm high) was found in sand-dunes. Both show the marks of grass temper or of sitting in the grass in the unfired state.

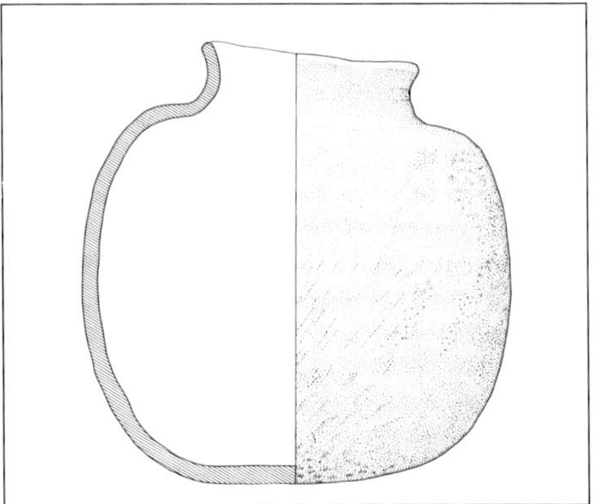

Fig. 10: Crogan (24 cm high) of nineteenth-century date from Lewis, showing characteristic profile and asymmetric shape, the marks of scraping down from the final stages of manufacture before firing, and the slight scar left by a fastening at the neck.

Thomas, then on the Admiralty survey of the coasts of Orkney, Shetland and the Hebrides. Thomas himself was a Corresponding Member of the Society of Antiquaries at the time and a prolific contributor to the Society's *Proceedings*. Thomas tended to concentrate on houses and shielings, and Mitchell on goods, chattels and tools such as ploughs, spinning and weaving instruments, querns, mills and pottery. The latter made the first collection of crogans and Barvas Ware, which he presented to the National Museum of Antiquities of Scotland.

In the second of his Rhind Lectures, delivered to the Society of Antiquaries in 1876, and subsequently published as the second chapter of his book *The Past in the Present*, Mitchell described his 'discovery' of both crogans and Barvas Ware:

> When I visited the Island of Lewis in 1863, I had the advantage of the company of Captain F. W. L. Thomas. In driving from Uig to the village of Barvas on the west coast, we passed a stone-breaker sitting at the roadside eating his dinner out of a vessel which struck us as remarkable. We found it, on closer examination, to be even a stranger thing than it seemed to us, as we first caught sight of it. We waited till the stone-breaker had eaten its contents, and then we carried it off; but we had acquired little information regarding its history, because the stone-breaker and we had no language in common.
>
> Before reaching Barvas we had a detour to make and some business to transact. When we got there, we found that our acquaintance of the roadside had preceded us. He had hurried home to tell of the profitable sale he had made, and while our horse was feeding, we were visited by many people carrying vessels like the one we had bought, and offering them for sale.
>
> They are called *Craggans*, and we learned that, at a period by no means remote,

they had been made in many of the villages of the Lewis, though at the time of our visit their manufacture was chiefly, if not entirely, confined to Barvas (Mitchell 1880: 25-6).

When they returned by arrangement after two days, Mitchell and Thomas were shown by a Mrs MacLeod her traditional pottery-making methods. They were told that it was women's work to make the pottery. She had also prepared for them (apparently being 'proud of her skill and anxious to display it') the rustic versions of commercial pottery, teacups, teapots, milk jugs and sugar basins. These imitative objects they subsequently dubbed 'Barvas Pottery' and 'Barvas Ware'; and this type of pottery, sold as souvenirs, continued to interest tourists and scholars for the next half century or so (Fig. 6).

Mitchell's interests and turn of phrase are important pointers to contemporary ideas, and this 'discovery' of crogans and Barvas Ware and also its subsequent neglect are symptoms of wider prevailing ideas and attitudes. His lectures reveal that he and Thomas were examining contemporary observable phenomena which could be deemed to throw light on prehistoric material and techniques. Mitchell developed his view of the pottery as he collected more of it and placed it in the National Museum of Antiquities for posterity. His implied viewpoint, which was more anthropological than archaeological in that it rested on assumptions such as the continuity, inheritance and unbroken succession of the particular phenomenon of the making of crogans, was expressed succinctly in terms of their

> . . . archaic character chiefly in respect of a certain rudeness in their form and purpose, but they are in reality not archaic, having all been made and used in this country by persons of this time. They have therefore been called neo-archaic, and the study of them throws light on the study of many objects which are really archaic' (Mitchell 1897-8b: 181).

Mitchell undoubtedly impressed his listeners: in a Presidential Address to the Inverness Scientific Society in the following year, the Inverness architect, Alexander Ross, summarised the gist of Mitchell's case, saying:

> In many respects the science dealing with ancient remains was going through a transition phase, for the ordinarily received classification had been rudely shaken by the lectures of Dr Arthur Mitchell, who had shown that the rudest manufactures and implements might co-exist with the most advanced art' (Ross 1875-80: 49).

This is not the place to try to describe or explain the history of archaeology, but reference should perhaps be made to the quickening of pace in archaeological studies in the second half of the nineteenth century, owing to the enormous influence of Darwinian theories of evolution and progress. The theory of evolution was not Darwin's own invention, but the publication of *The Origin of Species* in 1859 made an impact on the popular as well as on the scholarly mind, and took the ideas on evolution out of the narrow battle of Christian orthodoxy against science. It is not without significance that the sub-title of Mitchell's Rhind Lectures was 'What is Civilisation?'. His theory was that evolution and progress took place unevenly; that men co-existed in different stages of 'civilisation' from the primitive to the sophisticated, although their powers of intellect might well be similar. Hence, although Mitchell could not converse with the roadman from whom he bought Barvas pottery in 1863 because of the language barrier, he recognised his qualities and similarly the intelligence of the maker of that pottery who, for all her primitive material culture, was 'full of shrewdness, a theologian in her way, well versed in church quarrels and in the obligations of the Poor Law, and quite able to become well versed in a score of other things if the need and opportunity had arisen' (Mitchell 1880: 32).

After Arthur Mitchell's early essays, little effort was made further to record or investigate the Hebridean crogan ware, even for comparative purposes. The keepers of the National Museum of Antiquities such as that great pioneer keeper, Joseph Anderson (in office from 1869 to 1913), directed their energies and interests elsewhere, and his successors in office were more interested in Roman archaeology in accordance with the intellectual fashion of the day (cf. Anderson 1890: 138). The results have been twofold: in the first place, much ethnological information which could have been recorded in the field at that time cannot now be recovered, and in the second, little care was taken to record information in the catalogues and to classify the pottery itself. Although the crogans and Barvas Ware were correctly accessioned in 1863, they were wrongly described in the printed Catalogue of 1892. This initiated an unfortunate process of cumulative error in cataloguing which has been allowed to continue unchecked as the pottery collections of the National Museums have grown, and which is now being rectified while it is still possible to gather the remaining oral information about the pottery in the field.

Crogans and Barvas Ware did, however, catch the attention of ceramics collectors after the publicity that it received from Mitchell and his colleagues. The pottery's inclusion in the large two-volume work, *The Ceramic Art of Great Britain,* published in 1878, played an important part in this. The author, Llewellyn Jewitt, who was also a well-known tourist-guide writer, explained that his first source of information on handmade Hebridean pottery was a Scottish archaeologist (Jewitt 1878: 522-23). Barvas Ware continued to be made in some quantities until the time of the First World War, a trade sustained, according to a parliamentary report of 1902, by 'curio hunters'. It was advertised for sale in the national press, it sold in Stornoway, and it was sent for national exhibition in Edinburgh in 1908 and Glasgow in 1911. When the Cambridge Celtic scholar Edmund Crosby Quiggin spent two months learning Hebridean Gaelic in Lewis in 1907, his young wife—it was in fact their honeymoon—was able to photograph, despite the obvious technical

Fig. 11: Hugh MacNeil of Balevullin, Tiree, demonstrating in 1942 stages of making a small crogan. His mother, Flora MacKinnon (*c.* 1840-1920), was one of the last crogan-makers in Tiree, and had inherited the tradition from her own mother. (Photos: *by Mr George Holleyman, Brighton, by whose kind permission they are reproduced here.*)

difficulties then of using a camera in a windowless interior, some newly fired teapots on a central hearth in Barvas (Fig. 7). Thereafter, interest in the pottery waned and the archaeologist Dr E. Cecil Curwen commented in 1938: 'With a branch of Woolworths established in Stornoway it is not altogether surprising that in 1937 the writer failed to trace a single specimen of Barvas Ware in the island—apart from what was already in the Callanish Museum' (Curwen 1938: 282). Curwen did not seem to be aware that the continuing manufacture of Barvas pottery was not so much a symptom of deprivation as he suggests (since it was not being made for local use), but was rather a practical response to the odd trade which had developed between the 1860s and the First World War.

Now, in the second half of the twentieth century, crogans and Barvas Ware have passed out of use and are no longer made. The term *crogan* has itself survived in active use in colloquial phrases, mainly to describe food containers such as preserve jars, for example *crogan sioraip, crogan silidh, crogan trèicil* and *crogan meala* demonstrate. The term *crogan* has also commonly been applied to stoneware jars of a standard mass-produced type, that is, cylindrical containers with a slipware glaze finish. These have always had the same style of everted rim as the traditional crogan on which a soft or loose cover could be tied. Jam and preserves were sold until recent years in these jars, which, having been fired at a very high temperature, were tough and durable and could be used for many years for jam-making and for storing other foodstuffs. By extension, the term was used for other forms of food containers: for instance, Donald MacIntyre of South Uist and Paisley referred in one of his songs to *briosgaidean is feòil nan crogan*, 'biscuits and tinned meat' (MacMillan 1968: 291, 397).

The same term, *crogan*, or *cragan*, was used in vernacular Gaelic to describe unglazed earthenware dug up from early settlements or Neolithic burials (e.g. Thomas 1886: fol. 2f). Two accounts, one early nineteenth century and one mid-twentieth century, describe the circumstances of loss and discovery by which *crogain*-like vessels were preserved from an earlier age. The 'Morrison Manuscript', compiled in the early nineteenth century by Donald Morrison, *An Sgoilear Ban,* describes how a MacLeod chieftain of the early seventeenth century buried a treasure of gold in the island of Lewis: the treasure in 'a blackened clay pot' was dug up in 1813 (Macdonald 1975: 32). The same source describes a find of silver in Lewis in 'a black pot' but there is no information on the age of this material (*op cit.*: 78). A clay vessel discovered by chance in the grounds of Stornoway Castle in 1954 contained a hoard of coins, the dates of which suggest burial about 1670 (Kerr 1954-6: 222-3). The crogan (Fig. 8), approximately 11 cm in height and 11 cm in diameter, is in every respect similar to the later crogans whose manufacture we are able to document. This example suggests that at least from the seventeenth until the twentieth centuries therefore, the style and technique of manufacture remained unchanged. This archaeological evidence also provides important confirmation that

Martin Martin's contemporary references in fact relate to crogans as we know them from surviving nineteenth-century examples (MacLeod 1934: 85-6).

The method of making crogans, whether it was the survival of a prehistoric technique or not, has been recorded in some detail in several sources since its first description in 1764. The Reverend Dr John Walker, the 'Moderate' minister and botanist, then described the process of pottery-making in Coll in his report to the Annexed Estates Commissioners (McKay 1980: 171). The clay was dug, usually by hand, from the glacially deposited beds of boulder-clay, and kneaded by hand or beaten with a stick to reduce it to a plastic state, or as one commentator described it in 1833, 'as smooth as glazier's putty' (Cameron 1845: 134). It was formed into a vessel with the fingers, on the ground or on a board, and then left to dry out and cure for a day or two either in the sun or by the hearth (e.g. Fig. 10). For crogans with a narrow mouth, a stick could be used to scrape down the inside, and the very thin walls of many surviving crogans suggests that some such simple spatula was used (e.g. Fig. 11). When it had dried, the vessel was placed in the fire and peats were built up round it and filling it, forming a simple kiln. In Tiree, dry whin and seaweed were said to have been used for firing (Fleming 1923: 205). While the earthenware was red hot, the fire was moved away from it and fresh, skimmed milk was poured into and over the pottery. Accounts differ as to the exact details of this part of the process, but it was said to be done in order to prevent the crogan from being too porous: it put a simple waxy glaze on the finished surface (McGregor 1879-80: 146; Mitchell 1880: 26-8).

The value of clay deposits in different colours and consistencies in areas such as Lewis was long recognised. Tradition today describes how it was used for house-building by bedding stones in the clay as a form of mortar, to which burnt shells might be added as a lime or calcareous element. Before the state-instigated house improvements of the present century, clay was often used for making the floors of houses, and was the favoured material for a smooth threshing floor in the small Hebridean barns as well as in barns on the mainland.

Elsewhere in Scotland there is some evidence of small-scale industry based on local clay deposits, before the Industrial Revolution overtook it. In describing the soils of the Forth basin in the late eighteenth century, an agricultural writer commented: 'In many places, the clay is excellently fitted for making bricks, tiles and a coarse kind of crockery ware' (Belsches 1796: 15). The development of brick and tile works on clay deposits was common in South and East Scotland but rare in the Highlands and Islands. There were exceptional cases. A brick and tile works was established at Garrabost in Lewis in the 1840s as part of the estate improvements of the incoming landlord, Sir James Matheson: about £6,000 was expended on it but it proved to be a costly failure (Macdonald 1978: 41-2). This small industry used the same red clay that had customarily been used for making crogan pottery. The parish minister referred to this tradition in 1833, immediately prior to the setting up of the brickworks: 'Of the red clay, the indigenous islanders make vessels called Craggans, in which they keep their milk and carry water from the springs' (Cameron 1845: 117).

Although this craft was carried on in each generation by only a few families in the Hebrides, and the products mainly used for domestic purposes, it was not to be regarded as contemptible. The pottery was practical, and suited the economic requirements of time and place, and was a necessity in an age when the Hebrides were suffering severe economic decline. At the same time there were traditions of artistry and higher status that could indicate a decline in the social scale. A song composed about 1875 praises a locality in Point, Lewis, well endowed with its own natural resources of clay, water and fuel, and seems to suggest an aristocratic background for such Hebridean pottery:

> *'S chreadh dheanadh cupan gu deoch thoirt do'n rìgh*
> *R'a fhaighinn an taobh Cnoc Chusbaig.*
> [And there is clay to make a cup fit for a drink for a king,
> To be found beside Cnoc Chusbaig] (MacKenzie 1936: 27).

Another Gaelic praise-song, from Islay, makes a similarly prestigious reference, in that a man of aristocratic lineage is praised in a conventional fashion for his ability to turn the clay into fine red cups (Campbell and Collinson 1969: 146). Good pots were, in fact, admired; a nineteenth-century Lewisman described how the well-formed and well-finished crogans were passed round from house to house to be admired (Thomas 1866: fol. 3). Confirmation of such social attitudes is provided by the occurrence of pottery and crogan ware in the houses and castles of medieval clan chiefs or heads of kindred, indicating that the praise was more than simply literary hyperbole (e.g. Turner and Dunbar 1969-70: 182-5).

No account of crogans would be complete without considering the functions of the pottery in relation to elements of diet. In spite of the vagaries of climate, parts of the Hebrides were of relatively high fertility, especially in the late medieval period. Here, as elsewhere in Scotland, oat and barley crops were of prime importance in feeding the population. In the historical period, therefore, the main constituents of diet, apart from dairy products, have been oatmeal, barley meal, fish and, less frequently, meat. Domestic cooking utensils were few, but pottery vessels must have been common at least in some areas. There were two ways in which they were used for cooking: the pot was placed in the fire itself of stones heated in the fire were put into the pot to boil the contents. Crogans were probably also used in the process of 'graddaning' to dry or parch the grain. This process of drying grain in the house hearth was known as *earraradh*, as opposed to *ealchadh* which described the process of drying grain in the kiln. A Gaelic song collected in Lochaber in the middle of the nineteenth century refers to the three processes of grain drying, implying that there was a marked difference in quality between kiln-dried grain, *ealchadh*, burnt grain, *gradan*, and parched grain, *earraradh* (Macpherson 1868: 116-17; for further details, see Fenton1982: 85-106). A Gaelic song collected in Lochaber in the middle of the nineteenth century implies such differences in quality between the three types of dried grain

The late seventeenth-century Skyeman, Martin Martin, remarked on the fine red clay in Lewis and on the pottery vessels made by the local women, 'some for boiling meat, and others for preserving their ale, for which they are much better than barrels of wood' (MacLeod 1934: 86). The Reverend John Lane Buchanan, a Church of Scotland missionary minister in the Western Isles in the 1780s, observed that the islanders made a kind of coarse crockery ware which was used for boiling water and for dressing victuals (Buchanan 1793: 112). The storing of ale in pottery containers must have been common while ale was the commonest drink in the Highlands and Islands (e.g. MacLeod 1934: 295). It may be no accident that the phrase *crogan leanna* is still current in Gaelic though most frequently used now to refer to disposable metal beer and lager cans.

Dairy products such as milk, butter and cheese were a vital element in Highland and Island diet. Much of the work of butter- and cheese-making was carried on when the cattle and sheep were on the hill grazings in the summer months. While the menfolk stayed in the farming or crofting townships to cultivate the arable crops in the summer months, the womenfolk and children occupied the shielings in the moors and hills to look after the animals. It has been mentioned above that the shieling system survived longest in Lewis which was also one of the last areas in which pottery vessels were made and used.

A plentiful supply of containers for milk, butter and cheese was essential for the shieling economy. Wooden vessels have been commonly used in the last hundred years or so, and the more modern shieling huts were built with recessed stone shelves to keep wooden containers cool. Hardly any shieling sites have been excavated so it is not possible to assess confidently the importance of clay vessels for dairy products. Tradition describes the crogans being used to transport milk and butter from the shieling to the township across the moor, loaded in a creel on the woman's or child's back and wrapped in damp moss to keep them cool and safe from damage (Mitchell 1880: 46-7; Ross 1875-80: 92). The term *crogan ìme* for a butter container is still in common use; and the phrase *blas a' chragain* is based on the experience that the contents, such as butter, at the bottom of the crogan acquired a sour taste from the earthenware and were rancid. The idiomatic phrase *ghabh e blas a' chragain dheth,* for example, indicates that the subject has tired of the object or it has gone sour on him. Organic residues in pottery and the tainting of food have been described elsewhere (Cheape 1988: 22-3).

Wooden containers of staved construction, or carved out of the solid, became common in the Highlands in the eighteenth century and the former, craftsman-made type, rapidly acquired prestige value. This is reflected in an account of the dairy work on the West Highland estate of Gairloch at the turn of the nineteenth century, in which 'coarse earthenware' had been supplanted by wooden dishes, churns, pails and casks. This was on an improved farm with a herd of sixty cows and followers which were sent to the shielings during the summer. The implication may be that the small crofters had still been using clay vessels here around 1800, even though the area was better wooded than the almost treeless islands (Mackenzie 1922: 14).

Before such later forms of wooden staved vessels came to be commonly used for churning, during the eighteenth century, for example, skin bags or clay vessels were used as churns in many areas of the Highlands. These older methods lingered on until between the wars in some parts where wood was less abundant or where economic circumstances prevented the acquisition of such craftsman-made gear. One or two examples of clay churns have survived, such as those in the Glasgow Museums and Art Galleries and the National Museums of Scotland. One of these, from the island of Coll, measures 36 cm in height and 33 cm in diameter (Mann 1907-8: 326). Although these churns appear to be the largest of surviving Hebridean crogans, they are otherwise similar in shape and characteristics to the crogans except for a deliberately formed perforation in the side, as in the example from Coll. These holes were presumably necessary for the escape of the gases generated after the churning was begun. The method was partly to fill the vessel with milk, to tie a cloth or piece of skin tightly over the circular mouth and to rock the vessel backwards and forwards until the butter was made. A late eighteenth-century account from Skye describes the work as occasionally taking up to nine or ten hours (Mitchell 1897-8a: 16). This was a task generally performed by women and, characteristically, was accompanied by song to lighten the task. (A short account of butter-making in Melness, Sutherland, about 1870, describes a sheepskin bag containing the milk being thrown from one to another in the 'ceilidh house' until the butter formed [Gow 1981: 385]).

Crogans were used undoubtedly also for milking, although this is a detail which is barely recorded in historical sources. The few references which we have derive from Tiree where the making of pottery survived until the mid-twentieth century (Fig. 10), the quality of the clay deposits there approximating to good china clays. These describe their former use as 'milking pails', and their residual use in the late nineteenth and early twentieth century in the treatment for tuberculosis which was then rife in island communities. For this, small globular clay vessels were being made, into which milk was drawn directly from the cow; they were then warmed in the fire and the milk given to consumptives. Milk treated in this way was known as *bainne gun ghaoth,* or 'milk without wind' (Mitchell 1880: 28). This description was almost certainly not folkloristic fancy and was confirmed by the memories of an older generation in the 1970s when recorded by the School of Scottish Studies.

Fig 12: Set of Barvas Ware made in 1935 by Mrs Catherine MacLean, Brue, Barvas, for A. D. Lacaille(Wellcome Institute). The cream-coloured milk glaze is still prominent on these unused pieces. Mrs MacLean (Catriona Mhurchaidh Dhomhnaill Iain 'ic Iomhair) inherited the tradition of pottery-making from her mother, of Park, Barvas, who was probably the last person to be involved in the making of Barvas pottery on a large scale. (Photo: *Natioal Museums of Scotland.*)

Possibly owing to the lapse of time, 'milk without wind' was then sometimes described as a mild dietary cure rather than a specific (Sinclair 1971: 28; Cameron 1845: 134). The properties of warm milk in crogans are also praised in fifteenth- and early sixteenth-century descriptions (Gillies 1911: 20; Thomas 1879-80: 391).

Apart from the storage of liquids such as water, milk and ale, crogans were used for preparing and keeping fish oil for lighting. The process was described as it existed in Skye in the 1820s when flat-based crogans holding three to four gallons were used. When the creels of fish were brought up from the boats on the beach, the women gutted them and threw the livers into crogans where the mixture was left to decay into a partially liquid state. They then put the decayed livers onto the fire to dissolve them completely, poured off the pure liquid oil into another crogan, and threw away the refuse. The oil was described as being dark like port wine, but thin and effective. It was put into the lamps with a wick made of the pith of rushes (MacGregor 1879-80: 145-6).

Crogan pottery was not a unique survival on Europe's north-western seaboard. Similar traditions survived to be recorded in Brittany and Denmark, for example, with curious elements both of comparison and contrast. The black ware of Denmark, the so-called 'Jutland pots', were made in most parts of the peninsula, but survived until the twentieth century in western Jutland only. As with crogan pottery and Barvas Ware, their manufacture was always the work of the womenfolk. They were also formed by hand without a potter's wheel, scraped down and smoothed with simple tools and were slowly dried outside or on the hearth. But they were fired in a sealed kiln, not a fire of peat or turf: this gave them their distinctive black colour rather than the reds and browns of earthenware which has oxydised while firing (Steensberg 1939: 113-146).

In all these accounts, a keynote is the role played by women. In the same way that certain tasks in the family and in the community were the exclusive province of the womenfolk, the making of crogans and Barvas Ware was always carried out by women, a fact given specific mention in 1695, and as true when a potter made what might have been the last crogans and Barvas Ware to order in 1935 (Fig. 12). Common elements in the historical sources are that only a few families made pottery in the Islands, that it was the preserve of the women, and that the technique was handed down from mother to daughter. In the same way as the extemporising of song and verse in the *orain-luaidh* or chorus songs, the making of crogans was an art and skill of women which has been disregarded, or under-valued; there was no term in Gaelic for the women crogan-makers (e.g. MacDonald 1741: 53). Their numbers were probably never significant. Although the first-hand descriptions, by visitors, of pottery-making in the late nineteenth and early twentieth centuries do consistently suggest that the numbers of women potters had dwindled (implying that there were once many of them), this goes against the evidence that their number in fact was always relatively small. Where there were good deposits of clay, a local family would maintain the art through successive generations from mother to daughter, supply generally being sufficient to satisfy demand, until the domestic revolution of the nineteenth century introduced alternative utensils.

Today, crogans and Barvas Ware are appreciated in museums by archaeologists and historians as manifestations of a continuity from a past revealed otherwise only by the excavator's trowel. They are now only curiosities in the islands where they were made. *Crogain* have been transformed in speech into items of our disposable culture, and the 'clay cups fit for a royal table' fossilised as an image in song.

ACKNOWLEDGEMENTS

Any work which purports to take a retrospective glance at aspects of Scottish tradition from a modern standpoint and neglects the word of mouth must surely be the poorer for it. The accumulation of material on which this article is based has been helped immeasurably by advice and information sought from and generously given by the following people to whom I wish to record my grateful thanks: the late Mr Donald Macdonald, Mr Alex Murdo Morrison, Rev. William Matheson, the late Mr John A. Smith, the late Mr Eric Cregeen, Mr George Holleyman, Dr Margaret Mackay, Miss Morag MacLeod, Mr Graeme Cruickshank, Professor Alexander Fenton, the late Dr R. B. K. Stevenson, Mr George Dalgleish, Mr Trevor Cowie, Mr A. D. Cameron, Mr Iain MacDonald, Mrs Roderick MacDonald, Mrs Betty MacRae, Mrs Mina Smith, Miss Joan MacKenzie, Miss Hope MacDougall, Mr James Shaw Grant, Mrs Rosemary

MacKenzie, Mr Donald Mackay, Miss Anne MacSween, Mr Patrick Topping, Dr Jessie Sym, Mrs Thelma Aitken and Mr Alasdair Begg.
For the illustrations, I wish to thank Mr Anthony Shearman, City Librarian, Edinburgh Central Library, and Mr Ian Larner and Miss Doreen Moyes of the National Museums of Scotland. I would also like to thank Miss Helen Jackson of the National Museums for her drawings of crogan pottery (Figs. 8, 9 and 11).

REFERENCES

ANDERSON, J.
1890 'Notice of the Excavation of the Brochs of Yarhouse, Brounaben, Bowermadden, Old Stirkoke and Dunbeath in Caithness.' *Archaeologia Scotica* Vol. 5: 131-98.

BELSCHES, R.
1796 *General View of the Agriculture of the County of Stirling.* Edinburgh.

BUCHANAN, J. L.
1793 *Travels in the Western Hebrides from 1782 to 1790.* London.

CAMERON, REV. J.
1845 'The Parish of Stornoway.' *The New Statistical Account* Vol. 14: 115-40.

CAMPBELL, J. G.
1902 *Witchcraft and Second Sight in the Highlands and Islands of Scotland.* Glasgow.

CAMPBELL, J. L. and COLLINSON, F.
1969 *Hebridean Folksongs.* Oxford.

CARMICHAEL
1941 *Carmina Gadelica* Vol. 4. Edinburgh.

CHEAPE, H.
1990 Food and Liquid Containers in the Hebrides: A Window on the Iron Age. In Fenton, A. and Myrdal. J. (eds.) *Food and Drink and Travelling Accessories. Essay in Honour of Gösta Berg,* National Museums of Scotland, Skansen and Nordiska Museet, Edinburgh: 6-27.

CURWEN, E. C.
1938 'The Hebrides: A Cultural Backwater.' *Antiquity* 12: 261-89.

FENTON, A.
1982 'Net-drying, pot-drying and graddaning: Small-scale grain drying and processing techniques.' *Saga och Sed.* Uppsala: 85-106.

FLEMING, J. A.
1923 *Scottish Pottery.* Glasgow.

GILLIES, H. C.
1911 *Regimen Sanitatis. The Rule of Health.* Glasgow.

GOW, G.
1981 'Making Butter in the Ceilidh-House.' *Tocher* 36: 385.

JEWITT, L.
1878 *The Ceramic Art of Great Britain, From Pre-historic Times down to the Present Day* Vol. 2. London.

KERR, R.
1954-6 'A Hoard of Coins from Stornoway.' *Proceedings of the Society of Antiquaries of Scotland* 88: 222-3.

MACDONALD, A.
1741 *A Galick and English Vocabulary.* Edinburgh.

MACDONALD, D.
Lewis: A History of the Island. Edinburgh.

MACDONALD, N. (ed.)
1975 *The Morrison Manuscript. Tales and Traditions of the Western Isles.* Stornoway.

MCGREGOR, REV. A.
1879-80 'Notes on Some Old Customs in the Island of Skye.' *Proceedings of the Society of Antiquaries of Scotland* 14: 143-8.

MCKAY, M. M.
1980 *Rev. Dr John Walker's Report on the Hebrides of 1764 and 1771.* Edinburgh.

MACKENZIE, O.
1922 *A Hundred Years in the Highlands.* London.

MACKENZIE, W.
1936 *Cnoc Chusbaig.* Glasgow.

MACKENZIE, W. C.
1904-5 'Notes on the Pigmies Isle, at the Butt of Lewis.' *Proceedings of the Society of Antiquaries of Scotland* 39: 248-58.

MACLEOD, D. J. (ed.)
1934 *A Description of the Western Islands of Scotland by Martin Martin.* Stirling.

MACMILLAN, S. (ed.)
1968 *Sporan Dhomhnaill.* Scottish Gaelic Texts Society, Glasgow.

MACPHERSON, D. C.
1868 *An Duanaire.* Edinburgh.

MANN, L. M.
1907-8 'Notices of a Pottery Churn from the Island of Coll with remarks on Hebridean Pottery.' *Proceedings of the Society of Antiquaries of Scotland* 42: 326-9.

MILLER, H.
1874 *The Cruise of the Betsy* (11th edition). London.

MITCHELL, A.
1880 *The Past in the Present. What is Civilisation?* Edinburgh.
1897-8a 'James Robertson's Tour.' *Proceedings of the Society of Antiquaries of Scotland* 32: 11-19.
1897-8b 'A Description of Some Neo-Archaic Objects.' *Proceedings of the Society of Antiquaries of Scotland* 32: 181-94.

NICOLSON, A.
1881 *A Collection of Gaelic Proverbs.* Edinburgh.

ROSS, A.
1875-80 'Ancient Industries in Scotland.' *Transactions of the Inverness Scientific Society* 1: 47-50.

SINCLAIR, D.
1971 'Bainne Gun Ghaoth.' *Tocher* 1: 28.

SMITH, W. A.
1875 *Lewsiana, or Life in the Outer Hebrides.* London.

STEENSBERG, A.
1939 'Primitive Black Pottery in Jutland.' *Folk Liv* 3: 113-46.

STEVENSON, R. B. K.
1945-6 'Jottings on Early Pottery.' *Proceedings of the Society of Antiquaries of Scotland* 80: 141-3.

THOMAS, F. W. L.
1879-80 'Traditions of the MacAulays of Lewis.' *Proceedings of the Society of Antiquaries of Scotland* 4: 363-431.

THOMAS, F. W. L.
1886 Papers and Correspondence. *Society of Antiquaries of Scotland Manuscripts No. 28,* National Museum of Antiquities of Scotland.

TURNER, D. J. and DUNBAR, J. G.
1969-70 'Breachacha Castle, Coll: Excavations and Field Survey 1965-8.' *Proceedings of the Society of Antiquaries of Scotland* 102: 155-87.

YOUNG, A.
1955-6 'Excavations at Dun Cuier, Isle of Barra, Outer Hebrides.' *Proceedings of the Society of Antiquaries of Scotland* 89: 290-327.

Notes and Comments

'Bunning': A Contemporary Office Custom

The city of Edinburgh has enjoyed a long association with financial enterprises of one kind or another. Of particular significance is the insurance and life assurance industry, which today employs a substantial proportion of the city's workforce. The success of the industry is apparent to any Edinburgh resident, who will most likely be familiar with at least some of the insurance and life assurance head offices located either in St Andrew Square and its environs, or in newer buildings in less central areas. It seems that earlier generations of Edinburgh people would also have been aware of various forms of insurance operating within the city. In the medieval burgh, for example, burial guilds and mutual insurance societies seem to have played an important role within the merchant and artisan clases, and we know that by the eighteenth century commercial companies were to be found specialising in fire insurance.[1] It was not, however, until the second half of the nineteenth century that commercial life assurance, which now dominates the insurance scene and contributes so much to the city's economy, came to prominence with the dropping of premium costs to within the reach of the ordinary citizen. By the twentieth century insurance had become something that directly touched most people's lives.

Clearly then, Edinburgh's insurance and life assurance offices are of great potential interest to the economic historian. But their significance does not end there, as such offices also provide fine hunting grounds for the ethnologist. Even a preliminary investigation of these workplaces, such as the author conducted in four companies, reveals a wealth of vital, contemporary folklore, the exact nature of which varies from office to office and indeed varies from division to division within one office. Most head offices contain a large and generally young workforce, with roughly equal numbers of men and women (at the non-managerial level at least) who are usually highly educated and fairly frequently understimulated by their work. In such conditions it is only natural that a large corpus of folklore should come into existence and be maintained.

It is amongst one's peers in the employment hierarchy that most transmission of folklore seems to occur in these offices. Senior management tend to keep themselves apart from the rest of the workforce, especially in social and informal terms and indeed could be said to form their own occupational community. The same applies to groups of workers such as catering and messenger staff. The clerical workers and their immediate supervisors, who comprise the majority of the workforce and who are the focus of this brief study, interact continuously with each other, both at the formal and informal level. Because some offices have over three thousand employees, two-thirds of whom fit into the clerical or supervisory category, one tends to find that it is a smaller group than the body of clerical workers as a whole which is of more significance for the individual in terms of social interaction and the transmission of folklore. This group can be defined as one's immediate colleagues (usually between five and ten individuals), those one trained with (who may not be in the same part of the office as oneself), and those one knows from sports and other social events. Rarely does this group exceed thirty members in total.

The significance of such a group can be easily seen by looking at the example of one frequently found office custom. A whole range of customs is of course to be found in insurance and life assurance offices, including customs associated with the decoration of workspace, with recreation, with dress, calendar customs and customs associated with the individual's rites of passage, but it is the custom of giving gifts to colleagues to mark rites of passage in one's own life which we will look at here. Usually those involved in this custom do not refer to it by any special title, but some informants from Scottish Widows Fund and Life Assurance Society, Dalkeith Road, have named it 'bunning'. As the Widows' title indicates, it is often the case that those celebrating a birthday, or the announcement of an engagement or wedding, or celebrating the birth of a child, have to buy cakes or 'buns' for their colleagues to eat at work, usually their immediate co-workers and sometimes other members of the group at a local pub either after work or at lunchtime. In this case the individual who is celebrating will put out a message via computer mail inviting colleagues to come to a certain pub at a certain time. For birthdays the invitation is generally given only to group members, but for weddings and engagements the invitation is wider, often being addressed to all those working in the same department as the individual, or even the whole office. However, it is usually just the members of the group who turn up, which is frequently a matter of considerable relief to the person paying for the drinks.

One does of course receive as well as give at rites of passage. The computer is again used, this time by a close friend of the individual, to distribute a message to all or part of the office asking for contributions to a collection, out of which may be bought a card or present or both (presents are always given on eighteenth and twenty-first birthdays, and also at the announcement of weddings). Another friend will be responsible for collecting the money, and a third will choose and buy the gift. Usually it is only members of the group who will respond to such a message, but it is considered impolite not to ask others.

Here then we have an example of modern insurance and life assurance office custom. The author would be interested to know if equivalents of 'bunning' are, or were, to be found in other types of office, or indeed in other types of workplace. If you have any information on this topic please write to Susan Storrier, School of Scottish Studies, University of Edinburgh, 27 George Square, Edinburgh.

NOTES

1 See G. Clayton, *British Insurance*, London, 1971.

SUSAN STORRIER

Brose an Bannock Day

The following information was recorded by Margaret Bennett on 5 May 1985 at Ardvaser, Skye (School of Scottish Studies Archive, SA 1985/41), from Gladys and Charles Simpson, Keith, Banffshire. It was transcribed by the late Bill Salton.

G.S.: I had never even heard of Shrove Tuesday when I was a child, it was just always Brose and Bannock Day we called it. But my mother called it Fastern E'en, I think. We had brose made with what I thought was the water the turnips had been boiled in. But I think there may also have been beef boiled in it, you know, too, because I have a further recollection of the grown-ups having beef with their potato and turnip later, whereas we had the brose and then turnip and potato and then the bannocks. But I have that recollection that the grown-ups might have had beef with the potato and turnip.

M.B.: Now, at what time of the day would you have the brose?

G.S.: The middle of the day . . . Dinner-time was the middle of the day. Sometimes we had the bannocks at dinner-time and sometimes the bannocks at tea-time. But the bannocks would be special bannocks. You know, not like the usual pancakes. They would have spices in them and be big. The whole size of the girdle. And we would get them on a plate with syrup.

M.B.: Was it a batter rather than a dough?

G.S.: Oh yes! A batter like a pancake batter, but I suppose very similar to a pancake batter but with spices mixed in.

M.B.: Did she put eggs in it?

G.S.: Oh yes! Yes! Flour, eggs, sugar. Well, I would say if she had about half a pound of flour she would have two eggs maybe. And milk, you know. We just put the whole thing on a plate. We got one each.

Professor Alexander Fenton adds to this note:

'When I was at school in Auchterless, not far from Keith, in the late 1930s-40s, one of my fellow scholars would occasionally write on the blackboard:

Beef brose an bannock day
Please gie's a holiday.'

So *beef* brose it was.

MARGARET BENNETT

Carryanchor Night

The following Burghead custom was described by two Morayshire women, Mrs Marne Neillie and Mrs Doreen Shepherd, who have lived in Edinburgh for many years. They were recorded by Margaret Bennett and Emily Lyle who initially made contact in order to interview them about the better-known custom of the burning of the clavie (see Shepherd *et al*: 1992). Amy Stewart Fraser, who included a mention of the carryanchor custom (citing Doreen Shepherd) in *Dae Ye Min' Langsyne* (1975: 177), was incorrect in placing it on the night before Hogmanay as Mrs Shepherd informed us.

Marne Neillie: A few days before Hallowe'en the young people of the village went to the beach and collected a piece of seaweed. You know the long piece of seaweed that looks like a club with the fronds on the end of it? The fronds were taken off and the carryanchor . . . that is the carryanchor. This piece of seaweed was brought home and dried off. Very often in your mother's oven, if she allowed it. Well of course there was no gas or electricity at this time so it was an easy thing just to open the oven and slip it in without anybody noticing. And by the night before Hallowe'en they were very dry and very hard, and we used to run around the doors just banging on the doors to warn people that the next night was Hallowe'en and we would be round. But there was never any singing or rhyme or anything like that. We just banged on the doors. And most of the people didn't renew their doors, the painting on their doors, until after Carryanchor Night, because they knew that if it was newly painted and they got a bang on it they would have to do it again . . .

Doreen Shepherd: Also that night before Hallowe'en people knew that you would be round. And if someone had had their door painted, and they were canny folk, somebody would be behind the door. And as you came along they had a bucket of water and let fly at you. I remember one old 'meanie' she was, was known to do that every year, but we just learned to keep away from here. And there was another, a strange woman . . . It was said that people—that fishermen—didn't like to meet her on their way to the harbour because she had an evil eye. Somehow or other we children knew there was something odd about her. Do you remember that year? The house stood with another on a bit of green. On its own so that you could go right round it. So we took it in turn to bang her door and run round the back and then, of course, she came to the door and nearly caught us. We took to our heels like grim death and away down the road. We never did it again because I suppose we were frightened of her. There was an element of fear in that. I don't know any other village along the south side of the Moray Firth that had that custom of Carryanchor at all . . .

D.S.: In Elgin they went round the shops shouting 'Eelie-o-lo-lo gie's nuts'.

Emily Lyle: Did you meet people from Elgin that told you this?

D.S.: We went to Elgin Academy for our secondary education and our friends there told us about what they did on Hallowe'en.

M.N.: And by the time that we were ready to catch a bus the younger children were already out shouting 'Eelie-o-lo-lo gie's nuts'. But that must have been on Hallowe'en itself.

D.S.: Yes, that was actually Hallowe'en night. They didn't know anything about Carryanchor at all, the Elgin people . . .

E.L.: On the Carryanchor Night, how many of you went out together?

D.S.: A whole lot of us. In fact there were about eight of us, all of us the same age. And about the same time of schooling. As we got older we went around a lot together. Yes, six to eight it was.

E.L.: And did you all have a—what did you call it?—this thing you had in your hand?

D.S.: We called it 'carryanchor'. The actual object was a carryanchor.

Margaret Bennett: Did you knock with it or did you knock with your hands?

D.S.: You banged with it. A good wallop on the door. And then ran for your life.

M.N.: As a matter of fact, it's been known to have a door split. You know these doors that are in four panels? The boys, you see, would give it a good bang. And if it was one of those thin plywood things it would easily split down. It's been known.

D.S.: It was tolerated wonderfully well really.

M.N.: I suppose because our parents did it too in their day. . . .

D.S.: It was just making a good crack on the door.

M.N.: It wasn't vandalism.

E.L.: If you were inside the house, just sitting there by the fire—

D.S.: They knew what it was and you just said, 'Ach, that's another lot past'.

M.N.: And it didn't go on for very long.

D.S.: No, the early part of the evening.

M.N.: The early evening and then it was time for us to go home and get to bed. At least to be inside.

(School of Scottish Studies Archive, SA 1985/136, 191).

ACKNOWLEDGEMENT

We are grateful to the late Bill Salton for transcribing the tape.

REFERENCES

FRASER, AMY STEWART
1975 *Dae Ye Min' Langsyne*. London and Boston.
SHEPHERD, DOREEN *et al.*
1992 'Burning the Clavie at Burghead.' *Tocher* 44: 91-103.

MARGARET BENNETT AND EMILY LYLE

'It Sits Heich, It Cries Sair'

'Perhaps there were a couple of riddles that I remember . . .

To ma riddle, to ma riddle, to ma rot, tot, tot,
I met a man in a reid, reid coat,
A staff in his hand and a stane in his throat,
To ma riddle, to ma riddle, to ma rot, tot, tot.

And the answer to that was a cherry. And another one I remember was:

It sits heich, it cries sair,
It hes the heid but it wants the hair.

And that was a rooster'
(School of Scottish Studies Archive, SA 1976/256 A4-5)

When I recorded these two riddles from Alec Smith in Sydney (derived ultimately from his native Buckie), both the answers he gave seemed satisfying. It was only recently that I realised, through reading Stewart Sanderson's note 'Two Scottish Riddles', that the answer to the second riddle is an unusual one; in all the cases quoted by Sanderson the answer given is 'bell' or (once) 'townclock'. However, the riddle has been judged unsatisfactory when taken with these answers. Archer Taylor observes in his head-note to nos. 3-4 'Head, No Hair' in *English*

Riddles from Oral Tradition (1951: 11) that '[the riddler's] reference to a supposed "head" of a bell is confusing and obscure'. Sanderson (1967: 105) agrees with Taylor that the import of the reference to the 'head' is unclear and tentatively offers two possible explanations:

> Firstly, the riddlers may visualise the bell as having a position up at the 'head' of a bell-tower ('has the head'). Alternatively (but admittedly a far-fetched explanation), since 'head' or 'heid' is pronounced [hi:d] there may be a punning allusion to the idea that people pay heed to the bell.

It seems to me that the rooster—which undoubtedly has a head—provides a better fit than the other solutions offered. The 'cries sair' would then refer to the cock's loud crowing, and the 'sits heich' (or 'stands high', as in two versions) to the position taken up by the cock, as, for example, on top of a dunghill. The high position taken by the cock is noted in two Polish riddles mentioned by Taylor (1951: 229) which say that the cock 'stands on a fence in a red jacket' or 'stands on a hill in a red bonnet'. The idea of the cock's head not having hair is found, with reference to the beard only, in a set of riddles given by Taylor (1951: 193) as nos. 539-540. No. 540d, from Jamaica, runs:

> As I was going through Bramble hall,
> An old man gave me a call;
> His beard was flesh, his mouth was horn,
> And this old man was never born.
> —Rooster.

This riddle includes mention of the sound made by the rooster and provides a distant parallel to the 'sits heich' riddle if this is interpreted in the sense given to it by Alec Smith.

REFERENCES

SANDERSON, STEWART F.
1967 'Two Scottish Riddles.' *Folk Life* 5, 104-7.

TAYLOR, ARCHER
1951 *English Riddles from Oral Tradition*. Berkeley and Los Angeles.

EMILY LYLE

FOOTNOTE:

In my schooldays in Auchterless, not too far from Buckie, riddles were still in active service. The versions I learned of the two riddles discussed by Dr. Lyle were:

'Come-a-riddle, come-a-riddle, come-a-rot–rot-tot-tot,
A little wee man in a reed, reed coat,
A staff in eez han an a steen in eez throat
Gin ye tell me ma riddle I'll gie ye a groat'

'Hings heich, cries sair,
Has a heid, bit nae hair (or, bit wints e hair)'

The first was a cherry; the second was unequivocally understood to be a bell on a church steeple.

ALEXANDER FENTON

Nasg—a West Highland Tethering Device

The following description of a West Highland tethering device of birch twigs and wood, *nasg*, was recorded from the late Donald McColl, Gorten, Acharacle, North Argyll, in June 1975 by Donald A. MacDonald and Alan Bruford.[1]

The first meaning of *nasg* in Dwelly's Dictionary is 'Tie-band, wooden collar for a cow, formerly of plaited or twisted birch or other twigs'. The meaning of Old Irish *nasc* according to the RIA Dictionary is 'a fastening, tie, spancel, ring, etc. in wide sense'; it also means a champion's honorific chain or collar or a legal bond, and nine other modern Scottish Gaelic meanings are given by Dwelly. The ninth meaning, 'wooden ring of a sieve or fan' (contributed by Rev. D. M. Cameron, Ledaig) is the one known to DAM from his childhood in North Uist, meaning the circular wooden rim of the traditional pierced skin riddle. The present sort of *nasg* appears in the Scottish National Dictionary as *nask*, and in the aphetic form *ask*, reported from Caithness only. The Old Irish references indicate that a form of *nasc* was worn by cows and was considered essential farm equipment. It may well be that the material and form of the implement as described here had not changed substantially from the Dark Ages until this century, when rope and iron can be got with less effort than birch twigs.

The Gaelic text has been transcribed from the School of Scottish Studies Archive tape SA 1975/58 B by DAM, and translated, introduced and annotated by A.B. in consultation with DAM A few repetitive phrases in Donald McColl's rapid Gaelic have been omitted and shown by dots . . .

DAM: Bha rud eile bha sibh a' dol a dh'innse dhuinn cuideachd: sin agaibh a'

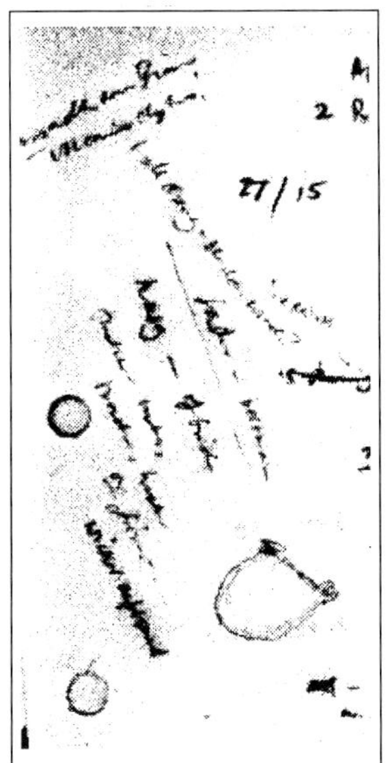

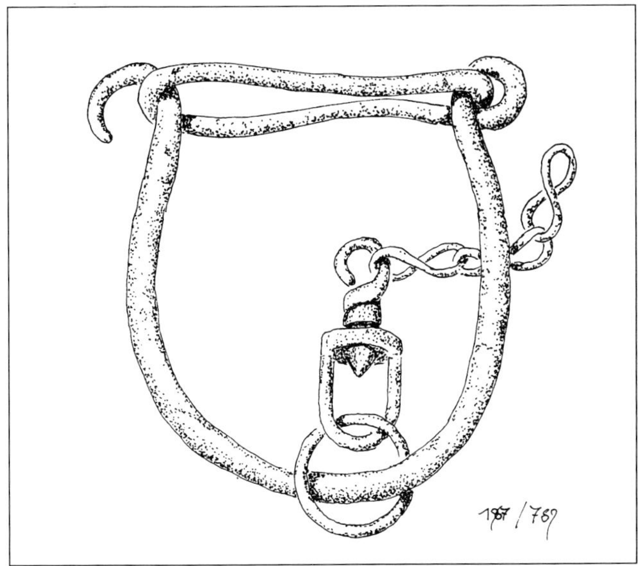

1. A rough sketch made by Dr. A. Bruford at the time of the interview, probably based on Donald McColl's own drawing.

2. A late nineteenth-century restraining device of iron from Angeln, Schleswig-Holstein, used for sheep but similar to devices (*bowsels*) used in Scotland for cattle. Its basic features—attachment of the tether chain at its base, ring and hook for the retaining bar or loop at the top—are functionally the same as for the *nasg* described here. Sketch by Felix Lühning (see note 4).

seòrsa nasg[2] a bha iad a' deanamh air a' chraobh bheithe airson a bhith ceanghal bheothaichean.

DMcC: O, nasg . . . *Well,* chan eil mi cinndeach ciamar a bha iad 'ga dheanadh . . ., ach 's e beithe bhiodh aca, slatan caol,[3] fhios agad. Agus bha iad air an tionndadh, tha fhios agad, mu chuairt, mu chuairt; chan eil fhios 'am ciamar, có-dbiubh bha bior air choireiginn aca dhan tionndadh mu chuairt, no dé . . . ach bha iad air an toinneamh na chéile. Bhiodh, och, gràinnean shlatan còmhla, bheil thu faicinn, agus bha iad cho ruighinn, a laochain, dìreach 's a ghabhadh iad . . . Agus chuireadh iad dul air a cheann furasda gu leòr.

Agus bha 'nasg,[4] 's e, that fhios agad, dìreach pìos de shlat. Dh'fhaoidte gum biodh i mu—ó, cha bhiodh móran 's òirleach de thiughad innte, bheil thu faicinn . . . agus croman, croman beag mar sin air an aon cheann agus forc mar sin air a' cheann eile. Agus chuireadh iad an ròp barraich seo my chuairt air a' forc a bh'ann a seo, agus bha dul air a cheann eile gu rachadh e fairis air a' chroman a bh' air an taobh eile. Bhiodh i, ó, dh'fhaoidte a réir . . . cho mór 's a bhiodh am beothach, ach 's e daonnan, tha fhios agad, beothaichean òga a bha air an ceanghal mar sin. Agus bha sin an ròp a bha 'sa' nasg, bha e 'ga cheanghal ri maide, agus bha dula chruinn air a' cheann sin aige, agus bha e air a cheanghal ris a' nasg . . . *Well,* bha e cruinn, fhios agad, dh'fhaoidte gum biodh gràinnean òirlich de leud ann a réir dé mheudachd a bha 'sa' phost . . . air a robh e ceanghailte, agus ruitheadh e sìos no suas . . . air a' mhaide seo: dh'fhaodadh e éirigh no laighe, bheil thu faicinn? Cha robh a' nasg a' cur dragh sam bith air. Agus mhaireadh sin na bliadhnachan 's na bliadhnachan 's na bliadhnachan: chan eil fhios dé 'n ùine a mhaireadh e.

DAM: A nis a' rud a bha seo a bha dol timcheall air a' phost . . ., dé 'n dùnadh a bh' air a seo?

DMcC: Bha e dìreach air a thoinneamh, bheil fhios agad, leis na slatan beithe—bha e air a thoinneamh gus an deanadh iad dìreach rud cruinn mar sin,[5] bheil thu faicinn, agus bha e cho làidir, a laochain, cho làidir ri ròp 'sam bith. Bha e na bu làidire na iomadh ròp.

DAM: Bha *ring* a bha seo a bha timcheall air a' phost, bha i sin dùinte: cha ghabhadh i sin fosgladh ann?

DMcC: O cha ghabadh sin fosgladh—cha ghabhadh, o cha robh: bha i sin glaiste, bheil thu faicinn an dòigh a bha iad air a dhèanadh, chan fhosgaileadh i idir . . .

DAM: Agus a nis a' ròp a bha eadar a' fàinne bha sin agus a' nasg . . . 'n ann air beithe bha 'ròp a bha sin air a dheanamh cuideachd?

DMcC: 'S ann, 's ann, 's ann. O, chuile gearradh dheth den bheithe. 'S ann.

DAM: Agus 's ann 'na choileir timchioll air amhach a' bheothaich a bha e 'dol, an ann?

DMcC: 'S ann . . . nam biodh peansail agam: . . . ceanghal ann a seo an dòigh nach fhosgaileadh e, agus bha lùb air ann a seo a rachadh fairis air a' chromag seo, bheil thu faicinn. Agus seall, dal a bha thu 'ga fhosgaladh, *well,* rachadh seo a-staigh na b'fhaide, bheil thu faicinn, 's cha robh a duilich, fhios agad, a thoirt a-staigh na b'fhaide agus . . . gheibheadh tu an dula far a' chromag a bha seo. *Well,* a nise, bha seo am pìos eile den bheithe air a thoinneamh ann a seo: bha e air a cheanghal ann a sin ann an dòigh nach fhosgaileadh e, 's bha e dol a-nunn, agus bha seo . . . a' maid' seo ann a seo, bheil thu faicinn: nise bha seo air a chur mu chuairt ann an dòigh eile nach fosgaileadh e, agus ruitheadh e'n àird 's a leis air a sin . . .

DAM: Agus ciamar a bha seo air a cheanghal ann a sheo . . .?

DMcC: *Well,* bha e air a cheanghal dìreach ann an dòigh nach fhosgaileadh e, fhioss agad. Bha e air a thoinneamh 'na chéile ann an dòigh nach fhosgaileadh e, agus bha seo, bheil thu faicinn, bha lùb air a chur air gun gabhadh e cur fairis ann a seo, agus fhosgaladh—bha e furasda gu leor fhosgaladh, chionn . . . rachadh e staigh go chéil', fhios agad, agus an deaghaidh sin bha streun air 'ga cumail nach fhosgaileadh e . . . bha streun gu leòr air, bheil thu faicinn, ach ghabhadh e gluasad a-mach no a-staigh, tha fhios agad . . . a' nasg.

DAM: Agus chunnaig sibh fhéin seo?

DMcC: Och a laochain, . . . gràinnean mór bhliadhnachan, dar bha mi òg, bha sin aca: sin agad an dòigh a bha iad a' . . . *Well,* 'se bràthair mo mhàthar . . .

bhitheadh e 'ga dhèanamh ceart gu leòr. Tha mi creidsinn gur ann aig 'athair a chunnaig e e. Bheil fhios agad, 'san am sin, cha robh sian eile 'dol ach sin, 'seadh an am mo sheanar.

DAM: Agus a nis, a' ròp a bha siod, a' fear a bha null a siod, 's ann air beithe bha sin air a dhèanamh cuideachd, an ann?

DMcC: 'S ann, 's ann, 's ann.

DAM: Agus an cearcall a bha seo, 'se beithe?

DMcC: An cearcall a bha sin, bha sin, 'sè, 'a ann den bheithe bha sin air a dheanamh cuideachd.

DAM: Ach bha 'm pios a bha seo, bha e nas gairbhe na 'n còrr?

DMcC: O bha, bha. Chan eil e go deifear dé fiodh a bha seo. Dh'fhaodadh gur e darach, 's dh'fhaodadh rud 'sa' bhith ann.

DAM: Seadh. Dh'fhaodadh. 'Se fiodh eile bha 'sa' choileir mar gum bitheadh?

DMcC: 'Se. 'Se deifear fiodh a bha sin mar bu bhitheanta. Cha chreid mi gu robh 'm beithe a sin uair 'sam bith, ach bha e bitheanta bhiodh darach aca, fhios agad? Bha.

DAM: Ach bha e 'n còmhnaidh 'na seòrsa V ann a shiod, a robh?

DMcC: Bha, bha V ann, *well,* airson gun cumadh e, fhios agad, nach rachadh e far a' chinn: bha e 'ga chumail, bheil thu faicinn, gun fhosgladh a sin . . . bha. Och, bha iad furasda gu leòr fhaighinn: gheibheadh tu gu leòr nasgan air feadh an àite, far an robh coille, gheibheadh tu gu leòr . . . O, bha e math, 's cha thachdadh e idir iad . . . Bha e sàbhailte gu leòr.

DAM: Agus a nis, robh iad a' coimhead airson pìos, nam b'e darach no fiodh mar sin a bha seo, robh iad a' coimhead airson pìos fiodh' aig a robh an cumadh a bha sin gu nàdurrach . . .?

DMcC: O *well,* bheil fhios agad, bhiodh iad 'ga lùbadh, bheil thu faicinn, 's tha fhios, dh'fhaoidte gu robh iad 'ga *steam*adh uaireannan cuideachd, fhios agad. Bhiodh iad 'ga lùbadh agus tha *chance* gu robh iad 'gan ceanghal ri chéile, bheil thu faicinn: bhiodh iad 'ga lùbadh 's a' cur ceanghal orra nach gluaiseadh iad, gus an tigeadh a' chumadh sin orra, bheil faicinn? 'S è, sin agad mar bhà.

DAM: A *well,* tha sin math.

DMcC: Bha e uamhasach math. Bha e cho math ri ceanghal 'sa' bith agus bha e sàbhailte. Bha e sàbhailte, cho sàbhailte 's a ghabhadh. Bha.

DAM: Bha: cha biodh e 'teannachadh mu amhaich a bheathaich idir . . . Cha bhiodh e 'fàs teann idir mu . . .

DMcC: O cha robh, tha fhios agad, bha gu leòr . . . a rùm ann: cha robh e *tight* idir orra. Cha robh.

TRANSLATION

DAM: There was something else you were going to tell us about too: that was the kind of ring[2] they used to make from birch wood to tie up cattle.

DMcC: Oh, the *nasg* . . . Well, I'm not sure just how they made it, but it was birch they used, slender[3] twigs, you know. And they were wound, you know, round and round: I don't know how, whether they had some sort of pin to twist them round with or what, but they were twisted together. There would be, och, several twigs together, you see, and they were just as tough, my lad, as they could be. And they could put a loop on the end of it easily enough.

And the *nasg* [proper],[4] you know, that was just a bit of wood. It would maybe be about—oh, it wouldn't be much more than an inch thick, you see, with a hook, a little hook like this on one end, and a fork like this on the other. And they'd put this birch rope round the fork here, and there was a loop on the other end so that it went over the hook on the other side. It would be, oh, I suppose big enough to fit the beast, but you know it was always young cattle that were secured like this. And then the rope from the *nasg*, it was tied to a stake, and there was a circular loop on that end of it, and it was fixed to the *nasg*. Well, it was circular, you know, it might be a few inches across, depending on the size of the post it was tied to, and it could run up or down on this stake: it [the cow] could stand up or lie down, do you see? The *nasg* didn't hamper it at all. And that would last for years and years and years—there's no knowing how long it might last.

DAM: Now, this thing that went round the post, how was it fastened?

DMcC: It was just twisted out of birch twigs—it was twisted till they simply made up a circle like this,[5] do you see, and it was as strong, my lad, as any rope could be. It was stronger than many a rope.

DAM: This ring that was round the post, it was closed; it couldn't be opened?

DMcC: Oh, that couldn't be opened—it couldn't, oh no: this one was locked together, you see, the way they made it, so that it couldn't open at all . . .

DAM: Now the rope that went between this ring and the *nasg* . . . was it birch this rope was made of too?

DMcC: Yes, yes, yes. Oh, every bit of it birch. Yes.

DAM: And it went round the neck of the beast like a collar, did it?

DMcC: Yes . . . if I just had a pencil . . . (as he speaks, making a sketch which unfortunately cannot now be found). . . fixed here in such a way that it wouldn't come loose, and there was a loop on it here that would go over this hook, you see. And see, when you were undoing it, well, this would go in a bit further, you see, and it wasn't hard, you know, to push it further and . . . you would get the loop off this hook here. Well now, this was the other piece of birch wound up here: it was fixed here so that it wouldn't come loose, and it went over here, and this . . . this stake was here, you see: now this was put round it in another way that wouldn't come loose, and it could run up and down on this.

DAM: And how was this fixed [to the collar] here . . .?

DMcC: Well, it was just fixed so that it wouldn't come loose, you know. It was twisted together so that it wouldn't come loose, and then, you see, there was a loop on it so that it could be put over here, and taken off—it was easy enough to take it off, because the ends could be pushed in together, you know, and afterwards the strain on it kept it from opening: there was enough strain on it, you see, but it could be moved out or in, you know, the *nasg*.

DAM: And you've seen this [in use] yourself?

DMcC: Och, lad . . . for a good few years, when I was young, they had this: this was how they . . . Well, it was my mother's brother . . . he made them right enough. I believe he saw his father with it. You know in those days there was nothing else to be had but that, I mean in my grandfather's time.

DAM: And now, that rope there, the one that went across [the collar] there, that was made of birch too, was it?

DMcC: Yes, yes, yes, yes.

DAM: And this loop, that was birch?

DMcC: That loop there, yes, that was made of birch too.

DAM: But this bit, that was more solid than the rest?

DMcC: Oh yes, yes. It didn't matter what wood that was. It could have been oak, or it could have been anything it was made of.

DAM: Yes. It could. This collar was made of another [kind of] wood, so to speak?

DMcC: Yes. That was a different sort of wood generally. I don't think it was ever made of birch, but they usually had oak, you know? Yes.[6]

DAM: But it was always a sort of V shape there, was it?

DMcC: Yes, there was a V in it, well, to hold it, you know, so that it would not go over the top: it kept it, you see, from coming off there . . . yes. Och, they were easy enough to get: you could find plenty of *nasgs* throughout the district, where there was woodland you would find lots . . . Oh, it was fine, and it wouldn't throttle them at all . . . It was safe enough.

DAM: And now, did they use to look for a bit, if this bit was oak or some such wood, did they look for a bit of wood that had that shape naturally . . .?

DMcC: Oh well, you know, they used to bend it, you see, and certainly, I dare say they would steam it sometimes too, you know. They would bend it and possibly they'd tie [the ends] together, you see: they'd bend them and bind them so that they couldn't move, until they took that shape, do you see? Yes, that's how it was.

DAM: Ah well, that's good.

DMcC: It was extremely good. It was as good as any sort of tether and it was safe. It was safe, as safe as it could be. Yes.

DAM: Yes: it wouldn't tighten round the cow's throat at all . . . It would never get too tight round . . .

DMcC: Oh it wasn't, you know, there was plenty of room: it wasn't tight on them at all. No.

NOTES

1 A short feature on Donald McColl, who died in 1977, appeared in *Tocher* 34 (1980: 248-251).
2 At the beginning of the interview DAM was thinking of the *nasg* in terms of something like the circular one he knew, a continuous collar made, as for instance Dwelly's definition suggests, of birch twigs. See note 4 below for the actual meaning to Donald McColl.
3 The Gaelic adjective *caol* is also used as a noun to mean the osiers or saughs used in making wicker baskets; its use might be taken to imply that the birch twigs here were of a similar thickness, but they may well have been thinner.
4 *Nasg* is here primarily the name of the U- or V-shaped branch of wood which formed the greater part of the collar, though it may also include the birch-twig withe permanently fixed to it, closing it at the top and the fixture beneath attaching it to the tether-stake, which Donald usually simply refers to as *ròp* ('rope'). A parallel appears to be an example from East Holstein, illustrated by A. Lühning, 'Stopping the cattle from running away', in H. Cheape (ed.), *Tools and Traditions. Studies in European Ethnology presented to Alexander Fenton,* National Museums of Scotland 1993, 118 (Fig. 3). This example has openings through which a pin goes, instead of hooks over which the fastening band goes as in the iron version (Fig 2).
5 Both the larger loop here and the smaller one at the other end would presumably be made by twisting round the end of the withe and knitting the twigs in among the strands further back, much as the end of a basket handle is made.
6 Oak seems to have been preferred, no doubt for strength, and perhaps also because many of its branches would naturally have the beginnings of the sort of curve needed for the collar. These practical reasons probably meant more than any survival of druidic beliefs in the tree's magical pwers: powers of magical binding in recent times have been more closely associated with the more flexible *buarach* or fetter which bound the cow's hind legs together for milking.

ALAN BRUFORD AND DONALD A. MACDONALD

Clawbare, otherwise Ruchlaw West Mains, Stenton, East Lothian (O.S. NT 617 729)

'Ruchlaw West Mains is sometimes known as Cla-bair but the meaning of these words is obscure, and the name is not agreeable, for some reason, either to proprietor or tenant' (Lang 1929, 189).

The farmers in the area of Stenton, East Lothian, today (1992) know the farm by the name of Clawbare or Clawbair (they have no particular spelling for the name), especially the family of Jeffrey, branches of which farm Bielgrange, Deuchrie and Halls, and whose descendants have been in this area since the nineteenth century. The farmer at Ruchlaw West Mains today, Mr Dobson, knows of the name but does not use it as much as the Jeffreys (he and his family have farmed here since the late

1950s). Mr Dobson stated that a field immediately north of the farm is known by the names of both 'Old Clabair' and 'South Blakelaw' (the latter being the name of a small settlement between the farm and Stenton, of which only a couple of walls remain, now built into the field boundary dykes). However, a neighbouring farmer, Mr Kinnaird of Pressmennan, knows this field only as 'Old Clawbare' (he knows of no particular spelling), and the field north of it (which is on his property) as 'Blacklaws' or 'Blakelaws'; he and his family have farmed at Pressmennan since the 1930s.

There is a Gaelic word, *clàbar*, meaning 'filth, dirt, nastiness, mire, mud, clay; a puddle' (MacLeod and Dewar 1887, s.v.), and most of the local farmers agree with the description of clayey ground.[1]

At West Register House, there is a map of the roads in this area, dated May 1750, which has both 'Clabar House' and 'West Mains' at the location of Ruchlaw West Mains.[2] This map is possibly related to a dispute over a right of way near Stenton in 1748: various people were cited as witnesses to a committee of justices of the peace. One of these witnesses was James Young who was described as having lived at 'Ruchlaw West Mains or Clawbare' for the first twenty-two years of his life, he being aged sixty-seven at the time of this dispute. However, whether the place was 'Clawbare' in the late seventeenth century, when James Young was a youth, or at the time of this dispute (1748) is not made clear.[3]

In a 1799 map of East Lothian, the farm is named only as 'Clawbare'.[4] However, in no other maps, past or present,[5] nor in appropriate estate papers,[6] nor in Stenton Parish Records, is the farm referred to other than as Ruchlaw West Mains (if mentioned at all in some of the earlier maps).

Incidentally, Ruchlaw West Mains took its name from being part of the estate of Ruchlaw, by Stenton. It was formerly known as the West Mains of Stenton.[7] (It is not west of Ruchlaw, but almost due south).

There are records of another Clawbare in East Lothian, near East Linton, some three or four miles north of Ruchlaw West Mains, although there is a problem in identifying exactly where this land was.

The first record was in May 1819, of 'parts of the lands of Ruchflatt or Porks now known by the name of Clawbare or Barebones', a description which remained in use in various documents dated to 1919/20, when Ruchflatt or Porks became used instead.[8] An earlier record of these same lands of 'Ruchflatt or Porks' dated February 1738 made no mention of the other names.[9]

These records all implied that these lands were part of the farm of Phantassie, by East Linton, but the farmer there today (1933), Mr Hamilton, knows of no such name of Clawbare (or Ruchflatt or Porks), though there is an Under and Upper Barebones lying west of the town, two fields about O.S. ref. NT 583 766.[10] There is also a reference to these two fields in a book published in 1890, though nothing is said about any other names (Martine 1890: Prestonkirk Parish), and to one field called Barebones in this general area on an undated map (but which pre-dates the local railway, so before the 1840s).[11] The farmer, Mr Hamilton, suggested the name of Barebones was 'because the soil in the fields is shallow in places over rock'.[10] Perhaps this Clawbare was a modern English descriptive name—'claw/bare', though the comparable Gaelic name *clàbar* should not be forgotten.

Lastly, there is a field by the name of 'Claw Bear' on the farm of Aitchisonbank, some two miles north of Gretna, Dumfriesshire, O.S. ref. NY 318 702.[12] The history of this name is not known to this writer.

NOTES

1 From interviews with farmers and landowners in the Stenton area, May-June 1992, including Mr and Mrs Dobson, Ruchlaw West Mains, branches of the Jeffrey family at Bielgrange, Deuchrie and Halls farms, Mr Kinnaird, Pressmennan Farm, and Mr Blair of Clint.
2 Scottish Record Office: RHP 56/1.
3 Biel Muniments, Scottish Record Office, GD6/1274 (No. 3).
4 William Forrest's Map of East Lothian, 1799.
5 Map of East Lothian, surveyed by Mr J. Adair, for John, Marquis of Tweeddale (late seventeenth century); Johan Blaeu's 'Atlas Novus' of Scotland (mid-seventeenth century); maps and plans held in the Buchan Sydserff of Ruchlaw Papers, SRO, GD1/494; precursors to the Ordnance Survey from 1850s onward, and O.S. maps to date.
6 Especially Buchan Sydserff or Ruchlaw Papers, SRO, GD1/494, in particular Nos. 113, 117, 121 and 126.
7 As recorded in several documents, including General Register of Sasines, RS2/1 f.208; Particular Register of Sasines for Haddington & co. RS26/2 f.329; Inventory of Ruchlaw Writs, held in Buchan Sydserff of Ruchlaw Papers, SRO, GD1/494/84 (and others).
8 Abstract of Sasines for Haddington, vol. 1781-1820 Nos. 2298, 2300, and miscellaneous references in various volumes to vol. 1919 No. 385, vol. 1920 No. 13.
9 Register of the Great Seal of Scotland (RMS) (SRO) C.2/96 f.50v.
10 Correspondence with Mr Hamilton, farmer, Phantassie Farm, East Linton, Jan.-Feb. 1993.
11 SRO RHP 3682.
12 Place names survey of Aitchisonbank-Goldilelea (1982), held at School of Scottish Studies.

REFERENCES

LANG, MARSHALL B.
1929 *Whittingehame.* Edinburgh.
MACLEOD, NORMAN and DEWAR, DANIEL
1887 *Dictionary of the Gaelic Language.* Edinburgh.
MARTINE, JOHN
1890 *Reminiscences of Fourteen Parishes of the County of Haddington.* Edinburgh.

DAVID SYDESERFF

The Earth Hound—a Living Banffshire Belief

In 1950, the *People's Journal* of 24 June contained a paragraph about 'yird pigs' or 'earth huns'. They were said to be 'really rats and . . . only found in graveyards' (*PJ*, 24 June 1950). Further investigation turned up a reference by the Reverend Walter Gregor in 1881, the oldest one so far identified. He spoke of 'a mysterious dreaded sort of animal, called the "yird swine" . . . believed to live in graveyards, burrowing among the dead bodies and devouring them' (Gregor 1881, 130).

> More information came from the archives of the Department of Natural History of the National Museums of Scotland. A letter written by A. Smith, Rayne School, Wartle, Aberdeenshire, dated 11 December 1917, to James Ritchie in Edinburgh, relates how the father of one Archibald, Gardener at Warthill, 'remembered quite well his father turning up one (an "earth hund") in its nest when ploughing in the haughs of Deveron about 50 years ago. He (the father) tried to kill it with his foot, but it bit and cut his boot, and he killed it with a "swingle-tree" and brought it home. It was brown in colour somewhat like a rat, but had a long head like a dog's—(hound's), and a tail bushier than a rat's, but he could not say how bushy. Their nests were from time to time turned up by the plough, but the animals themselves were very rarely seen, reputed to frequent churchyards. This was in the immediate neighbourhood of a churchyard which was eventually disused owing to the firm belief that it was infested with earth-hunds. They invariably lived in the immediate neighbourhood of water, and their nests were in haughs.
>
> 'Archibald saw this one himself, has quite a distinct recollection of it, and says all the neighbours were interested to see it, and all agreed it was an earth-hund from its appearance, though it did not transpire whether any of them were acquainted with the animal before. . . . He describes it as being something between a rat and a weasel, and about the size of a ferret, head very like that of a dog, and I think he said the tail was not very long. At a casual glance it would be mistaken for a rat, but was quite unlike on close examination.'

There is also a note by the same writer, with the same date, but posted on the following day. It reads as follows:

> 'Had occasion unexpectedly to visit Mastrick on W.S. business about 10 p.m. tonight. Did not see the old man, who was presumably in bed. Asked about the supposed earth hund, with undernoted result.
>
> It was not this season but 2 years or so ago it was killed.
>
> It was turned up by the plough (by Jas. McIntosh, I think).

> It ran along the furrow some distance before it was killed.
> His recollection was that it was about the size of a rat. Asked about colour, he thought it was like a dark rat. It had feet like a mole, and a tail about half as long as a rat's.
> Head was long and nostrils very prominent, suggesting a pig's. Head somewhat like that of a guinea-pig.
> It had noticeable white "tusks'', whatever that might mean—(probably incisors). Other members of the family added the latter details.
> Some reference, vague, was made to some large heap or heaps occurring on the farm credited by their father to earth-hunds.
> Mastrick is about 10 minutes' walk from here, and curiously enough is close to the churchyard. . . .'

Even today, there seems to be a belief in these creatures. In April 1990, when A.F. visited a friend in Keith, that sprawling three-part Banffshire town, conversation turned to the earth hound. 'They're atween a rat an a rabbit,' he said. 'They live in graveyards. They howk doon an cleek intae the coffins. . . . Aye, I'll tak ye tae far they are.' We drove through Fife Keith, along the Dufftown road and then by side roads, rising through forestry plantations and bare hillside through the Haugh of Glass and then a couple of miles on to the Hill of Dumeath, stopping on its shoulder just before Beldorney Castle.

Below us was Walla Kirkyard. Instead of a road to it, there was only a wide fenced-off strip of field, giving access down a steepish slope in dry conditions, but surely not in ice or snow. The kirkyard stood on the edge of the River Deveron, alone, remote from any church.

We walked amongst the stones. The oldest dated to 1741. There were new graves in an extension against the old wall. My friend looked intently around the stones where someone had cleared weeds and bared the earth, searching for scrapes and scratch marks, but Walla Kirkyard revealed none of its mysteries. No earth hound appeared, no reeking burrows were seen.

It is part of the North-east sense of humour that a grim topic can be pursued in all apparent seriousness, and this A.F.'s friend did. If he did not in his heart believe in earth hounds, at least he never dropped his mask.

REFERENCE

GREGOR, REV. WALTER
1881 *Notes on the Folk-lore of North East Scotland.* London.

ALEXANDER FENTON AND DAVID HEPPELL

Appalachian-Scottish Studies, East Tennessee State University

An exchange agreement between East Tennessee State University and Edinburgh University was signed in 1989, to encourage and promote comparative study on the similarities and differences between Scotland and the Appalachian region, through the exchange of cultural links between scholars and tradition bearers of the two regions. In 1989 and 1991, the School of Scottish Studies hosted students from Tennessee. In 1992, from 7-13 July, honours students Owen Hand, Alyne Jones and Jane George, together with lecturer Susan Storrier, representing the School of Scottish Studies, contributed to the course on Appalachian and Scottish Culture, which was co-ordinated by Dr Tom Burton, Professor of English at ETSU.

The programme assembled by Dr Burton encompassed the broad spectrum of Scottish and Appalachian culture, with a variety of lectures. Dr Michael Montgomery of the University of South Carolina discussed the languages and dialects of Scotland, showing how these may have influenced Appalachian speech patterns. Dr Edward Cowan from the University of Guelph, Ontario, explored the Scots, from the 'forging of a nation', through its people, religion and popular culture, to the 'myth of Scotch America', in a series of spirited and lively lectures. Susan Storrier contributed illustrated lectures, ranging from 'The Land and Early Peoples of Scotland' and 'Traditional Society and its material base in Modern Scotland', to 'Rural and Urban Vernacular Architecture'. Alyne Jones presented a beautifully illustrated lecture on 'Galloway—land of the people' and an informative study on Riccarton Junction—a railway village in the Scottish Borders.

Owen Hand traced the industrial history of Paisley and the famous 'Paisley Pattern', with examples of Paisley shawls, and he also held the audience spellbound with a lecture on 'The Seal Legends of Scotland'. Jane George's lectures on 'The Royal and Ancient Game of Golf' and 'The Roaring Game of Curling', highlighted the central place which these two traditional sports have played in the lives of Scots.

The Appalachian input was in the form of story-tellers, ballad singers and ballads. Barbara McDermitt, an American scholar and former PhD student at the School of Scottish Studies, discussed the similarities and differences between superstitions in traditional tales, told by story-tellers in Scotland and Appalachia. With such a strong narrative tradition in the Appalachian region, an 'unofficial' as well as an 'official' audience with Ray Hicks, one of the tradition bearers in the art of story-telling, proved to be among the highlights for the Scottish students. Tom Burton provided an academic and scholarly approach in his lecture on 'The Traditional Scots Ballads in Appalachia'. On a trip to Beech Mountain, North

Caroline, the three Scottish students also heard ballads 'in situ', sung by two tradition bearers, Hattie Presnell and her sister Rosie-Jane.

There were several outings to places of local interest. The Museum of Appalachia is a 'living' open-air museum relating to the pioneering lifestyle of the early settlers and the Scottish students found it to be a rich source of ethnological interest. A trip to Grandfather Mountain, North Carolina, for the Highland Games, proved an eye-opening and overwhelming experience. The ubiquitous tartan, worn in a multiplicity of forms on a variety of shapes and sizes, made the 'tartanless' Scottish students feel like displaced persons in the cast of 'Brigadoon'! It has to be said that although these games are unique and a spectacular affair, they are in stark contrast to the majority of the local community types of games with which we are more familiar in Scotland.

Wherever we went we were given generous hospitality and a warm welcome. On our last evening, a public concert was held at ETSU, with the musical talents of Owen Hand and Alyne given top billing. They were supported by local singers, musicians and story-tellers. This proved to be an apt ending to a successful exchange of cultures.

Having been given the opportunity, through the School of Scottish Studies and the financial assistance of ETSU, to go to Tennessee and be a part of the course and with the experience gained in lecturing as undergraduates, we feel this has been of great benefit, not only to us as students, but we hope also to the students at ETSU. The links which have been forged with ETSU will be continued in the future, through greater sponsorship by bodies interested in maintaining links in a shared heritage.

OWEN HAND, ALYNE JONES, JANE GEORGE

Postgraduate Work in the School of Scottish Studies, the Department of Scottish History and the Department of Celtic, 1992-93

The following list, giving the name of the postgraduate and an indication of the thesis subject, shows the wide range of work being covered by the School of Scottish Studies, the Department of Scottish History, and the Department of Celtic.

SCHOOL OF SCOTTISH STUDIES

Audrey B. Main. A study of the modern Scottish theatre as a social phenomenon, examining how twentieth-century Scottish dramatists perceive and represent the family, community, gender relations and the workplace.

Margaret Bennett. Hebridean Traditions and the Eastern Townships of Quebec.

Frank Bruce. Scottish Comedians and Comediennes, 1900-1940.

Antoinette Butler. See Department of Celtic.

Shari A. Cohn (Department of Psychology; jointly with the School of Scottish Studies). An Investigation of the Scottish Tradition of Second Sight and Other Psychic Experiences in Families. The three basic aims are: (1) to study and explore the Scottish tradition of second sight through interviewing people about their experiences; (2) to examine family histories of second sight to see if they support the belief that this ability is hereditary; (3) to see if second sight is related to eidetic imagery.

Hugh P. Hagan. Community Identity in Port Glasgow/Greenock. The thesis examines the cultural history of the community in this urban industrial region, including aspects of housing, work, religion, gender roles and leisure pursuits, over the period 1850-1950, with particular reference to Irish and Highland influences.

Mark C. Hanford. The Role of the Wizard in Scottish and Icelandic Traditional Narratives.

Mary Harman. The History, Social Organisation and Material Culture of St Kilda.

Heather D. Holmes. Potato Harvesting in the Lothians, 19th-20th centuries.

Michael Kennedy. See Department of Celtic.

Allan A. MacDonald. The Relationship between Gaelic Song and Ceòl Mor.

James R. MacDonald. Folk History and Tradition of the Scottish Immigrants to North Carolina.

Thomas McKean. See Department of Celtic.

Neill Martin. The Melodic and Non-melodic in Folk Song with particular reference to the Greig-Duncan Folk Song Collection. The work centres on verbal contests and exchanges, both literary and non-literary. These include bardic contests, flyting, repartee and ritual exchanges as part of seasonal and social customs, for example weddings. Celtic tradition dominates, but parallels from further afield are sought, particularly to support a structural analysis of the phenomena.

Howard Y. Mitchell. The Lives and Lore of Staff and Patients in some Scottish Hospitals, from the 1850s. The thesis examines the lives of the mentally handicapped in Scotland from the 1850s and charts the influences which led to the building of large hospitals for this group. Lennox Castle Hospital is the basis of a community study involving the patients and the groups of staff employed there.

Gillian Munro. Fisherwomen or Fishermen's Wives? A Study of Change in the Lives of the Women of Gardenstown, Banffshire. Based on field notes and recordings, the thesis draws on the methodologies and the theory of ethnology and of social anthropology.

James R. Souness. A Survey of Thatching in Scotland.

Gary J. West. Farmhouse, Cottage and Bothy in Highland and Lowland Perthshire during the Nineteenth and early Twentieth Centuries. The emphasis is on social organisation and modes of lalbour. It looks at the recruitment, organisation and living conditions of the labour force, the role of women and children and the concepts of exchange and charity labour.

Yusuke Uno. A Comparative Study of Scottish and Japanese lullabies focusing on the Relationship between Text (words and tune) and Context (historical, social and cultural background).

DEPARTMENT OF SCOTTISH HISTORY

Sharon Adams. Church and State, c.1590-1640, with particular reference to the south-west.

Bob Akroyd. William Gladstone and Lord Rosebery and the Scottish and Irish Home Rule Movements. The strength and effectiveness of the first Scottish Home Rule Movement, particularly 1880-1895. Within Liberal politics as a whole and in Scotland specifically, Rosebery and Gladstone are clearly pre-eminent, and any study of Scottish politics at this time cannot fail to assess their specific roles and ideas.

Winifred Coutts. The Work in the College of Justice in 1600. Litigation as source material for social and economic conditions in Scotland in 1600; types of cases brought before the Court of Session and the participants therein.

Polly Davidson. Extreme Right Wing Groups and Ideas in Scotland, c. 1918-1939.

Flora Gilfillan. David Hume of Godscroft. An examination of his work, his life and his significance in Scottish history. A comparison of the published and manuscript editions of the *History of the House of Douglas*, with due reference paid to his other works.

Ruth Grant. George Gordon, Sixth Earl of Huntly: A Study in a Sixteenth Century Politique, c. 1576-1610. Examination of Huntly's position as both a strong regional magnate and as a figure in the central government within the context of his international intrigues. The aim is to determine the extent to which both his regional and government positions when combined with his international Catholic activities affected not only the foreign policy of James VI, but that of Elizabeth I of England as well.

David Henderson. Economic Consequences of the Union of the Parliaments. A one-year research project analysing how the 1707 Union affected the regional economies of Scotland and whether these regional differences translated into varying degrees of anti-English sentiment or Jacobitism.

Karen Hunt. The Governorship of the 1st Duke of Albany. The rationale of the thesis is to provide an in-depth analysis of a man whose career spanned three decades and was central to the affairs of Scotland in the late fourteenth and early fifteenth centuries. Moreover, with the early Stewart period itself often represented as an unfortunate hiatus between the golden age of nationalism in the early fourteenth century and the return of James I in 1424, the thesis will also discuss certain aspects of later medieval life, including kingship, political ideas, law and order, the economy and international relations, and attempt to establish these issues within the continuum of history. However, the main thrust of the thesis will be to examine the many contentious issues that punctuated the career of Scotland's first governor and to establish this complex figure as a credible and viable force in the political life of late medieval Scotland.

Andrew Jennings (jointly with the Department of Celtic.) Norse and Gael in the West of Scotland from 795 to 1000. A multi-disciplinary study of the settlement of the Norse and their interaction with the Gaels during this period. Particular reference is made to the people called Gall-gaidhil, and the historical links between the Hebrides and Dublin are examined.

Andrew Lang. George Dempster of Dunnichen. A comprehensive biography of George Dempster of Dunnichen (1732-1818), the noted landowner, agricultural reformer, Member of Parliament and director of the East India Company. He was also closely involved in the introduction and establishment of the cotton spinning industry in Scotland.

Allan MacDonald. The Politics of Kirk, Crown and Congregation in Scotland 1584-1610. An examination of relations between the Kirk and the state involving the crown's attempts to control the Kirk, as well as ecclesiastical involvement in central government; relations between secular and ecclesiastic jurisdictions at a local level; the role of the political community in ecclesiastical affairs; the influence of the Kirk on the laity. Running through all these things is the question of the role of the so-called 'Melvillian' ministers and their political influence within the Kirk in spite of their numbers.

Douglas Watt. The Highland Nobility and their Lawyers in Seventeenth-Century Scotland. A study of the ruling grades in Highland society in the seventeenth century focusing in particular on the developing relationship between Highland chiefs, their legal representatives and the institutions of central government.

DEPARTMENT OF CELTIC

Antoinette Butler (jointly with the School of Scottish Studies.) A historical survey of the development of the drama in Scottish Gaelic. The origins are traced within the indigenous culture to whatever can be called dramatic in the broadest sense of the word, e.g. dance, mime and even preaching. The literary origins in catechism and ecclesiological dialogues in the eighteenth and nineteenth centuries are examined. It is then shown on the basis of Irish models and following Irish nationalistic aspirations how Scottish Gaelic plays came to be written for the stage. The thesis is brought up to date by examining how Gaelic drama has evolved and how it may have been influenced by foreign models. The establishment of Gaelic broadcast plays is also taken into account.

Joseph Calise. 'Picts' and related terms in Celtic literature.

Ann Carrington (jointly with the Department of Fine Art). The hunt and horses in Celtic epigraphy and literature.

Michael Davies. Irish translation literature with special reference to the Charlemagne cycle. The aim of this project is to provide an edition of Chanson de Geste 'Fierabras', preserved in a unique manuscript, T.C.D. MS 667. This Latin adaptation was translated closely into Irish during the period around the year 1400. Following the edition, a comparison will be made with other extant versions of the 'Fierabras', and an attempt will follow to set the Latin/Irish texts in their European setting. Coupled with the motives for translation, the texts will be considered alongside contemporary trends in the Irish literary scene.

John Melville Galloway. The Gaelic language and employment: history and prospects.

Anja Gunderloch. Gaelic and Irish Fenian literature. A study of active textual development in Scottish and Irish Gaelic ballad tradition after c. 1550. Different versions of a body of well-attested heroic ballads are investigated in order to establish patterns of transmission and development, with reference both to patterns with ballads and to the different manifestations of versions in Ireland and Scotland. The emphasis of the thesis lies on the Scottish evidence, using published as well as manuscript sources.

Kevin Hind. Gaelic language and linguistics.

Andrew Jennings. See Department of Scottish History.

Michael Kennedy (jointly with the School of Scottish Studies). Highland settlement in Prince Edward Island.

Sheila Kidd. Nineteenth-century Gaelic literature: the literary works of Rev. Alexander MacGregor.

Joan MacDonald. Early Modern Gaelic literature: classical Gaelic poetry composed in Scotland, with special reference to the works of Neil and Donald MacMhuirich.

Thomas McKean (jointly with the School of Scottish Studies). The Life and Songs of Iain 'an Sgiobair' MacNeacail and the Role of a Songmaker in a Hebridean Community.

Robert Mullally. Aspects of the historical phonology of Irish and Scottish Gaelic. The thesis traces some of the major phonological developments in Gaelic from the so-called 'Common Gaelic' period onward and is based mainly on synchronic accounts of modern Gaelic dialects.

Terence Rosecrans. Studies in the concepts of Celtic origins and identity.

Donald William Stewart. Eighteenth-century Scottish Gaelic poetry.

Carol Zall. The repertoire of a Scottish Gaelic Story-teller.

Book Reviews

The Good People: New Fairylore Essays edited by Peter Narváez. Garland Publishing, New York and London: 1991. ISBN 0-8240-7100-X. 519+xiv pages.

The word 'fairy' can conjure up a wide range of differing interpretations. It has been applied to creatures as dissimilar as the 'good people' of traditional folklore and the tooth fairy of popular children's culture. This is due in part to the ambiguous nature of fairies themselves and in part to the popularity of the word for describing a host of analogous beings. The confusion only increases when we begin to compare material from different cultures separated linguistically, geographically or temporally. This collection of fairylore essays does not attempt to reconcile this ambiguity or offer any consistent definition for the word 'fairy'. Rather the individual essays concern a wide variety of apparently unrelated supernatural beings. The three consistent themes which run throughout this collection are the issues of context, function and belief.

In order to understand any branch of fairylore it is first necessary to consider the social and historical factors which have influenced its development. To this end we must begin by studying fairylore in the context of the tradition-bearing community. This is the purpose of three of the essays in this collection. Alan Bruford attempts to disentangle the Norse and Celtic influences which have shaped accounts of supernatural beings in Orkney and Shetland. Robin Gwyndaf describes the Welsh land of the fairies including their appearance, activities and possessions. Linda-May Ballard seems more interested in the human world. She gives a short history of Reachraí (Rathlin Island) and emphasises the social context and function of the legends. Both Gwyndaf and Ballard begin with accounts of their informants and methods of recording and illustrate their essays with numerous texts.

Typically fairies have personified the potentially hostile forces outside the community. They can reward proper behaviour, but are quick to punish improper behaviour or take advantage of a momentary lapse of caution. Fairylore has often functioned to explain good or bad fortune and to reinforce accepted standards of behaviour. Richard P. Jenkins compares acts of aggression by witches and fairies in this context. He discovers that fairy aggression is often interpreted as punishment for deviance from accepted domestic relations. Peter Narváez investigates accounts of fairies leading berry-pickers astray in French Newfoundland. He argues that fairies can serve to maintain geographical as well as moral boundaries to the community.

Fairylore can also function to explain inexplicable phenomena. Three of the essays focus on fairylore as folk explanations of physical disorders. Susan Schoon Eberly and Joyce Underwood Munro offer convincing arguments when they compare accounts of fairy changelings with disabled or 'failure to thrive' infants, though Eberly may overstate her case when she attempts to explain brownies and solitary fairies as disabled or mentally retarded adults. Barbara Rieti uses the theory of 'folk explanation' in her study of 'the Blast' in Newfoundland, but she emphasises the narrative value of the stories in accounting for their popularity.

Any attempt to explain fairylore is essentially a matter of translating supernatural accounts into our own belief system. Peter M. Rojcewicz offers the most ambitious explanation of fairylore when he compares fairy encounters with sightings of UFOs. He draws in accounts of 'nonhuman others' from around the world and attempts to explain them all as manifestations of Jungian archetypes. While Rojcewicz is careful to avoid any comment on the validity of these accounts he suggests that archetypes may 'possess . . . the ability to cross over from the psychic to the physical realm' and appear 'in the world as an external event, and occasionally even as a quasi-physical object'.

Estimating a community's level of belief in a supernatural tradition can be one of the most difficult problems facing a folklore collector. This is especially true when the tradition has maintained some metaphoric value in the absence of actual belief. In describing 'The *Lutin* tradition in French Newfoundland Culture' Gary R. Butler discusses this problem in relation to a disappearing tradition. Paul Smith's essay on 'The Cottingley Fairies' examines how media forces and a desire to believe helped to perpetuate a fairy hoax. Margaret Bennett takes up the issue of belief on a more optimistic note when she visits Balquhidder, the home of Robert Kirk who wrote *The Secret Commonwealth of Elves, Fauns and Fairies*. Bennett's interviews with school children offer hope for the future of fairy beliefs in the Scottish Highlands.

The issue of belief appears most often in the essays concerning fairylore in contemporary societies. In a culture where the validity of fairylore is no longer accepted fairies can become a symbol of innocence and naiveté and have been relegated to the field of children's culture. This is the focus of two essays on the tooth fairy. Rosemary Wells regards the tooth fairy ritual as a rite of passage, but she stresses that it is the loss of belief, not the loss of teeth, which marks the transition from childhood to the adult world. Tad Tuleja quotes Wells's research and his essay is largely redundant. His primary independent contribution is the assertion that the tooth fairy ritual functions to indoctrinate children into the capitalist system of monetary exchange.

Often the fairy faith has had to co-exist with other systems of belief. Two essays in this collection concern the relationship between fairylore and orthodox Christianity in bicultural societies. In 'The Fairy Belief and Official Religion in Ireland' Diarmuid Ó Giolláin describes that relationship as a conflict between the hegemonic culture or the state and subordinated local cultures. Conversely Ann Skjelbred emphasises the influence which Norwegian beliefs in *huldre*-folk have had on Christian beliefs, in some cases serving to legitimate Christian rituals.

David Buchan contributes the only essay in this collection to discuss ballads. He applies talerole analysis to ballads of encounters with otherworld beings. Noel Williams offers an etymological study of the word 'fairy', drawing on texts from the fourteenth to the nineteenth centuries. Finally, Patricia Lysaght examines the biography and repertoire of a single story-teller from Ireland. Unlike the traditional Irish Gaelic-speaking male story-teller, Dr Lysaght's informant is a woman from outside the Gaeltacht, specialising in 'short realistic stories dealing with fairies, ghosts and other supernatural beings'. Focusing on a single story-teller allows Dr Lysaght to deal with questions of belief in specific terms and brings 'formation of repertoire dominants' to the level of favourite types of stories.

The largest group of essays in this collection concerns Celtic fairylore. There is an even mix of Newfoundland traditions and fairies in contemporary culture with only one essay from Scandinavia. The essays are written at a range of different academic levels, but none is so technical as to be inaccessible to the general reader while most will provide the serious scholar with some interesting points to consider. Collectively they serve to question, or even disprove, some of the accepted beliefs of fairylore: that fairy beliefs represent a dying tradition, or that fairies are rooted in the European soil and are never found in North America. They open up new avenues of research and provide informative reading for anyone with an interest in fairylore or folklore in general.

MARK HANFORD

Homes

The Scottish Development Education Centre (Old Playhouse Close, Moray House College of Education, Holyrood Road, Edinburgh EH8 8AQ) has produced an Active Learning Pack for six to twelve-year-olds under the heading *Homes*. The pack contains a set of Notes for Teachers, a range of full-colour photographs and work sheets. Its interest for Scottish education is two-fold. First of all it includes a section on the homes of two families of travelling people, the Reid and Sutherland families. These are seen alongside families and homes from Sarawak and North-west China, unity lying in the concept of what is a home. Secondly, it draws attention to a new phenomenon in Western societies—their increasing multiculturality. In the Centre's words, 'Development Education fosters skills, knowledge and attitudes which promote justice and equality in a multicultural society and an interdependent world.' The *Homes* pack matches this thinking, and can help to inculcate understanding and awareness at an early age.

The Farmsteadings of the Bathgate Hills, by Nils White. West Lothian District Council, 1991. 44pp, 44 photographs, 7 diagrams and map. £1.95. Available from local bookshops, Tourist Information Office and W.L.D.C.'s Planning Department, County Buildings, Linlithgow. ISBN 0 907 952 038

Based on a comprehensive survey of fifty farmsteadings in the 'heart of West Lothian', this booklet charts a process of transformation which continues to the present day.

Originating during the eighteenth and nineteenth centuries each farm has subsequently undergone a series of alterations, additions and adaptations. The author links these changes in design to changes in agricultural technology, such as the replacement of animal power by mechanical, and to more general changes in social attitudes, such as the increasing separation of the farm house from workers' dwellings. This process is brought up to date by consideration of the present use of buildings, 40 per cent of which are no longer used for farming.

The emphasis of this study is firmly on the locality. The Bathgate Hills are bordered to the north by Linlithgow and to the south by Bathgate and Uphall. Elements of upland and lowland farming were practised, giving the area a character which contrasts both with neighbouring industrial areas and with more palatial farmsteads of East Lothian.

The main farm buildings, such as the barn, byres, dairy, horse mill, stables, bothy and farmhouse are all fully described and well illustrated. Less common features of farm buildings, such as owl holes, beeholes and loupin-on-stanes, are also noted. In addition, there are more complete and detailed descriptions of the farmsteadings at Cauldhame and Brunton.

The relationship between farm buildings and their local environment is explored through examples of building materials used, such as the locally collected or quarried blue-grey whinstone and red pantiles manufactured within the county. Construction techniques may also display local character, for example the fine cornice work featured in farmhouses belonging to the Lochcote estate. Innovations are similarly considered in terms of the pace at which they were adopted within this district.

The booklet shows the extent to which traces of the past are still visible in existing structures. However, the pace of change in the countryside continues to increase and alternative pressures on the use of land and rural buildings are now creating much uncertainty concerning developing trends.

This timely contribution from Nils White and W.L.D.C.'s Planning Department will help to inform future decisions as well as serving as a useful guide for both visitors and locals.

ANDREW MORRISON

The Culbin Sands—Fact and Fiction, by Sinclair Ross. Centre for Scottish Studies, Aberdeen, 1992. xi+196pp. £7.95. ISBN 0 906265 16 9

Sinclair Ross, the Sherlock Holmes of geomorphology, has produced an excellent and meticulously researched account of the Culbin story in *The Culbin Sands—Fact and Fiction*. The story is immediately compelling and one quckly shares the author's determination to get to the bottom of the sand dune mystery. Did the Barony of Culbin really disappear one night in 1694 in one of the most vicious sandstorms ever to be recorded (inaccurately?) in Scotland? Mr Ross traces the many written accounts of the great storm theory and discovers that the few original facts have been so embellished over the years as to make the popular account quite unreliable. In fact his research concludes that the land devastation was created by a gradual advance of sand caused by patterns of bad weather, and accelerated by the damage done in stripping vegetation from the old shingle ridges. Although the original estate was known as the garden and granary of Moray, the extent of the arable land and the information on the grain rents available were grossly exaggerated. The first serious attempt to reclaim the sandy wastelands by planting trees was made by R. Grant of Kincorth as long ago as 1837, and there have been many schemes since with varying degrees of success.

In addition to the Culbin Sands mystery, which is central to the book, there are two chapters dealing respectively with Agriculture and Farm Life in Seventeenth-century Moray and the Buildings on the Old Culbin Estate. In the former chapter the author provides a good account of tenant farmers' rights and obligations (the obligations were much more numerous) and paints a good picture of just how primitive the countryside was at that time—very poor standard buildings and houses, few fences and walls and the almost impossible task of keeping the animals alive over the winter months. The chapter on the buildings gives an interesting account of the various styles of cruck-framed houses. The book concludes with an account of the families of Murray and Kinnaird.

The text is supported by numerous illustrations and graphs and there is a comprehensive bibliography and several appendices. The technical data will not be lost on the expert and it need not detract from the enjoyment of the general reader.

MALCOLM CANT

Evidence for Old English. Material and Theoretical Bases for Reconstruction. Edited by Fran Colman. John Donald Publishers Ltd., Edinburgh, 1992. £32.00.

This is the second volume in an occasional series, *Edinburgh Studies in the English Language* (general editors: John Anderson and Norman Macleod). The series is thematic, the present volume being devoted to the examination and interpretation of problems presented by the surviving corpus of Old English data. The papers cover a range of phonological and syntactical questions; they are ordered alphabetically by author rather than by subject matter. The editor maintains that fact is dependent upon theory, but this cannot be true (any more than theory can depend upon fact) until the relevant facts are discovered and noted. It is refreshing to find among the contributions to this volume warnings against the dangers, all too often incurred, of recycling ready-made data packages. There is here recognition that even though all the manuscript sources for Old English have long been known about and adequately catalogued there still remains much to be gleaned from them as well as from the complementary sources of coins, runic inscriptions and place names.

1. Cynthia Allen, 'Old English and the Syntactician', points out that editions of OE texts, often assembled from several different manuscripts, are frequently inadequate for linguistic research. Rightly advocating recourse to the original manuscripts she offers as a preliminary towards a syntactic study of Ælfric's prose a check-list collated with N. R. Ker's *Catalogue of Manuscripts Containing Anglo-Saxon*, Angus Cameron's list of texts for the *Dictionary of Old English* and the major editions.

2. Ann King, 'Interpreting Old English Written Data', offers a thoughtful analysis of OE <a>~ <o> variation in words of the *man, hand* type and warns of the dangers of drawing wide-ranging conclusions from inadequately scrutinised data. Her own conclusions, though understandably cautious, are well argued and backed by extra-linguistic historical evidence and palaeography.

3. Willem Koopman, 'Old English Clitic Pronouns', also takes as his starting point a critique of another scholar's work, producing some modifications to Van Kemenade's thesis that OE personal pronouns may be regarded as clitics. Some initial definition of terms here would have been useful for those unfamiliar with government-binding theory.

4. Roger Lass, 'Front Rounded Vowels in Old English', gives a very useful conspectus of knowledge and opinion to date with some new insights and several considered conclusions ranged in order of preference.

5. C. B. McCully, 'The Phonology of Resolution in OE Word-stress and Metre', examines the device of resolution in OE metrics and argues for a biplanar analysis, stress and time occupying different planes. McCully's 'template' for the phonology of OE metrics seems to confirm the phonological reality of Sievers' metrical 'Types'.

6. Donka Minkova and Robert Stockwell, 'Poetic Influence over Prose Word Order in Old English', consider different views of Old English verse syntax and its influence on changes in prose word order. The conclusion finds that OE main clauses became more like Dutch and German (i.e. verb second) and that only much later did English change into an atypical West German language in this respect.

7. Matti Rissanen, 'Computers are Useful—for *Aught* I know', introduces the OE section of the *Helsinki Corpus of English Texts* showing the new possibilities provided by a computerised corpus specially constructed for structural and lexical studies. The OE sub-corpus consists of half a million words of text, both poetry and prose, and is arranged with reference to date, dialect, text type and author. Rissanen's worked example suggests that the survival of *aught* was supported by the high frequency of the negative form *not/naught*.

8. Veronica Smart, 'Die-Cutting and Diatopic Variation', presents evidence about local and centralised die-cutting which dramatically affects how the linguistic

evidence from coins should be viewed. She examines the <LIOF-> variant as a Kentish feature which has spread beyond its usually accepted area of use in its occurrence on the late Anglo-Saxon coinage.

9. Anthony R. Warner, 'Elliptical and Impersonal Constructions: Evidence for Auxiliaries in Old English', redefines the label 'auxiliary' with respect to OE as 'a grouping of "less verbal" verbs . . . with some strictly syntactic properties'. He gives evidence to support this categorisation from elliptical and impersonal constructions.

10. W. van der Wurff, 'Another Old English Impersonal: Some Data', focuses on the combination adjective plus infinitive in OE and presents data from a fresh corpus study to illustrate the constraints operating on certain sub-types.

In spite of some unevenness in format, font size and system of reference, this is a nicely produced book with a good range of material and variety of approach. As a time when the study of Old English in university departments is increasingly threatened, it is encouraging to see that those who do still teach it are continuing to reassess the rigour of their research methods and to reaffirm with new discoveries the vitality of their subject.

MARGARET LAING

Books Noticed

Books included here may also be reviewed in a later issue of *Scottish Studies.*

They are grouped as far as possible according to the subject categories of the International Ethnological Bibliography (edited by Dr Rainer Alsheimer, University of Bremen, FB 10 (Kulturwissenschaft), Postfach 330 440, D-2800 Bremen 33, Germany).

01 *Ethnology as a Science.*

Bibliography.

Jaap Kerkhoven en Paul Post, *Volkskunde en museum: een Literatuurwijzer* (Publikaties van het P. J. Meertens-Instituut, Deel 14, Amsterdam 1992. [A review of books and articles from several countries on current and recent thinking about open-air museum and cultural historical museum activities.]

Sources.

M. Cox, *Exploring Scottish History. A Directory of Resource Centres for Scottish Local and National History in Scotland* (Scottish Library Association and Scottish Local History Forum 1992), 161 pp. £6.95. [An indispensable guide to sources and resources for amateur or experienced researchers. If the book is not readily available in bookshops, purchasers should contact Elaine Finnie, Secretary, S.L.H.F., c/o Huntly House Museum, 142 Canongate, Edinburgh EH8 8DD.]

History, Theory and Methods.

Simon J. Bronner, *Creativity and Tradition in Folklore. New Directions.* Utah State University Press, Logan, Utah 1992. [A volume of essays in honour of Professor W. F. H. Nicolaisen, grouped under the headings Ballad and Song, Narrative, Language and Cultural Knowledge, Community and Identity.]

02 *Regional Ethnology:* Celtic Language Area.

Alexander Carmichael, *Carmina Gadelica. Hymns and Incantations,* presented by John MacInnes, Floris Books, Edinburgh 1992. 684 pp. £11.99. [This one-volume English edition of what was formerly available only in bilingual volumes, is very welcome. Carmichael's gathering of oral traditions is an irreplaceable record of religious texts with a strange blend of pagan and Christian imagery. MacInnes's Preface puts them in the context of the life and folklore of the Gaelic community.]

Derick S. Thomson, ed., *The Macdiarmid MS Anthology. Poems and Songs* mainly anonymous from the collection dated 1700 (Scottish Gaelic Texts Society), Scottish Academic Press 1992. 340 pp. £15.00.

03 *Ethnicity, Identity, Living Styles*

General.

Malcolm Chapman, *The Celts. The Construction of a Myth.* St Martin's Press 1992. 342 pp. £45.00.

Geoffrey W. S. Barrow, *Scotland and its Neighbours in the Middle Ages,* The Hambledon Press, London and Rio Grande 1992. 255 pp. £35.00. [A collection of eleven important articles that have appeared in scattered sources between 1969 and 1985.]

David McCrone, *Understanding Scotland. The Sociology of a Stateless Nation.* (International Library of Sociology), Routledge, London and New York 1992. 238 pp. £12.99 paperback, £40.00 hardback. [The first sociological analysis of Scotland's individual identity, in social, political and economic terms, and through its myths, legends and culture.]

William Warrell Fee, I: *Robert Humphrey and West Alexander, Pennsylvania. A Revolutionary War Soldier and His Town.* 1989.
II: *The Fee Family and the Daily Notes of Canonsburg, Pennsylvania. The Evolution of a Family, its Newspaper, and its Community.* 1990.
III: *Character(s). Dwight Humphrey Fee and Lucille Brockman Fee of Pittsburg, Pennsylvania.* 1900. [This three-volume study of the Ulster-Scot ethos as it developed in West Pennsylvania is available through the author at 3330 N. Leisure World Blvd., No. 174, Silver Spring, Maryland 2096, USA.]

Stephen J. Hornsby, *Nineteenth Century Cape Breton. A Historical Geography,* McGill-Queen's University Press, Montreal and Kingston, London, Buffalo. xxvi + 274 pp. £33.95. [A detailed examination of the patterns of economy, settlement and society, focusing on the impact of Scottish immigration, agricultural development, cod fishing and coal mining.]

J. I. Little, *Crofters and Habitants: Settler Society, Economy and Culture in a Quebec Township: 1848-1881.* McGill-Queen's University Press, Montreal and Kingston; London; Buffalo: 1991. 368 pp. including maps, tables and photographs (N.P.) [Study of Winslow Township, settled by Gaelic-speaking Highlanders from Lewis, and French-speaking colonists from the St Lawrence Seigneuries.]

Marianne MacLean, *The People of Glengarry: Highlanders in Transition, 1745-1820.* McGill-Queen's Studies in Ethnic History, McGill-Queen's University Press, Montreal and Kingston, London, Buffalo, 1991. [A study of Glengarry County, Ontario, and the process of Trans-Atlantic migration, strongly based on Scottish archive material.]

04 *Age, Family, Group.*

Women.

Lindy Moore, *Bajanellas and Semilinas. Aberdeen University and the Education of Women 1860-1920.* Quincentennial Studies in the History of the University of Aberdeen. Published for the University by Aberdeen University Press 1991. 164 pp. including illustrations, tables, figures. £8.95.

Children, Adolescence.

L. Jamieson and C. Toynbee, *Country Bairns. Growing Up 1900-1930,* Edinburgh University Press 1992. 245 pp, illustrations. £14.95. [A sociological study of individuals who were the children of 45 farm-servants, crofters and farmers, and whose stories have been tape recorded, analysed and presented.]

05 *Economy, World of Work, Occupations.*

Forestry.

William C. Wonders, *The 'Sawdust Fusiliers'. The Canadian Forestry Corps in the Scottish Highlands in World War Two.* Canadian Pulp and Paper Association, Montreal 1992. 130 pp, including 50 illustrations, and maps and figures. $13.00 (Canada). [Based on War Diaries of the C.F.C. Companies in the National Archives of Canada, historical sources in the National Library of Scotland, and field investigation and interviews conducted in the Scottish Highlands.]

Handicrafts.

Carolyn Murray-Wooley and Karl Raitz, *Rock Fences of the Bluegrass* Perspectives on Kentucky's Past, Architecture, Archaeology, and Landscape), The University Press of Kentucky 1992. x + 220 pp. $35.00. [Discusses geology and sources of stone, dyke construction, the predominantly Scotch-Irish origins of the dykers, a case study of a farming estate, and the contemporary situation. One of the best books on stone-walling that has so far appeared.]

Agricultural Workers.

David G. Adams, *Bothy Nichts and Days: Farm Bothy Life in Angus and the Mearns,* John Donald 1991. 90 pp. £9.50.

Seasonal Workers.

Anne O'Dowd, *Spalpeens and Tattie Hokers: History and Folklore of the Irish Migratory Worker in Ireland and Britain.* Irish Academic Press, Dublin 1991. 441 pp. £35.00.

09 *Food*

General.

C. Anne Wilson, ed., *Traditional Food East and West of the Pennines* (Food and Society 3), Edinburgh University Press 1991. 220 pp. £25.00. [Contains seven chapters by different writers, each expert on a particular area of food research, ranging from changes in traditional forms of food to provincial taste and the impact of printed material, such as recipe books.]

C. Anne Wilson, ed., *Waste Not Want Not, Food preservation from early times to the present day.* (Food and Society 4), Edinburgh University Press 1991. 165 pp. £22.50. [A survey by six writers of aspects of food preservation, pottery, necessities and luxuries, and the impact of industrial processes.]

C.Anne Wilson, ed., *Liquid Nourishment. Potable Foods and Stimulating Drinks* (Food and Society 5), Edinburgh University Press 1993. 171 pp. £29.50. [Nine contributors examine different kinds of liquid nourishment, from potage and soup to sherbets and alcoholic drinks.]

10 *Settlement, Cultural Landscape*

Other (Place Names).

Gregory Toner and Mìcheál B. O. Mainnín, *Place-Names of Northern Ireland*, Vol. 1, County Down I. Newry and South-West Down (The Northern Ireland Place-Name Project, Department of Celtic, The Queen's University of Belfast), Belfast 1992. £8.50 paperback, £20.00 hardback (standing orders £14.00).

A. J. Hughes and R.J. Hannan, Place-Names of Northern Ireland, Vol. 2, County Down II. The Ards (The Northern Ireland Place-Name Project, Department of Celtic, The Queen's University of Belfast), Belfast 1992. £8.50 paperback, £20.00 hardback (standing orders £14).

11 *Architecture, Building, Dwelling*

Dwelling House and Ways of Living.

Ian Gow, *The Scottish Interior*, Edinburgh University Press 1992. 174 pp. £25.50. [This is a survey of Georgian and Victorian Decor in the eighteenth and nineteenth centuries, 'a visual anthology of the domestic room in Scotland culled principally from the collections of the National Monuments Record of Scotland', ranging across the social strata.]

13 *Custom, Festival, Game, Spare Time*

General.

Margaret Bennett, *Scottish Customs from the Cradle to the Grave*, Polygon, Edinburgh 1992. xxii + 298 pp. [An unusual source book, comprising extracts from published sources, transcripts of recorded interviews, and analytical commentary.]

14 *Religion, Piety*

General.

Callum G. Brown, The People in the Pews, Religion and Society in Scotland since 1780. (Studies in Scottish Economic and Social History No. 3), Dundee 1993. 52 pp.

Forms of Devotion.

Christopher Bamford, trs., *The Voice of the Eagle. The Heart of Celtic Christianity. Homily on the Prologue to the Gospel of St John,* by John Scotus Eringena. Lindisfarne Press, Hudson, New York; Floris Books, Edinburgh; 1991. 192 pp. £8.95.

Institutions, Communities.

Anne Gordon, *Candie for the Foundling,* The Pentland Press Ltd., Edinburgh, Cambridge, Durham 1992. 720 pp. £17.50. [A book concerned with the social impact the Kirk has made on the lives of the ordinary people of Scotland, during the period before many of the Church's functions were taken over by the State. It covers Kirk Sessions and the poor, sickness and sins, witchcraft, marriage, baptism and death, and Sabbath observance.]

19 *Song*

Ballads and Epics.

Peter B. Freshwater, ed., *Sons of Scotia, Raise your Voice* (Friends of Edinburgh University Library), Edinburgh 1991. ix + 142 pp. £10.00. [This is No. 4 in The Drummond Book series. It is a selection of early nineteenth-century Scottish broadside ballads from a collection in Edinburgh University Library, with a very useful introduction.]

21 *Popular Prose and Reading Materials*

Accounts of Everyday Life.

William Alexander, *Rural Life in Victorian Aberdeenshire,* edited and introduced by Ian Carter. The Mercat Press, Edinburgh 1992. 168 pp. £6.95. [A selection from the published and very readable work of William Alexander, one of the best nineteenth-century guides to the social history and agricultural development of the Aberdeenshire countryside.]

Dorothy Hyslop Booth, *Echoes from the Border Hills.* The Pentland Press Ltd., Edinburgh, Cambridge, Durham 1992. 172 pp. £16.50. [This is a revised version, from the original manuscript, of Part iv of *Langholm As It Was,* by Robert Hyslop, 1912. It is an important account of the everyday life in the Borders over a century ago.]

M. L. Elder, *Ann Anderson 1833-1906. The Enduring Spirit. The Memoirs of a Country Lass from Aberdeenshire to Australia,* The Pentland Press Ltd., Edinburgh, Cambridge,

Durham 1992. 168 pp. £9.50. [An account compiled from detailed letters of an Aberdeenshire farmer's daughter who began as a kitchen lass in homes in North-east Scotland and in England and eventually became matron of Paramatta District Hospital in Australia. The 'below stairs' life of the Victorian servant and the harsh existence of a nurse, and the current state of medicine, are graphically presented in these pages.]

Elizabeth McGregor, *Before I was Ten.* Privately published, 1993. £5.00 (+ p. and p. £1 UK, £2.50 overseas surface). Available from Moira McGregor, 17 Charterhall Grove, Edinburgh EH9 3HU. [The early years of the 86-year-old author. Proceeds go to The Friends of Loch Lomond.]

Clodagh Brennan Harvey, *Contemporary Irish Traditional Narrative. The English Language Tradition* (Folklore and Mythology Studies, Vol. 35), University of California Press 1992. 138 pp. $18.00.

Other Literature and Reading Materials.

Priscilla Bawcutt and Felicity Riddy, eds., *Selected Poems of Henryson and Dunbar* (The Scottish Classics Series), Scottish Academic Press 1992. xxi + 241 pp. £9.75.

Philip Flynn, *Enlightened Scotland. A Study and Selection of Scottish Philosophical Prose from the Eighteenth and Early Nineteenth Centuries,* Scottish Academic Press, Edinburgh 1992. xxii + 356 pp. £22.50. [Essays from a variety of writers, on the mind, on morals, on creativity and aesthetic taste, and on society, with a general introduction.]

R. James Goldstein, *The Matter of Scotland. Historical Narrative in Medieval Scotland,* University of Nebraska Press, Lincoln and London 1993. 386 pp. £38.00.

Robert L. Kindrick, *Henryson and the Medieval Arts of Rhetoric* (Garland Studies in Medieval Literature, Vol. 8). Garland Publishing, Inc., New York and London 1993. $54.00. 359 pp.

Maurice Lindsay, ed., *The Youth and Manhood of Cyril Thornton,* by Thomas Hamilton. The Association for Scottish Literary Studies, Aberdeen 1990. xxii + 458 pp. (N.P.)

22 *Language*

Range of Sources

Margaret Laing, *Catalogue of Sources for a Linguistic Atlas of Early Medieval English* (Institute for Historical Dialectology, School of Scottish Studies, University of Edinburgh), D. S. Brewer, Cambridge 1993. 186 pp. £29.50. [A comprehensive inventory of the source material in English available for the study of Early Middle English, mainly for the period 1150-1300. Over 500 entries, with information on dates, lands, manuscript associations and language. Of interest to students of the English language, medievalists, demographers, social historians, palaeographers, codicologists and historical geographers.]

William Morrice Wilson, *Speak o' the North-East,* NES Publications, Huddersfield 1993. 343 pp. £9.75. [A record of dialect phrases, grouped according to themes, and including bairns' rhymes, riddles and proverbs, from the Turriff area of North-east Scotland.]

23 *Theatre, Circus, Media*

Popular Drama.

Brian Hayward, *Galoshins. The Scottish Folk Play,* Edinburgh University Press 1992. viii + 303 pp. £40.00. [A remarkably thorough assemblage of all known texts of the play, each localised and dated, with a commentary on the performance and its relationship to guising, and a discussion of the socio-cultural history.]

FOLKLORE

The Journal of the Folklore Society

Ed. Jacqueline Simpson, MA, DLitt

Folklore publishes articles and reviews on a broad range of cultural traditions, past and present. Priority is given to British folklore and ethnology and to material from Europe and the New World which offers relevant points of contact or comparison.

Folklore is published twice a year. The annual subscription is £18/$45 for individuals (special rates for students and pensioners), £25 for institutions. Available from: The Folklore Society, University College London, Gower Street, London WC1E 6BT.

Articles in vol. 104 (1993) include:

Alexander Fenton,
Folklore and Ethnology: Past, Present and Future in British Universities

Roy Judge,
Merrie England: Theatrical Morris

Bill Ellis,
The Highgate Cemetery Vampire Hunt: Anglo-American Connections in Satanic Cult Lore

Adrienne Mayor and Michael Heaney,
Griffins and Arimaspeans

Hugh Cheape,
The Red Book of Appin: Magic as Medicine and Medicine as Magic

Deborah Crawford,
St Joseph in Britain: Reconsidering the Legends